THE
YELLOW
FOOTPRINTS

Book 1

TIMOTHY RILLEY

©2025 Timothy Rilley
The Yellow Footprints

eBook ISBN: 978-1-965761-40-3
Paperback ISBN: 978-1-965761-41-0
Ingram Spark ISBN: 978-1-965761-42-7
Library of Congress Control Number: 2025904272

Cover Design by Angie Ayala
Interior Design by Marigold2k

Published by Spotlight Publishing House –
https: SpotlightPublishingHouse.com

THE YELLOW FOOTPRINTS

TIMOTHY RILLEY

SPOTLIGHT
PUBLISHING HOUSE

Goodyear, Arizona

Table of Contents

Dedication

This book is dedicated to the memory of my good friend LCPL Michael W. Havranek. Mike served with me in Boot Camp, and was the 1st Squad Leader of Platoon 2227, FOX Company, 3rd Training Battalion, MCRD San Diego, CA. Mike and I Graduated from Boot Camp together and were both Promoted to PFC out of Boot Camp. Mike was also Awarded the Highest Score attained on the Rifle Range at Edson Range with a Score of 239 out of a possible 250 which was Expert.

After Boot Camp Graduation, we were both transported to Camp Pendleton, California, where I attended ITR Training (Infantry Training Regiment) at San Onofre, Camp Pendleton, and Mike attended BST Training (Basic Squad Tactics) at Camp Margarita, Camp Pendleton. Mike was assigned an MOS of 0311 and his wish was to become a Recon Marine.

After we finished our training at Camp Pendleton, Mike and I both were given a 20 Day Leave to go home before reporting to our next Duty Stations. Upon termination of my 20 Days Leave, I reported to NAS Memphis, TN to attend Air Operations School before reporting to NAS Pensacola in Florida to attend Air Traffic Control School.

After Mike finished his 20 days Leave in Missoula, MT, he returned to Camp Pendleton to attend RECON Training before being sent to Okinawa, Japan and then on to Vietnam. Mike and I kept in touch by mail while I was going to school and he was attending his training to fulfil his dream of being a RECON Marine. After Mike completed his Training with the 1st Marines in Camp Pendleton and shipped out to Okinawa, Mike was assigned to 3rd Force Recon in Vietnam at the end of May, 1967.

On June 11, 1967, LCPL Michael W. Havranek was on his first Recon Patrol. Mike was about one of two CH-46's and 2 Huey UH1E Gunships in formation for insertion at their mission destination. Mike was with his seven man Force Recon Team, designated Sommersail-one, out of Dong Ha, Quang Tri Province.

Their CH-46 was shot down by rocket fire in the vicinity just inside the southern edge of the DMZ, and all seven members of his Team and the four crew members were killed. June 11th and 12th ground parties tried reaching the crash site but were driven back by small arms fire. LCPL Havranek's body was never recovered and has been listed as MIA since June 11, 1967. To date, only Mike's Dog Tags have been recovered.

Mike graduated from St. Francis Xavier Grade School and Loyola High School in Missoula, Montanna. Mike was born on May 30, 1948 and joined the Marines after High School and entered the Marines in September in 1966.

I think of Mike often and there were times I wished we had more time together or could have become better friends and spent our lives reminiscing about our time together in the Marines. Mike is my Hero and never had a chance to prove to the world what a wonderful guy he was and would have become.

Introduction

College Spring Break normally lasts just a week, however I decided to extend my Spring Break and stayed away for three weeks. That turned out to be a bad decision on my part. At the time I was fortunate enough to attend college on a basketball scholarship, but didn't appreciate how important it was to stay in school. When I finally returned to campus, I was locked out of my Dorm Room and kicked out of college.

The year was 1966 and the United States was involved in a military conflict in Vietnam and unless you were in school, suffered a disability, worked for a certain company, or had a job vital to our country's security, you were eligible for the draft.

I wasn't just eligible for the draft; I was a poster child for what a draftee looks like. I was 19, I was in great physical shape, I was single, I had no particular skills to speak of, and to be honest, it turned out I wasn't too bright. After getting kicked out of school and having my scholarship terminated, within two weeks I received my Draft Notice.

The envelope I received was very official looking and when I opened it and took out the letter inside, it said,

"GREETINGS, From the President of the United States."

So I did what every young red blooded American boy at the age of 19 did, I panicked. Even though I screwed up and got myself kicked out of college, I couldn't believe I had been drafted. Not me, at least not yet.

I had too many personal obligations that had to be attended to before I could give myself to my country in such a sacrificial way. My brother was getting married in May, and I was in the Wedding. My sister was getting married in June, and I was in her Wedding. Not with-standing the fact that I had made some pretty wild plans to enjoy the summer of 1966, and those plans would be ruined in more ways than anyone could possibly imagine if I let myself get drafted. Besides, my mother would kill me if I missed the family weddings.

Although I have admitted that at the time I was not very bright, I thought through my dilemma and looked at my situation from every aspect and came up with a plan. It wasn't much of a plan, but it was the only thing I could think of to keep me from being drafted. I tried to join the Navy. I forgot to mention that in my Draft Notice, they only gave me one week before I had to report to Fort Campbell Kentucky.

The truth of it all was, because I had been Drafted, the Army owned my ass. While I was trying to enlist in the Navy, I found out that I was out of luck because of my Draft status with the Army. The Army only gave me one week to get my affairs in order and then report for induction.

While trying unsuccessfully to enlist in the Navy, I met a Marine Corps Recruiter who showed me a way that I could beat the Draft, be able to attend both my brother and my sister's weddings and be able to stay home for the next four months and enjoy all of my summer plans.

This Marine Corps Recruiter explained in detail my only way out of the Draft. His solution, which after enjoying my summer, would make me a part of the greatest fighting force the world has ever known. The United States Marine Corps.

You have heard it said many times, "Once A Marine, Always A Marine." That expression is based on the days, weeks and months that Marines are trained, taught, brain-washed and molded into, "The Few The Proud, The Marines."

We were trained to be tough; we were taught to be fearless; we were brainwashed to be invincible and molded into men to be respected. It has also been said that "Not everyone can be a Marine," and although some think it a cliche, not everyone can be or wants to be a Marine.

In my 50 years since being in the Marines and sharing numerous conversations with so many other military veterans who served in other branches of the service, I have heard them say over and over, "I could have been a Marine, but…" They all had a "but" and a number of reasons why they chose not to be a Marine. Like I said, "Not everyone can be a Marine."

However, not once in all my years have I ever heard a Marine say, "I could have been in the Army, Navy or Air Force." There is a brotherhood in the Marines that is not found in any other branch of the service. That brotherhood all started on "The Yellow Footprints."

This book is about my journey from a civilian to becoming a Marine, and anyone who chooses to join the Marine Corps has to go through the same process, we all go to Boot Camp. No matter whether your journey takes you by way of Parris Island or MCRD San Diego, your first encounter once off the bus, passing through those coveted gates, has you standing on those Yellow Footprints.

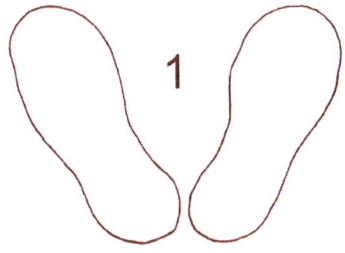

Boot Camp Begins

80% of Life is Just Showing Up

When the American Airlines Boeing 707 landed at the Los Angeles airport and rolled to a stop just outside the main terminal, all the Navy and Marine Corps recruits onboard were told to stay in their seats. This was my first Jet Airplane ride and all the way to California I kept asking myself if I made the right decision. Hopefully this journey I have chosen for myself to offset the bad choice I made not to return to school and to avoid the Draft will put me on the right course that will make a difference in my life.

The steps were rolled up to the front door just behind the cockpit, and after the door was opened, all the civilian passengers from Detroit made their way off the plane.

The Naval Officer traveling along with a Marine Staff Sergeant (SSgt) told all the remaining recruits who were either going to Navy or Marine Corps boot camp in San Diego to exit the plane in single file.

As the recruits filed off the plane and walked into the terminal, the Navy recruits filed to the left and the Staff Sgt had the potential Marine recruits file to the right. When the Naval Officer and Marine Staff Sgt were satisfied that everyone who was supposed to be present was in attendance, we then walked to the other side of the terminal. One line for the Navy personnel and one single file line for the potential Marine recruits.

There were no direct flights from Detroit to San Diego, therefore now in the LA terminal, we had to board another plane and fly to San Diego. We arrived at LAX at 1810 (6:10 pm) and we were to depart LAX to San Diego at 1930 (7:30 pm) arriving in San Diego at 2010 (8:10 pm). We were allowed to make a bathroom break and then get back in line. While in line, each recruit was given a boarding pass for PSA Airlines flying from LA to San Diego. As each recruit boarded the plane, the stewardess stood just inside the plane doorway and took our boarding pass. She tore off the small, perforated end of the boarding pass and gave us

back the tab with the seat number and directed each recruit to our seat.

There were 32 Marine recruits and 22 Navy recruits who boarded that PSA flight for San Diego. All the recruits moved to the rear of the plane filling the seats at the rear of the plane. There were 12 civilian passengers also boarding the PSA Flight to San Diego, and they boarded after all the recruits were seated. All 12 civilian passengers were seated in front of the plane. After everyone was in their seats, the stewardess closed the aircraft door.

The pilot made some announcements, and the steward-ess gave the safety briefing. The engines began to whine, and the plane began to move toward the runway for our departure to San Diego. The flight was uneventful and lasted 55 minutes from lift off to landing. This was my second jet airplane flight and was less exciting than I had expected. After landing, I waited for the steps to be rolled up to the plane. Once the door of the plane opened, the 12 civilian passengers departed the plane down the stairs while the Marine and Navy recruits were told to stay seated until given the command to move off the plane by the Naval Officer accompanying the group.

Once all civilians were off the plane, the Navy recruits were told to file out of the plane first in single file, but the Marines were told to remain in their seats by the Marine Staff Sargeant. Once the Navy Recruits were off the plane, two Marine Corps Drill Instructors (DI's) boarded the plane and walked to the rear of the plane where all the Marine recruits were still seated. In a very unmistakable voice, one of the DI's gave the following instructions. "When told to do so, you will stand and in a single file line, you will quick time down the aisle and off the plane, down the stairs, and fall in on the two Sgt's at the bottom of the stairs on the tarmac. Do you understand what I just told you?" We answered, "Yes Sir!"

The DI then gave the command in a very loud voice, "Now ladies, get-up and move, move. Quickly, Quickly, Quickly." With that, all 32 recruits jumped up and moved very quickly in a single file down the aisle, through the door and down the steps to the waiting Sgt's at the bottom of the stairway. As we hit the tarmac at the bottom of the steps, we were met by two rather large screaming Marine DI's who were yelling at the recruits to "fall in three ranks, one behind the other, let's move, move, move."

The yelling continued until all the recruits were off the plane and in a formation on the tarmac. Every recruit lined up in three single files. The Senior DI, who was also the DI who boarded the plane, moved to the front of the formation and spoke. "Through those doors, to your right, inside the terminal, you will find another group of recruits in formation. You will quick time to the end of the terminal, and join that formation, and you will not talk at any time.

When I tell you to "move out," you will double time through the terminal doors, turn to your right, and "**Fall-In**" with the group already waiting for your arrival. You will "**Fall-In**" quickly and quietly behind them and wait for further instructions. "Do you understand me?" The response from the 32 recruits was, "**Yes, Sir.**"

He then said, "**Move Out.**" "Go, go, go." The recruits took off running as fast as we could run, trying to stay three abreast. We made it thru the terminal doors, turned to the right and ran until we came upon a group standing in a four-column formation at the end of the terminal. The 32-man 3-column formation came upon the 4-column formation and were confused as to how to fall in.

The DI's were yelling and screaming at the 32 recruits trying to figure out what rank to "Fall-In" with. It took a minute or two for the 32 recruits in a 3-column formation to figure out where to go in a 4-column formation, but with the assistance of the yelling DI's, it was figured out pretty fast. The DI's were yelling at us the entire time we were running to join up with the group of recruits already waiting.

The new formation now consisted of 92 Marine recruits waiting to find out what we had to do next. There were now six DI's surrounding the formation. Yelling, "stop talking," "stop moving," "stand at attention," and it seemed like they wanted us to stop breathing. Then the Senior SSgt DI in charge stepped up directly to the middle of the formation. We were in a formation of four ranks facing forward with 23 recruits in each rank.

The DI then yelled, "There is a grey bus parked to my left, your right. When I tell you to do so you will face right and from the left to the right, you will run in single file to that bus, and you will board it and occupy every seat starting from the rear to the front. The rear seat runs across the width of the bus, the first six recruits will sit in those seats. The rest of you will sit two to a seat. When all the seats are full, you will continue to the rear of the bus, and you will sit on the knees of the two men in the last row of the aisle and then the next two will sit on their knees and so forth and so on until all of you are seated. Is that understood."

My head was spinning trying to understand every command we were receiving and scared to death not to make a mistake. I didn't in any way want to bring any attention to myself and if I screwed up in any way it would almost guarantee some type of dressing down from a DI and it wouldn't be pleasant. I made it a point to listen carefully to every command given and follow it to the best of my ability as I prayed and said to myself, "Please don't fuck up Tim."

The formation answered, "**Yes, Sir**." The DI yelled, "I can't hear you," and we yelled again, "**Yes, Sir**." Louder than we had just yelled. He said again, "I Can't Hear You." Again, we yelled louder, "**Yes, Sir**." He then said, "You will do this in silence, not a word is to be spoken, "Is this understood?" and we all screamed again, "**Yes, Sir**." He again screamed, "I can't hear you." And again as loud as we could, we yelled back, "**Yes, Sir**." He then gave the command, "**Right Face**."

The recruits attempted to all turn to the right. Believe it or not there were a few recruits who didn't know their left from their right, and a couple were forcibly turned to the right. The DI yelled, "Move Out, Move, Move!" We took off running towards the bus in single file, first rank from the left to right, followed by the next, then the third rank and then the fourth.

As we boarded the bus the other three DI's were yelling all the time, "Move, move, move, get the lead out," and the seats began to fill up and the recruits were silent, except for a few who just couldn't keep their mouths shut, some arguing, saying things like, "I was there first, move over damn it," and so on.

As the DI's continued to yell, the bus filled with the 92 poor souls who had no idea what was in store for them. When the chaos ended and there was no more movement, then silence. All I heard was heavy breathing and I swore I could hear my heart beating.

Two DI's boarded the bus and stood at the front making sure no-one was talking. JUST SILENCE! The bus consisted of one full seat across the rear which held six recruits. There were 16 seats on each side of the bus with each seat holding two recruits which totaled 32 recruits on each side of the bus.

With six recruits across the back seat and 32 recruits sitting on each side, that left 22 recruits without seats. Two recruits sat on the knees of the two recruits who were in the middle of the rear seat and then two recruits sat on their knees and then two more on their knees until the additional recruits were all seated on the knees of the recruits in the middle isle of the bus.

Once the bus was full and the DI's were satisfied that all 92 recruits were seated, the bus moved off the tarmac onto the route to MCRD Recruit Depot. The life-changing adventure that not one poor soul on that bus could possibly have imagined, had begun. I was one of the recruits sitting in the middle aisle with another recruit sitting on my knees. The pain was excruciating, and I was now thinking to myself, "What the hell have I gotten myself into?"

It was exactly 2200 hours (10:00 pm), when our bus passed through the main gate at MCRD. Taps were being played as the bus made its way to the Receiving Depot, and the lights throughout the base were out for everyone except Marines on duty and those individuals who were going to welcome the bus load of new recruits who just passed through the gates. The bus made its way around to the Receiving Depot building where all new recruits were dropped off to start their infamous journey through boot camp.

When the bus stopped the two DI's on the bus spoke up loud and clear to the 92 recruits who were crammed onto the bus, that brought them to their new home where traditions of the Corps has been made for over 191 years. All attention was directed to the two DI's at the front of the bus. The 22 Recruits sitting on knees in the aisle were very uncomfortable, but nothing was going to be comfortable for quite a while to come.

The DI's at the front of the bus gave the following "Command," "When you slimy, civilian, pukes run off this bus, you will find a spot on the yellow footprints just to the right as you leave this bus, and you will stand with your heels together on those yellow foot prints, at attention and do not talk or move." Do you hear me?" The 92 occupants on the bus yelled a response, "**Yes, Sir**." The DI responded, "I can't hear you." The bus responded again, but louder this time, "**Yes, Sir**." The DI then commanded in a load voice, "Move, move, move, move, now, now, now you pieces of civilian slime!"

The recruits scrambled off the bus as fast as their feet could carry them, without falling down or being trampled on. Those first off the bus were those sitting on each-others knees, then the seats from front to rear. Once off the bus we all went to our right as we left the bus through a covered walkway with a sign above which explained what it was to be a Marine.

At the end of the walkway we made a right turn to find four rows of yellow footprints, with 25 sets of footprints in

each row. There were a total of 100 yellow footprints facing forward. Each set of prints were heel to heel with the footprint at a 45-degree angle which is the exact position your feet are to be at, when at attention.

The yellow footprints were exactly 30 inches apart from the ones in front of or behind you, and 30 inches from each side, right and left. Each recruit found a set of footprints and stood on them as if in a unit formation at attention. The yellow footprints are a symbolic tradition in the Marine Corps of the transition from civilian to recruit, and the start of a new reality for the recruit.

Most recruits are terrified by the screaming drill instructors because of their continued yelling at the Recruits to stand up, shoulders back, heads up, chin down, thumbs along the seams of your trousers. The yelling was chilling, and it seems nothing is ever done fast enough or good enough.

There were a total of six DI's that were on all sides of the recruit formation as we were standing on the yellow footprints. The screaming finally stopped and the formation on the yellow footprints waits to see what comes next. The silence was deafening but didn't last long.

The next command given to the recruits on the yellow footprints by the DI In-Charge was… "If the man in front of you is shorter than you, change positions with the smaller man. The smaller man moving back and the taller moving forward." He said, "You will continue to do so until the taller recruit is in front and the shorter recruit is behind the taller one." Again, he said, "On my command," and he then said, "Now move, move, move, get it done,"

At that command, total chaos began with the other DI's yelling loudly, "Move to the front you idiot, don't you understand the English language you maggots?" They continued yelling at whoever wasn't moving the way the DI's expected him to move. It felt like nothing the recruits did was right and the DI's were letting us know it. Trying to get us lined up in the proper formation took longer than the DI's expected. The yelling was deafening, and recruits were pulled and pushed and pushed and pulled as the yelling continued at what seemed like an eternity.

We were finally in the formation the way the DI's commanded us, the taller recruits were in front and the shorter recruits to the rear. If the formation was to "Face Right," the end result was tallest recruit in the front and shortest in the back so it looked like a right angle of men, from front to rear. It took more time than the DI's wanted, so the yelling intensified.

When the DI's quit yelling and slapping recruits in the back of the head and thought this was as good as it was going to get, the order was now given to face half right. When we were all facing half right, we were told to get down in a push-up position and the DI started yelling, "Down, Up, Down, Up, Down, Up." You civilians pieces of garbage think you'll ever make a Marine? You have a lot to learn and a long way to go." The push-ups continued for a 25 to 30 count and the yelling continued. The DI commanded, "Get on your feet and get on those footprints you pieces of civilian shit, maggot infested, civilian pukes." The colorful words, phrases, and statements we were going to hear while in boot camp had just begun.

As the recruits stood up and tried to arrange themselves on the yellow footprints, again the DI's were yelling, "Stand up straight, shoulders back, head up, chin down, thumbs along the seams of your trousers." This continued for what seemed like an hour, but in actuality it was only about five minutes with the DI's moving through the formation and yelling at individual recruits who seemed not to understand the English language, or their left from their right, but in my opinion, they just liked to yell.

The senior DI in charge was a SSgt Owens, and as the formation needed to understand they had to listen and learn very fast or pay the price. SSgt Ownes then told the formation, "You will now go up this set of stairs in a single file, and follow the green line painted on the ground to a set of double doors. Once you go through the double doors, you will find a row of telephones on the wall, and you will cover down on those phones and you will call home to tell your parents you made it safely to the Marine Recruit Depot."

Once inside the building, there was a long wall with 20 pay telephones on the wall. Each recruit was to call home to talk to their parent and read the card hanging on each phone. The card read, "Hello mom or dad, this is………... I just arrived at Marine Corps Recruit Depot at San Diego, California. I am safe and will be starting training tomorrow morning. I will write to you soon. Please do not worry. I Love you, Goodbye."

My mother answered the phone and I read the message on the card and then hung up so the next person could call. Each recruit was allowed to make one call but if no one answered, they were allowed to make a second call. The call was limited to 30 seconds. The call was free, no coins were needed.

Once all the calls were finished, we were to return to our previous position in formation on the yellow footprints. There was some confusion, but SSgt Owens made sure all 92 recruits were back where they were supposed to be before he gave his next command. "You will now experience the first phase of learning how to look like a Marine. You will receive a Marine haircut." He continued, "You will follow in single file by squad when I give you the command and follow the blue line up the stairs.

I will then give you the command to move out, which means the first Squad will turn right, and will go up these stairs in single file and follow the railing until you reach the end and then stop.

Each squad will turn to the right and follow in order. Once you come to the end of the railing, you will not move until someone tells you to move, or sit when told to sit, do you understand?" The platoon responded loudly and in unison, "Yes Sir." We had to respond at least three more times before Staff Sgt Owens was satisfied we knew what we were supposed to do.

SSgt Owens then commanded, "1st Squad, Right Face, move out, Move, Now, Move you civilian pieces of shit." I was in the first Squad, second recruit in line, we all moved out, and we moved quickly.

The first squad turned right, and then moved out fast, and then was followed by the next squad and so on until all the recruits were on their way for a haircut. After stopping where we were to stop, one of the DI's began to herd us into the base barber shop.

There were six barber chairs along with six barbers, one behind each chair.

One by one the recruits were sent in and sat down, and in approximately 40 seconds or so, but no longer than a minute, the recruit was finished with his haircut.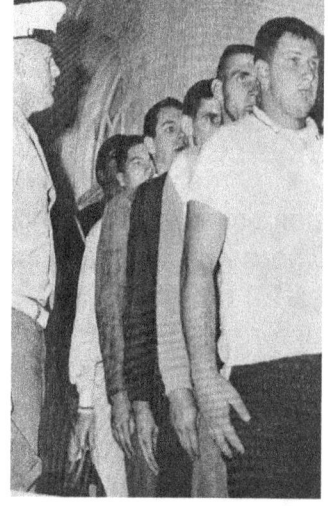

A recruit haircut was done with a clipper blade, and the end result was totally bald. With six chairs and six barbers, within 20 minutes every one of the 92 recruits was bald with their first, new, Marine haircut.

When the recruits were finished with their haircut, they were told to return to their spot on the yellow

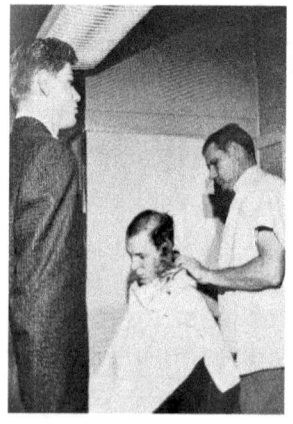 footprints. After all recruits returned to their spot on the yellow footprints Staff Sgt Owens introduced us to our permanent Platoon Commander and the two Drill Instructors who will train us while at Boot Camp.

There was total silence, and then a new voice we had never heard before echoed through the damp dark night. As we were standing on the yellow footprints in formation, in front of

us stood a six-foot six-inch, larger than life tanned DI. He had a round pit marked face and was a scary looking Indian in a Khaki Uniform with the green smoky bear hat on his head, which is the symbolic cover for Marine Corps Drill Instructors. The black leather belt around his waist indicates he's a Platoon Commander.

He began, "My name is Gunnery Sargent Wolfmule, I will be your Platoon Commander for the next 11 weeks, while here at MCRD for those of you who make it. You are all here thinking you will become Marines, but you have no idea what it takes to become a Marine. You are nothing but low down, civilian pieces of garbage, and do not even deserve to be on the same "Hallowed Ground" that Marines before you have walked on.

Someone turned their head to look at the GySgt where he was standing, and the GySgt responded in kind. "You do not look at me, you keep those slimy civilian eyes looking straight ahead, you piece of shit. If I think you are eyeball fucking me, I will rip your eyeballs out of your fucking head. I will tell you what to look at, when to look at it, and I will tell you every move you are to make while you are on my depot. Do you understand me?" The formation answered, "**Yes Sir**." It wasn't loud enough, and GySgt Wolfmule yelled, "I can't hear you maggots." Again we answered, "**Yes Sir**." as loudly as we could.

He continued, "You civilian pieces of garbage will go through a total transformation while you are here. We will take all that undisciplined civilian lady, baby fat off your body; we will wipe out that civilian way you act and think. We will change the civilian way you eat and sleep and walk and talk. We will break you down both mentally and physically. We will then rebuild you to meet my standards, and the standards of the Marines who served before you, and who bravely have built the majestic history of the Marine Corps."

"Some of you won't make it and will be dropped out of this Platoon. Those of you who survive and make it to graduation, will be stronger, smarter, meaner than ever, and able to do things you never thought possible. Then and only then will you know what it means to be a United States Marine. We will have to see how many of you pieces of civilian shit actually make it."

"Every day you will work, work, work, and then you will work some more. You will eat when we tell you. You will sleep when we tell you. You will go to the head only when we tell you, and you will not speak unless you are spoken to. Everything you need to know we will teach you. You will move only when we tell you to move, and if you don't, you will have my wrath fall upon you."

"This is my Marine Corps not yours. Since you have chosen to walk into my Hell, you may wish to regret it. You currently are the lowest form of life there is on this planet. You are a civilian slime, piece of shit. You are a boot, a Marine Corps recruit,.."

"While you are here at my Recruit Depot, I will be your mother, your father, your sister, your brother. I will not be your priest or your minister and I definitely won't be your friend. Some of you will be homesick, some of you will cry, some of you will wish you never joined the Marines, and will want your mommy, but mommy isn't going to be here to help you. I own your slimy ass, and if you don't hack it, I will send you home and hopefully not in a body bag."

"While you are here at my Marine Recruit Depot, and from this moment forward, the first words out of your mouth will be Sir, and the last word out of your mouth will be Sir, Do you understand me?" The entire formation answered, "**Sir, Yes Sir**." The GySgt then yelled, "I can't hear you." The formation again and louder replied, "**Sir, Yes Sir**." GySgt said, "I still can't hear you ladies" and one more time the whole formation screamed as loud as they could, "**Sir, Yes Sir**." "Every time you are given an order, you will repeat that Order, do you understand me." The response was as loud as the last, "**Sir, Yes Sir**."

"You are the lamest excuse for human beings I have ever met." If you get cut from my platoon you will go to Motivation Platoon, or someplace close to hell. I make Marines, ladies, and if by chance you make it you will have to earn it. If you fail here you will fail everywhere. If you succeed, you will wear the coveted Eagle Globe and Anchor and earn the title, United States Marine."

GySgt Wolfmule continued. "The other two drill instructors that will assist me in training your Platoon will be Sgt James and Sgt Martinez." Both Sgt James and Sgt Martinez stepped out to be seen by the entire platoon. Sgt James looked just like the Poster that depicted Smoky the Bear. He was an African American, five feet eight inches tall and you could see he was built like a brick shit house.

Sgt Martinez was a Mexican/American, five feet ten inches tall, dark hair, slender built but solid. Both Sgt James and Sgt Martinez were Vietnam Veterans and wore their Ribbons and Shooting Badges on their Khaki uniforms with pride and precision. Their shoes were spit shinned like glass, and both wore a green cartridge belt with a first aid pouch centered on the back and had the coveted "Smoky the Bear" campaign cover on their heads.

GySgt Wolfmule turned to SSgt Owens and told him to carry on. SSgt Owens replied, "Aye, Aye Gunny." He then approached the formation which was standing tall on the yellow footprints and told the formation "**At Ease**." This meant we could relax instead of standing at Attention. He then huddled with the other five DI's, and they held a conversation for approximately two or three minutes.

SSgt Owens then called the Platoon to "**Attention**." He instructed the formation, "When you are given the command to come to Attention, you will stand with your feet at a 45-degree angle heel to heel, your arms at your side with your thumbs touching the seams of your trousers. Your chest out, your shoulders should be back, your head and eyes looking straight ahead, and your chin slightly tucked to your chest.

On the Command of "**Right Face**," you will turn on your right heal and the ball of your left foot to the right and then bring your left foot back heel to heel and stand at "**Attention**." His next statement, "When I give you the command of "**Forward March**," you always start off with your left foot and continue to march to the cadence given you by the Sgt in charge." He then commanded, "**Right Face**," his next Command was, "**Forward March**." The entire Platoon started off by taking a step with their left foot and listened to SSgt Owens call cadence, "Left, Right, Left, Right."

The formation was no longer on the yellow footprints, and we marched to a warehouse. The formation was brought to a halt when SSgt Owens commanded, "**Platoon, Halt**." When we stopped, it wasn't in unison, it was choppy and sounded terrible. SSgt Owens said we would work on that. Now you also have to understand that every moment we either executed a movement or marched, the other five DI's continued to yell at anyone who didn't execute properly. Whether we executed properly or not, the yelling continued.

The formation was stopped outside a supply warehouse, where SSgt Owens instructed us that we were to follow the yellow line that led from our formation up to the warehouse entrance. We would "**Fall Out**" by squad, in a single file line and follow the yellow line into the warehouse where we would be given a sea bag and issued our initial uniform and certain toiletry items.

Each of us as we entered the warehouse was given an olive-green sea bag with a strap. We were to connect the strap to the grommet on the sea bag and carry it over our left shoulder. We then proceeded in a single file line past numerous stations where we were issued our gear. The first item of clothing we received were two green utility covers, putting one on our head.

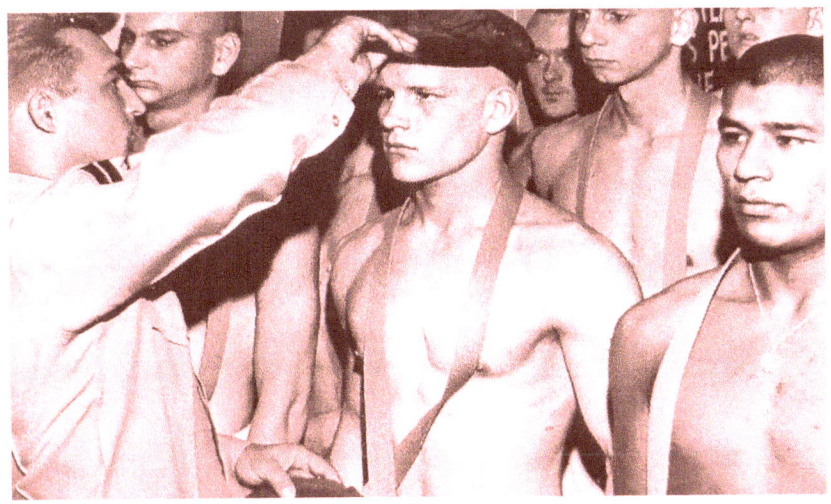

The rest of the clothing issue consisted of a belt you could wrap around your waist almost twice, a yellow sweatshirt, one pair of white tennis shoes, three white t-shirts, three pairs of white boxer shorts, one pair of red PT shorts, three pair of black socks, two pair of utility trousers and two utility shirts. All of those items were issued as we went up the left side of the warehouse.

At the end of the warehouse we crossed over to the right side of the warehouse staying on the yellow line and were issued a metal bucket. Next we got a bar of soap in a plastic soap dish container, a pair of shower shoes, a belt buckle, two combination padlocks, two towels, and two wash cloths.

After leaving the warehouse, we were to fall back into our Platoon formation. Now there were no yellow footprints to help line us up, so we experienced some confusion although there shouldn't have been much confusion as we came out the same way we went in. The DI's continued their yelling as some of the recruits were having difficulty getting back into formation properly.

Again SSgt Owens wasn't satisfied with our efforts to get back in formation, so when we were all back in our Formation, he had us place our sea bags and buckets at our feet and turn half right. We knew what that meant, and as the DI's yelled and screamed at recruits who couldn't follow instructions, SSgt Ownes had us give him 25 more push-ups.

After completing the 25 push-ups and back in formation, we were given the command to "**Forward March**." We were then marched over to another building still wearing our civilian clothes, carrying our sea bags over our left shoulder, and buckets in our right hand. As the platoon of recruits entered the next building by Squad in a single file, we were ushered up the stairs to a large room with eight rows of long counters that had individual cubicle compartments. Each recruit was ordered to stand in front of a cubicle.

There were eight rows with twelve compartments in each row that measured 24 inches in height, 24 inches deep and 24 inches wide. Under each compartment there was a shelf the same depth and width and contained a cardboard box. We were told to stand centered on each space remove our utility covers and place it in our sea bag and then place it on the floor by our left foot and the bucket by our right foot with DI's continually yelling and screaming at recruits who still couldn't tell their right foot from their left.

At the front of each cubicle was a strip of white tape about six inches long. There was a black marking pen and a 4 x 6 inch white mailing label. SSgt Owens then commanded each recruit to take the marking pen and print your last name on the tape, but do not touch the Label. The five DI's moved from recruit to recruit making sure they at least knew how to write their name.

When you finished writing your name on the tape you had to take one step back and raise your right hand, standing at attention and facing forward. When every recruit had his hand in the air, the DI's gave you an order to drop your hand to your side and step back to your cubicle. The next command given by SSgt Owens was to bend down and take the box from under their cubicle and place it in front of them in their cubicle. The box was 12 inches high by 12 inches wide, by 12 inches deep.

While standing in front of our cubicle, we were then ordered to empty all of our pockets onto the bench in front of us. Empty everything, wallets, money, jewelry, rings, watches, glasses, knives, guns, condoms, pills, gum, cigarettes, matches, lighters, brass knuckles, everything on your person. You were given two minutes to follow these instructions, and once all your pockets were emptied, again take one step back from your cubicle and raise your right hand. All the time the DI's were screaming instructions, and some recruits were being yelled at for not following the instructions given to them.

The DI's walked up and down each row and stopped and inspected what was laid out from all the recruits' pockets. Everything except our wallets and possibly glasses were considered contraband, and would not be allowed to be kept in the recruits possession.

The DI's made their way up and down each row, inspecting all the possessions that were placed on the bench, and DI's confiscated anything that they considered illegal. The rest of our belongings in the center of the cubicle, that was considered contraband, would be boxed and sent home. Wallets were gone through. Paper money, driver's license, and appropriate pictures were kept in the wallets. The DI's confiscated the illegal items and placed them in a bag for disposal.

Other items considered contraband that would not be allowed and placed in the box were watches, rings, jewelry, necklaces, coins, knives, etc. Wallets with paper money and pictures were placed to the side and would be allowed to be kept. If you wore glasses, you were instructed to make sure you were wearing them, otherwise they were placed in the box in front of you.

Once all contraband was delt with, SSgt Owens then told us we would remove our clothes, by the numbers. The first item to take off was the jacket or sweater you were wearing and hold it over your head. We were then told to place the jacket or sweater in the box. We were then ordered to remove our shoes and hold them above our head. Then we were told to put them in the box. Next, we were told to take off our socks and hold them above our heads. This continued with every article of clothing until we were stripped down naked, and each article of clothing was placed in the box. The DI's were yelling at the recruits the whole time they were placing each article of clothing into the box.

Once we were totally naked and all of our clothes and possessions were in our box, we were ordered to close the boxes, and tape them shut. It didn't matter if everything fit, you had to make it fit, and you had two minutes to fit everything you were wearing in the box and be able to close it and tape it shut.

Now each recruit is totally naked, has no personal articles of clothing or anything else except a wallet or a pair of glasses if they needed them to see, and were set to the side of the cubicle.

SSgt Owens again called the entire room to attention and commanded everyone to be facing towards their cubicles. Although we were all standing naked, SSgt Owens ordered us to take one step back and do an about face, (turn around). Now we were facing away from our cubicle. As we were standing at attention, each row of recruits were inspected by a Corpsman and a DI. They inspected our hands, our feet, our mouths, and we were ordered to lift our arms. We were then ordered to put our arms down to our sides and then ordered to do another about face.

We were now again facing our cubicle, and then told to bend over and spread our butt cheeks. What a sight, 92 recruits stark naked, bending over spreading our butt cheeks and having our butts inspected by the Corpsman and DI looking for contraband.

It may sound funny, that we had to do that, but there was a reason for it, and there were actually two recruits that were trying to smuggle contraband past the DI's by stuffing it in their butts.

Both recruits were trying to smuggle drugs in their possession by putting the articles up their butt. They had gotten caught, and were not treated kindly. Both were taken by the arm and were led out the door into another room. I saw them without turning my head, as they were led away still naked. The Corpsman took their sea bags and buckets and followed them into the next room.

After everyone was inspected, again we were brought back to "Attention," and then SSgt Owens instructed all of us to reach into our bucket and grab our shower shoes and soap container. Then we were to reach into our sea bag and grab one towel. When that was finished, we were to put on our shower shoes, stand at attention with our towel over our right arm, and the soap dish in our right hand. Again, the DI's walked up and down each aisle yelling at recruits to move faster, to open their sea bag, to grab a towel. You would be surprised how hard it was for some of the recruits to complete such simple tasks.

Once everyone had their towel over their right arm, the soap dish in their right hand and their shower shoes on their feet, you could have heard a pin drop. Then the recruits were told they would take a shower to wash the loose hair from their haircut, wash the civilian stink off their body and soap down every inch of their body, before rinsing off. Then dry themselves, wrap the towel around their waist and return to their place in front of their cubicle.

One more thing, there was to be absolutely no talking from anyone under any circumstances. Anyone caught talking would regret it for the entire time at the depot. The order was given for the first row to head to the showers, and then the second row, followed by the third and so on. When you got to where the showers were located, you could hang your towel on hooks on the wall outside the entire length of the shower. There were 24 shower heads, so no one had to wait long for a shower, and there was a soap dish under each shower head to place your soap on.

This was probably the fastest shower anyone took in the Marines. The water was ice cold. There were a few screams and a few comments just from reflex action from the cold water. There were two Recruits who were cornered by the DI's for talking, screaming, or complaining, and these two recruits were also led away to the other room where the two recruits were led earlier for trying to conceal contraband. I made every effort not to make a sound as I walked under the ice-cold water and soaped myself as quickly as possible, then rinsed off faster than any shower I had ever taken.

After everyone showered and returned to their cubicle where their civilian clothes had been boxed for shipment home and their name was marked on the tape, the whole platoon was standing with a towel around their waist, soap dish in our right hand and shower shoes on our feet. The next command was to reach into their sea bag and grab our utility cover, a pair of white boxer shorts and place their web belt around their neck and stand back at attention.

The DI's exchanged covers with some recruits whose cover didn't fit, and then had us continue getting dressed in a white t-shirt, a pair of black socks, a yellow sweatshirt, one pair of utility trousers, a belt and the belt buckle we were issued, and the pair of white tennis shoes.

We were told to place our soap and shower shoes back in our bucket and our towel back in our sea bag. It took about 15 minutes for everyone to be dressed by themselves and not by the numbers, and again the DI's walked up and down the rows yelling as they went, and making comments to recruits who just didn't seem to follow direction or instructions well, especially those trying to lace up their tennis shoes.

Next, SSgt Owens told us to write our name and home address on the mailing label, or an address where we wanted our civilian clothes to be mailed. The DI's gave us two minutes to finish the task. There was a DI walking up and down each row watching as we wrote our labels, yelling as he went.

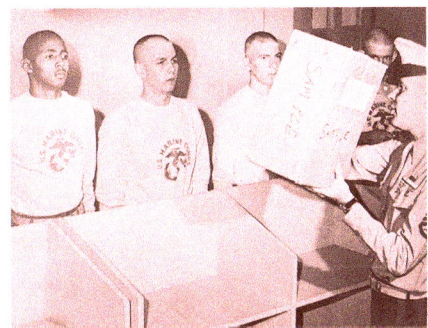

When you finished filling out your label, we were then told to take the address label and lick the glue on the back and stick the label on the front of the box and make sure the boxes were closed so no clothes would fall out of the box, then instructed to pass the box to our right until all boxes were collected and put into carts to be mailed to the addresses on the boxes.

We were then to take one step back and stand at attention, placing the marking pen to the right side of the cubicle. Again, the DI's walked up and down each row yelling and making sure instructions were followed. We were then told to take the piece of tape off the bench with our last name and place it on our sea bag, and were shown where it should go. As usual, there were guys who couldn't follow instructions and were either yelled at, slapped in the back of the head, or punched in the solar plexus.

By this time, it was around 0130 in the morning, and after everyone was dressed, the DI's had us turn to the left with the sea bag over our left shoulder and our bucket in our right hands, and from the front to the rear, the DI's double timed us down the stairs and outside to fall into formation. One recruit tripped on the stairs as he was running down them, and when he fell, he hurt his leg pretty badly. The

DI called for a Corpsman as the rest of the recruits passed him by. The corpsman called for an ambulance as the fallen recruit had a broken leg.

The entire platoon tried to remember exactly where they stood on the yellow footprints, because now there weren't any yellow footprints to stand on, and the guy you were standing next to didn't look like the guy you stood next to a couple of hours ago, plus we now had five recruits missing from the original formation and the DI's had their yelling down to a perfect pitch getting us organized.

Again we had the shorter man get behind the taller man until the Platoon of recruits was finally in the positions that the DI's wanted the Platoon in, with the tallest in the front and the shortest in the rear. The DI's were unhappy that we hadn't learned much in the four hours we'd spent at the depot and were told to face half right and again did another 25 pushups.

Now the Platoon is dressed all the same, green utility covers, yellow sweatshirts, green utility trousers, white tennis shoes and we all have a new green sea bag and a metal bucket. SSgt Owens turned over the Platoon to GySgt Wolfmule, Sgt James and Sgt Martinez. GySgt Wolfmule told the formation we had one more stop to make before we would end up at our new home while at the Depot.

GySgt Wolfmule attempted to march the Platoon of recruits in a military formation to another building about 200 yards away, with Sgt James and Sgt Martinez yelling and screaming the entire time. When we reached our next destination, we were ordered to place our sea bag on the ground by our left foot and carry our bucket in our right hand before we were to fall-out into another single file line. We then filed by and received a toothbrush and a plastic container to store it in, a razor, razor blades, a can of shaving cream, a vinyl pouch to carry our shaving gear and toiletries in, a small bottle of mouth wash, an inking kit, a scrub brush, a bottle of Wisk laundry soap, 2 padlocks and a red notebook.

After receiving our bucket issue, we were to fall back into formation and when the entire Platoon was back in formation, we were marched to another warehouse where we were issued a mattress, a pillow, two sheets, a pillowcase and two blankets. As I made my way through the line, I was given a mattress that was rolled up with the pillow in the middle and handed two blankets, one pillowcase and two bed sheets.

We all had our hands full as we tried to get back into the same formation. It shouldn't have been as hard as it turned out since we went in the warehouse in a single file and came out the same way we went in. It was apparent to me we were in for a long night.

Since I was one of the taller recruits, I was close to the front. I was actually the 2nd recruit to receive my gear, but I knew I was the second recruit in the 1st squad, so I knew exactly where to go when I came to get back to the for- mation. There were a few guys that had a tough time figuring out where their gear was. This confusion caused our DI's to be quite upset, so the yelling  and screaming and name calling continued and actually became scary.

When the entire Platoon of recruits figured out exactly where everyone was supposed to be, it was almost 0300 in the morning. Then GySgt Wolfmule had us face half left and get in the push-up position and we did push-ups for what seemed like an hour but was probably only 5 minutes. Once back on our feet, the yelling continued while we had to figure out how to carry a sea bag, a rolled-up mattress, two sheets, one pillowcase and two blankets, as well as a bucket to our next destination.

I put my blankets, sheets and pillowcase in my sea bag and carried it over my left shoulder. I carried the mattress with both hands in front of me and held my bucket in my right hand. It was amazing how many of the recruits had absolutely no common sense and had to be yelled at and ridiculed and dehumanized in order to do a simple task like putting their sea bag on the proper shoulder. If they didn't know their right from their left when it came to carrying a sea bag, we were in for a tough time.

To be honest, I thought if things kept going the way they have, Boot Camp would be a lot harder than it should be. I also learned that first night, that the DI's use what is known as the "mass punishment" process at recruit training. One person screws up and the entire platoon pays for it.

The entire time since I had gotten off the plane there was someone constantly yelling at us whether it was about moving faster, or staying in step or not writing fast enough, not undressing fast enough or not dressing fast enough, not showering fast enough or being quiet or not marching straight or not knowing how to carry everything we had to carry correctly. It had been a long day for all of us and I wondered if we were ever going to get to bed that night.

At around 0330, our formation finally made it to a row of Quonset huts which was to be our new home while we are at boot camp. Our Platoon was designated Platoon 2227. There were numerous rows of Quonset where our unit was billeted, and our platoon had four huts assigned to us plus one hut for the DI's. The sidewalk outside of our huts was known as Platoon Street.

When our Platoon reached our new Platoon Street, the four squads of our Platoon were each assigned a Quonset Hut. The 1st squad had 21 recruits and was in the Quonset across from the DI's duty hut, the second squad had 22 recruits and were in the next hut, the third squad had 22 recruits and were assigned the hut next to the DI's hut and the 4th squad had 22 recruits and was next to 3rd squad's hut.

We were now 87 recruits from the original 92. Two were bumped for trying to smuggle contraband, two were bumped for disobeying orders and acting like girls while taking our showers, but the one that was the most disturbing to me was the one who was hurt falling down the stairs breaking his leg and being transported to the base hospital. I found out later that once his leg healed, he would be placed in another Platoon and be able to complete boot camp.

As each squad went to their assigned hut, we were to choose our bunk beds. I chose the lower bunk just inside the door to the right. Under the bottom rack there were two-foot lockers, one for each bunk. The DI's had us roll out our mattress and pillow, hang our sea bags on the end of our bunks. We were to dump the items that were in our buckets into our footlockers and lock it with one of our padlocks and place the bucket under the lower bunk next to our footlocker.

Our sea bags were to be locked to the end of our bunks with the other pad lock we were issued. We then were to make our beds by putting on two sheets one blanket and the pillowcase on the pillow. By 0415 we were allowed to hit the rack and get some sleep. We were told to take off our new white tennis shoes, and our utility trousers and yellow T-shirt when we hit the rack to sleep. We were told to sleep in our white skivvies and a white t-shirt. In the morning when reveille sounds, we were to put on our utility trousers, yellow sweatshirt, a pair of black socks, our tennis shoes and our utility covers.

I kept my yellow sweatshirt on, and sloppily made my bunk so I could get some shut eye. Both Sgt James and Sgt Martinez were the DI's on duty our first night. Sgt James warned us all and said, "If I hear one peep out of any of these huts, if anyone talks, laughs or plays grab ass, the whole platoon will fall in on the platoon street and stand at attention until morning reveille." At 0415 the lights were turned out in our Huts and I think I was sleeping before my head hit the pillow.

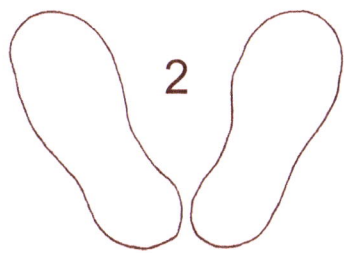

The First Morning

It seemed like I had just closed my eyes when I heard the bugle blow reveille and the DI's came into each hut yelling, "**Get up, get out of those racks and stand by your bunks**." Some Recruits didn't move as fast as Sgt James wanted and the yelling continued. Sgt James gave the instruction for all the Recruits to be wearing one pair of boxer skivvies, one white t-shirt, a pair of utility trousers with the web belt we were issued, the yellow sweatshirt, a pair of black socks, our tennis shoes, our utility cover, and to put our Red Notebooks in our left trouser pockets.

After we were dressed, we were ordered to report to Platoon Street. We were to "**Fall-In**" two single file ranks, one on the right side of the street and one on the left side. The ranks were to be the tallest to the front and the smallest to the rear.

It was 0500 Saturday morning in San Diego, and if I was home, it would be 8:00 A.M. and I would probably still be sleeping, or at least enjoying a hot cup of coffee instead of being yelled at and not knowing what was in store for me this day. I thought this was nuts.

There was total chaos in all four Quonset Huts while the Recruits tried to get dressed and organized. As the Recruits reported to Platoon Street, and "**Fall-In**" two single file lines, one on the right and one on the left of platoon street, they tried to line up the tallest to the front and the shortest to the rear. After one minute Sgt James started yelling to move it, move it, move it. All the recruits yelled, "**Sir, move it, Yes Sir.**"

After two minutes, only half of the recruits were on platoon street. Again, Sgt James yelled, "**You maggots have exactly 30 seconds to all be in formation on Platoon Street.**" The response was, "**Sir, Yes Sir.**" He began counting. "**15,14,13,12..........5, 4, 3, 2, 1.**" There were still a couple recruits not in formation, whether still trying to get dressed or not knowing what to do.

The Recruits standing on Platoon Street were standing at Attention and Sgt James ordered us to be Asshole to Belly button, which meant to be standing close to the man in front of you. However, we were still missing a couple of Recruits who were still not on Platoon Street and still in their huts, so now, there were consequences.

Sgt James had the recruits face half right or half left depending on which side of Platoon Street they were on, and then lean two, assume the push-up position. He made us do push-ups until every recruit was out of the huts and on platoon street. The four recruits who were the last to get out of their huts were made to stand while the rest of us did push-ups.

The DI would say, Down, and everyone would say, "**Sir, Down Sir.**" Then he would say, Up, and we answered, "**Sir, Up Sir,**" then he would say, Down, the answer was "**Sir, Down Sir.**" This continued UP, "**Sir, Up Sir.**" Down, "**Sir, Down Sir.**" Up, "**Sir, Up Sir.**" Down, "**Sir, Down Sir.**" for over 15 minutes. We must have done 50 push-ups.

The four recruits who were the last to "**Fall-In**" were standing watching as the rest of us did push-ups. The DI pointed out that we were doing pushups for the benefit of the four recruits standing. Each time someone fails to do what is required, he will be punished, but the rest of the platoon will be punishment as well. Then it is up to the platoon to square away recruits who don't follow orders.

Once Sgt James had us finish our push-ups, he told us to "**Fall-In**" one single file line right in the middle of Platoon Street instead of two lines. The entire platoon got into one single file line down the middle of our platoon street. Sgt James then commanded, "If the person in front of you is shorter than you, then change places. I want the taller man in front of the shorter man, Do it now and get Asshole to Belly button." This took about two to three minutes to get everyone lined up as perfectly and exactly as ordered. The whole time we were yelled at by both Sgt James and Sgt Martinez.

We were now standing in a single file line at attention facing the direction of the DI Duty Hut touching the person in front of you and being touched by the person behind you. Unfortunately it took two to three minutes too long to suit Sgt James. He made us stand there at attention for what seemed like half an hour. Reveille was at 0500, it was now close to 0545. So far the experience of being in Marine Corps Boot Camp was a big blur since we hadn't had any sleep for over 30 hours.

When Sgt James thought we had stood long enough, he had the whole platoon count off by two. One-Two, One-Two, One-Two, One-Two, until all 87 had sounded off. Sgt James then commanded, All "ones" move to the left side of Platoon Street, facing the front and stand at Attention. All the "two's" move to the right side of Platoon Street, also facing front, standing at Attention." Now the entire Platoon was standing at Attention in two lines again, the tallest at the front and the shortest toward the rear, and again Asshole to Belly button.

Sgt James then addressed the formation standing on the Platoon Street. He began, "This is what will be known as Platoon Street Formation." Every time you are ordered to "**Fall-In**" on the Platoon Street this is what it will look like. Know the person in front of you and the person behind you.

If you fail to "**Fall-In**" properly you will be dealt with severely. Do you understand?" We responded in unison, "**Sir, Yes Sir**."

Now that we knew where to stand when told to "**Fall-In**" on the Platoon Street, Sgt James told everyone to reach out with their left hand and touch the man in front of them on the shoulder. This caused people to push backwards, until what Sgt James commanded was done. Both formations adjusted the distance between themselves and the man in front of him, and Sgt James told us to always keep one arms distance between us every time we "**Fall-In**." Confusing, from Asshole to Belly button to an arms distance.

Sgt James now commanded the Platoon to stand at "**Attention**." He explained how the position of Attention should be executed. He began, "Place your left heel against your right heel and turn your feet at a 45-degree angle. Just like you stood on the Yellow Footprints. Keep your legs straight, but not stiff. Hips and shoulders level. Chest Lifted. Arms straight, but not stiff, your thumbs along the seams of your trousers with your fingers joined in their natural curl. Keep your head and body erect. Look straight ahead and keep your mouth closed and chin pulled in slightly. Stand still and never talk while in the position of Attention."

Sgt James then told Sgt Martinez to take charge of the platoon. Sgt Martinez told the formation, "When I give you the command you will "**About Face**." To execute an "**About Face**," there are two movements. First shift your weight to your left leg without a noticeable movement, then place your right toe half a foot behind and slightly to the left of your heel. Rest your weight evenly on the heel and ball of the right foot."

The second movement is to turn smartly to the right until facing the rear. The turn is made on the left heel and ball of the right foot. All movements are made from the position of attention. Sgt Martinez then commanded, "**About Face**." The entire Platoon attempted to "**About Face**," and the results were very chaotic. Sgt Martinez had us perform this movement another ten times, and it seemed to get better each time we attempted it.

After the tenth attempt to get it right we were again facing forward on the Platoon Street. Sgt James witnessed all our attempts to execute this movement and said out loud, "Well you can bet we will work on that." Sgt James then told Sgt Martinez to march us to the Grinder and get us in a Platoon Formation. Sgt Martinez gave us the command to "**About Face**," followed by the command to "**Forward March**."

When the command "**Forward March**," is given, you step off with your left foot on the command of "**March**," and then listen to the cadence of whoever is in charge. Sgt Martinez's cadence was "**Left, Right, Left, Right**," until we reached the Grinder. We marched until the entire 87 recruits were all on the Grinder, then Sgt Martinez gave the command, "**Platoon, Halt**." The command "**Halt**" is given on the left foot, we take one more step with the right foot and then bring the left foot even with the heel to heel at a 45-degree angle.

Sgt James was waiting on the "**Grinde**r" for Sgt Martinez to deliver the Platoon. Once the command of "**Platoon Halt**" was given, Sgt James then took charge of the Platoon and gave the following instructions. "You will now "**Fall-In**" in a "**Platoon Formation**" on me, which is exactly the Formation you were in while standing on the Yellow Footprints. When I give the command to "**Fall-In**," you will form four Ranks, tallest from the right smallest to the left. Do you understand me?" The entire Platoon answered, "**Sir, Yes Sir**."

"**Platoon, Fall-In**." So with that command, we fell out and began to "**Fall-In**" to a four-rank formation from our two single file columns, with Pvt Bowman as 1st Squad Leader, Pvt Herbert was 2nd Squad Leader, Pvt Mayers as 3rd Squad Leader and Pvt Wheeler as 4th Squad Leader. These were the four tallest recruits in our Platoon. The rest of the Platoon was trying to remember where they stood last night.

With a little help from Sgt Martinez, it took about two minutes to form four ranks by height, with the tallest to the right and the shorter to the left. Sgt James made a few adjustments by moving a few recruits from the third squad to the second and the first to the second and one from the third to the fourth before he was satisfied we were in the proper Platoon Formation.

Sgt James stood three paces from the formation, in front of the 11th recruit in the first squad which was about the center of the formation. He then said, "This is our Platoon Formation, stick out your left arms to touch the recruit to your left, and turn your head to the right and align yourself. Squad leaders keep facing forward." He informed us that this was now known as "**Dress Right, Dress.**" The four Squad Leaders stuck out their left arms to touch the recruit to their left, as the recruit moved right to touch his right shoulder to the fingers on the left hand of the recruit to his right, and this was done with every recruit in all four Squads.

"Whenever you are told to "**Fall-In**" anywhere other than on Platoon Street, this is the formation you will "**Fall-In**". There are four Squads, remember exactly what Squad you are in and who is to your right and your left. You will spend half your day in this formation. This formation is how you will get from one location to another. This morning you civilian pukes will be marched to morning chow. Before we go to chow, we will go through some close order drill commands."

"The first movement will be "**Right Face**," which is executed in two counts. The entire Platoon tried to follow Sgt James commands by the numbers, and we practiced both "**Right Face**" and "**Left Face**" about five times. The entire Platoon attempted a "**Right Face**". Then the command was "**Left Face.**" Again the entire Platoon turned back to where we started. Sgt James explained how to execute each movement. For example, the "**Right Face**" was executed by pivoting on the right heel and the ball of your left foot then bringing your left foot forward with heels together in a 45 degree angle. "**Left Face**" was just the opposite, using the left heel and the right ball of the foot.

After we Practiced some of our close order drill for about a half hour, Sgt James called the Platoon to "**Attention**" and then "**Right Face**," and in Platoon Formation, "**Forward, March**." We were on our way to the 2nd Battalion Mess Hall to eat our first Marine Corps breakfast. When we arrived at the Mess Hall, Sgt James called the Platoon to "**Halt**" and then had the first and second squads form a single file line in front of the Mess Hall on the left, then had the 3rd and 4th squads form a single file in front of the Mess Hall to the right and stand in line for morning chow.

We stood at "**Attention**" as we moved through the line to enter the Mess Hall. Sgt James told us to take a metal tray off the stack, plus a fork, knife and spoon from the bins and either a coffee cup or a glass or both and set the tray down on the serving line. He told us to continue to stand at "**Attention**" and side step through the chow line. As we move to our left through the chow line we would hold our trays up so the servers could place food on our tray as you passed from right to left.

Our first breakfast consisted of, scrambled eggs, bacon, sausage, fried potatoes, oatmeal, grits, fruit, toast, milk, juice, coffee. You took what you wanted by putting your tray in front of the server at each station. There was a sign over the door of the Mess Hall as you entered, "Take all you want, But eat all you take." When you reached the end of the chow line, Sgt Martinez guided us to a bunch of tables with benches to sit on. We could seat twelve recruits on each side of the tables. On each table was salt, pepper, and hot sauce. We were told to find a spot and to stand at "**Attention**" until told to sit.

There were 24 Recruits to a table, so with 87 recruits, we filled up three and a half tables. We were told to stand at "**Attention**," until given permission to sit. When the entire platoon was standing at their table, Sgt Martinez yelled,

"**Seats,**" and the entire platoon responded, "**Sir, Seats, Yes Sir,**" and sat down with a bang in unison. Sgt Martinez told us we had 20 minutes to eat our breakfast and told us to begin.

I didn't realize just how hungry I was until I took the first fork full of my scrambled eggs. As we ate, other platoons went through the Mess Hall and went through the same process as our platoon. They stood at Attention until their D I gave them the command to "**Sit.**" I tried not to gawk or look around while I ate. My breakfast was gone in no time and my tray was totally clean. After my food was gone, I sat there at "**Attention**" waiting for the next command.

When 20 minutes were up, Sgt Martinez walked up to our tables and said, "Platoon 2227, On your feet and exit the chow hall." We responded, "**Sir, Yes Sir,**" and got up and moved out. We were told to dump any food left on our tray into the garbage cans before leaving the Mess Hall and then place our trays, glasses, cups and silverware onto the dishwashing station just inside the door. I don't think anyone had anything left on their trays.

Once we finished morning chow, we were told to "**Fall-In**" Platoon Formation outside the Mess Hall to be marched back to our Platoon Street to enjoy our first Head Call. Once we were back on Platoon Street, Sgt Martinez had us "**Fall-In**". Everyone scrambled to remember where they were supposed to be standing and who they were supposed to be standing behind. When the chaos ended everyone was facing forward at "**Attention.**"

Sgt James didn't like the speed in which the platoon followed the last command, so he said," "**Lean Two**" (*get in the "Push Up" position*). The left column turned half right and the right column turned half left and the entire platoon responded. "**Sir, Lien Two, Yes Sir.**" The Platoon got down in the push up position. Sgt James said, "**Down.**" We answered, "**Sir, Down Sir,**" Up, "**Sir, Up Sir,**" Down, "**Sir, Down Sir**", this continued for another 15 minutes.

Sgt James and Sgt Martinez walked throughout the recruits yelling at us to, "**Get your knees off the deck**", kicking guys who weren't doing it right, constantly yelling that we were lazy, soft, civilian pukes. Then after he thought we had enough, he yelled, "**Fall-In**," again everyone jumped up and found their position on the Platoon Street, got their distance and stood at attention.

While we stood at attention, Gunny Sgt Wolfmule came from the Duty Hut with a RED magic marker. He started at the front of the left column on platoon street and marked the number 1 on the recruits yellow sweatshirt. He then marked the next recruit number 2, and so on until he had marked all the recruits sweatshirts in the left column of Platoon Street ending with the number 44.

Any recruit who looked down to see what the Gunny was doing, got hit in the stomach by the Gunny with an explanation of, "Who told you to move, keep your eyes straight ahead." When he finished with the last recruit on the left, he continued with the last recruit on the right side of platoon street. Before marking the next recruit, he said, "If you move or eye ball fuck me, I'll rip your head off your neck." He then continued to mark the next recruit as being 45. He continued until he had marked every recruit in the right column. My number was 85 as I was the 5th tallest recruit in our platoon.

Gunny then talked with Sgt James and Sgt Martinez for a few minutes and then he told Sgt James to "**Carry On**" with the "**Plan of the Day**," and left the Platoon Street. Sgt James told the first two recruits in the left column marked with the Number one and number two on their sweatshirts to go into their Hut and carry out Recruit Number 1's rack and bring it onto the Platoon Street. He then had Number 6 and 7 go into the Hut and bring out Number 6's Rack and carry it onto Platoon Street. Our bunks were referred to as our "*Rack*."

A "**Rack**" (*Metal Bunk Bed held together with bolts, with springs for the base and a 4-inch mattress*). The bottom rack was 24 inches off the floor and the top rack was five feet off the floor. Once both the racks were delivered to the Platoon Street, Sgt James and Sgt Martinez had everyone crowd around both racks to observe how a rack is made up. The "**Rack**" had an upper and a lower mattress, and each had two sheets, a pillow with pillow case and two blankets.

Sgt James proceeded to make the first upper bunk according to regulations and began by laying the first sheet on the mattress making sure there was enough sheet to tuck under the top of the mattress, and enough to tuck under the foot of the mattress. By tucking the sheet under the mattress on both sides at the top of the mattress, he made a 45 degree fold with the side of the sheet making what is called, "hospital corners," then tucked the sheet under the mattress repeating the same procedure at the foot of the mattress making hospital corners on both sides at the foot of the bed.

He then laid the second sheet on top of the first sheet making it even with the top of the mattress and leaving the same amount of sheet to hang over on both sides centered on the mattress. Next, he laid the first blanket on top of the second sheet, lining it up with the top of the mattress with the top of the second sheet equal on both sides.

With the blanket and second sheet even with the top of the mattress, he made a four-inch fold with the second sheet and blanket together, folding them three times. By making the fold exactly 4 inches wide, the first sheet and blanket were now 12 inches from the top of the mattress. Then he tucked the fold with blanket and second sheet under the mattress firm and tight. The foot of the mattress has the blanket and sheet tucked under and folded with hospital corners.

The pillowcase was put on the pillow, then centered on the mattress and laid even with the 12-inch fold. Then the second blanket was folded in half and laid over the pillow at the head of the bed and tucked in tightly. The second blanket was known as a duster. When made properly, the top blanket should be tucked in tightly so you should be able to bounce a quarter off the bed. At the end of the bunk facing right on the frame, you place a towel that is folded in half long ways and laid two inches from the left side of the bunk with a washcloth on top of the towel and equal to the fold.

After Sgt James made up the upper bunk, Sgt Martinez made up the second upper Rack exactly the same as Sgt James. Because there were 87 Recruits, everyone needed to see how they were made up. Once everyone had a chance to see how to make the upper Rack, Sgt James and Sgt Martinez made up the lower Racks again exactly like the upper except, the head of the Rack on the upper always faced to the right, and the bottom Rack was just the opposite and faced to the left.

So when all the bunks are made, all the bottom bunks would face to the left and all the top bunks would face to the right. The towels and wash cloths would be hanging at the end of all bunks on the end of the right bunk frame as you looked at each rack. The towels and wash cloths would always be to the left of the frame of both the top and bottom bunks.

Once Sgt James and Sgt Martinez had made up both the top and bottom bunk, he had the Recruits whose bunk they had just made up, return their Rack back to the Hut that it was taken from and then had us "**Fall-In**" on the Platoon Street. Except for the possible one hour sleep we got last night, all of us had been up for over 30 hours.

When the two recruits returned to the Formation on Platoon Street, Sgt James made a point to tell the entire platoon that he had hoped we had paid attention to how he made both Racks. He told us when we were dismissed, we would "**Fall-Out**," back into our Huts, and we had 30 minutes to make our Racks the way he just showed us, and when our rack was made we would "**Fall-In**" back on the Platoon Street. He then gave the command to "**Fall-Out**."

Again, nothing but chaos as everyone made their way to his Hut and began to make their bunk the way Sgt James and Sgt Martinez showed us that morning. We were told No Talking and reminded we only had 30 minutes to complete the task of making our racks. Time ticked away, as everyone was busy trying to make his rack as well as they had been instructed. Once finished making his Rack, each recruit made his way back to the Platoon Street to "**Fall-In**" and stood where he believed his spot was on the Platoon Street at "**Attention**".

With less than a minute left in the time we were given, Sgt Martinez counted, 15, 14, 13, 12, ...4, 3, 2, 1. Surprisingly, everyone had returned to the Platoon Street. GySgt Wolfmule came out of the DI Duty Hut and made his way to the Platoon Street and stood next to Sgt James. Sgt

James then told everyone that once he put us **"At Ease**," we were to take our Red Notebook out of our pockets and study our General Orders.

There were at least seven or eight Recruits who did not have their Red Notebooks in their pockets. Gunny had the entire Platoon **"Lien Two**," and the Recruits who didn't have their Red Notebooks were told to go into their Huts and get them and **"Fall-In"** as the rest of the Platoon did pushups.

When the Recruits returned, they got down and did push-ups with the rest of the Platoon as Gunny yelled and made sure he knew who the eight recruits were who didn't have their notebooks. After 10 minutes and at least 50 pushups, Gunny got us back on our feet and back into Formation. He then Commanded, **"Platoon, Attention,"** and then Sgt James and Gunny Wolfmule walked into the first Hut to Inspect how well we made our Racks.

At least ten minutes passed while we stood studying our Red Notebooks. Gunny Wolfmule walked out of the 1st Hut and walked directly towards the second Hut, as Sgt James walked to the front of the Platoon Street and said, "Pvt Rilley, identify yourself." I held up my right hand and said, **"Sir, I'm Pvt Rilley Sir**." He told me to **"Fall-Out"** and stand in front of him. I left my position on Platoon Street and ran over to where he was and stopped in front of him.

Sgt James grabbed me by the throat and said, "Don't you know how to Report yet Private?" I found it hard to answer with his fingers digging into my throat but managed to say, **"Sir, No Sir**." He let go of my throat and then said, "Anytime you are given an order to Report Private, you stand at Attention and yell out, your last name and say you are Reporting. Do you understand me Pvt." I answered, **"Sir, Yes Sir**." He punched me in the gut and then said, "Then Report properly Private." I stood tall at **"Attention"** and answered, **"Sir, Private Rilley Reporting, Sir**." He then said, "That's better." He then addressed the formation, "Everyone who bunks in Hut #1, step into the middle of the Platoon Street."

He then grabbed me again, but by my sweatshirt this time. Although I was probably six or seven inches taller than Sgt James, he turned me around so everyone from Hut #1 standing in the middle of Platoon Street could see who I was and he said, "This is Private Rilley, he is now in charge of Hut #1. I want all you maggots from Hut #1 to put away your notebooks and **"Fall-Out"** and go to your Hut and stand by your Rack." He then yelled, **"Do it Now."** The 20 Recruits standing in the middle of Platoon Street answered loudly, **"Sir, Yes Sir,"** and ran to Hut #1.

When all 20 recruits returned to Hut #1, every rack was torn up with bedding laying on the deck except one. Each recruit stood next to their rack, Sgt James grabbed me again by the back of my neck and said, "Private Rilley, is in charge of this Hut, he will show you how to make your racks, and you have just 45 minutes to re-make your racks and **"Fall-In"** on the Platoon Street. "Do you understand me?" Hut #1 responded, **"Sir, Yes Sir."** Sgt James said, **"I can't hear you."** We responded again, louder this time, **"Sir, Yes Sir."** He then left and all the recruits in Hut #1 began re-making all the racks with my help.

My Rack was the only one still made and not thrown on the floor. I guess making my bed at home every morning paid off. The fact that Sgt James put me in-charge of Hut #1, was the first recognition that I did something right and impressed my Drill Instructor without my having to volunteer. I thought I better take this responsibility seriously, and help those that weren't doing it right, make their Rack. There were a couple of Recruits that got it right, but there were a couple that had no concept of how to make their Rack. I almost had to make some Racks totally myself. Not having a watch, we had to guess at the time.

After Sgt James left Hut #1, he walked into Hut #2 and witnessed the same mess he witnessed in Hut #1. All the racks but one were thrown all over the deck of the hut. Gunny Wolfmule left Hut #2 and made his way to Hut #3. Sgt

James left Hut #2 and went back to the platoon street and ordered Private Havranek to identify himself. Learning from what had happened to me earlier, Pvt Havranek fell out of Formation and stood in front of Sgt James and said, "**Sir, Private Havranek, Reporting as Ordered Sir.**"

Sgt James then ordered all recruits who occupy Hut #2 to stand in the middle of the Platoon Street. He then grabbed Havranek by the sweatshirt and turned him around so the recruits standing in the middle of Platoon Street could see who he was and said, "This is Private Havranek, he will be in-charge of Hut #2. All you maggots in Hut #2, '**Fall-Out**' and go stand by your Rack." The 21 Recruits in the middle of Platoon Street responded, "**Sir, Yes Sir**," and took off running to Hut #2.

This process continued through Hut #3 and Hut #4. Private Gagnon was chosen to be in-charge of Hut #3 and Private Wilson was chosen for Hut #4. After all four Huts had been ravaged by Gunny Wolfmule, the Recruits worked feverously to get all their Racks remade within the 45 minute time limit given by Gunny Wolfmule. The four Recruits who were chosen to be in-charge of each Hut worked with their Recruits to re-make their Racks correctly.

Not knowing the time, after all the racks in Hut #1 were re-made, all the recruits in Hut #1 returned and "Fell-In" on the Platoon Street. Sgt James came to the front of Platoon Street and yelled, "You have just one minute to finish and Fall-In on Platoon Street." Then we heard him counting, "10, 9, 8, 7, 6, 5, 4, 3, 2, 1." As he was counting, Recruits were running from all three Huts finding their place on Platoon Street. It was a mad dash, with everyone in formation as Sgt James yelled ONE.

When all the Recruits were back in Formation on Platoon Street, Gunny Wolfmule told Sgt James he would re-inspect the Huts and our Racks while we were at noon chow. Apparently there wasn't enough time left in the morning training schedule to stand inspection again, so

Sgt James told Sgt Martinez to take us to noon chow and afterwards return us to the Platoon Street. We repeated the same procedure that we went through for morning chow.

Once outside the Mess Hall, we were split into two single file lines and then proceeded through the chow line. The procedure of grabbing our metal trays for noon chow was the same as we went through for morning chow. For lunch they were serving meat loaf, mashed potatoes, green beans, gravy for the meatloaf, bread and butter, peaches, Jello, milk, iced tea or water. Once through the chow line, we again stood at our table until we were told to sit.

We again were allowed 20 minutes to eat and then Sgt Martinez told us to finish up and get out. We left our metal trays and silverware at the dishwashing station before leaving the mess hall and **"Fell-In"**. We had already experienced a full day and it was only 1245. I was tired since only having one hour sleep, and glad there was no down time, or I wouldn't have been able to keep my eyes open.

After noon chow when Sgt Martinez had us back on Platoon Street, Sgt James told us to return to our Huts. If you Rack was torn up you have 30 minutes to remake it and stand at Attention next to your Rack. If your Rack hasn't been torn up retrieve your sea bag, your footlocker, your bucket and **"Fall-In"** back on the Platoon Street. The entire Platoon ran to their individual Huts to see if their rack had been torn up and then retrieve their gear and get to the Platoon Street.

To my surprise there was not one rack torn up in Hut #1. I unlocked my sea bag from my Rack and put it over my left shoulder, I placed my bucket on top of my footlocker and carried them out onto the Platoon Street. Again, there was total chaos in all four Huts retrieving all our gear and falling in on the Platoon Street. All the time Sgt James and Sgt Martinez were yelling at us to get the lead out and to get in formation.

Not one Rack had been torn up, allowing all Recruits to follow Sgt James instructions and report with all our gear to the Platoon Street. Once all the Recruits were on both sides of the Platoon Street, he gave us instructions to face inward to the middle of Platoon Street, place our footlocker at our feet and set our bucket on the ground behind our footlocker. Then Sgt James had us take a seat on our buckets and remove the padlock off our footlockers

After taking our seats on our bucket, it took a little time to get all the combination locks open on our footlockers; we were given two padlocks, one for our footlocker and one for our sea bag, and each had a different combination. Some of the recruits had trouble with their combinations.

Sgt James was going to tell us where everything we were issued was supposed to go in our footlockers, so he told us to listen closely to all the instructions we were about to get. Last night when we arrived at our Hut, we were told to just dump the contents of our bucket issue into the bottom of our footlocker and then lock it with one of the combination padlocks.

Sgt James told us to take the items we dumped last night from our buckets, and put them by our feet. Each footlocker was 18 inches tall, 16 inches deep, 24 inches long and 18 inches wide with a 4-inch tray that sat on the inside. It had a hinged latch that we could use to lock with a padlock to secure our contents. Sgt James told us to open our footlocker and remove the 4-inch tray and lay it on the ground next to our bucket.

Now with the tray on the ground, at our feet, Sgt James told us where to place each item in our footlocker, one at a time by the numbers. The items that we dumped into our footlockers last night will now be placed in our footlockers properly. He said, "First, place the scrub brush and the inking kit on the right side of the tray. Next, place your green Marine Corps handbook, and red notebook on the left side of the tray and place your shower shoes by your feet."

Once all the footlockers were checked to make sure all items were where they were supposed to be, Sgt James then told us to pick up our inking kit and to close our footlockers and to sit back down on your buckets. Sgt James then had us assemble the inking kit by the numbers on top of our footlockers. Everything we did was done by the numbers so everyone did everything the same at the same time.

Sgt James and Sgt Martinez walked up and down the Platoon Street making sure we were doing it properly. The ink kit had all the letters of the alphabet, and some letters had more than one, i.e. there were three A's, three I's two R's, two S's, etc. The instructions were to assemble your Stamp pad with your Last Name, and then your first and middle initials only. The top of the stamp had a handle making it easy to hold as you used it to stamp your name on all your uniforms.

Once all the ink stamps had been properly assembled, Sgt James had us open the black indelible ink pad and lay it on the footlocker next to the stamp. "Now take your sea bags and dump the contents onto the ground between your feet."

Next we were to take out one pair of boxers shorts and lay them on our footlocker. Sgt James and Sgt Martinez were walking up and down the Platoon Street to insure we were following instructions. Then, by the numbers, we marked our names on the bottom of the right leg of our boxer shorts.

It was inevitable that someone would put their inking kit together wrong. There were two individuals who apparently didn't listen or couldn't follow instructions properly, and put their names on the ink stamps backwards and two others who had their names upside down. Sgt James had them do 25 pushups while the rest of us watched, and luckily they only stamped one pair of boxer shorts with their mistake. Sgt James had to fix the mistake on their stamp before moving on to stamping our next item.

With the mistakes fixed, we finished marking our boxer shorts, then the t-shirts on the back inside of the neck. We stamped our names on our utility blouses over the right pocket and on the waist band of the utility trousers. We stamped our name on the utility cover on the inside of the headband. We stamped our name on the inside of the web belt, buckle side as near the end as possible.

We stamped our name on our sea bag near the handle. We stamped the inside tongue of our tennis shoes, and our Red PT shorts as well as our yellow sweatshirts. We then marked our Towels at the bottom right on both towels and also on our wash cloths on the bottom right. We marked our shower shoes, and there would be more items to be marked once other gear was issued.

He showed us how to fold and place your sea bag, in the right corner in the bottom of your footlocker. We then folded our utility trousers and utility shirts and place them on top of the sea bag. Sgt James continued, "Next place your red PT shorts in the bottom left corner, and fold and place your boxer shorts and t-shirts in top left corner of your footlocker. Place your socks between your sea bag and your boxer shorts and t-shirts." When we were all finished marking our clothing with our new stamp pads, we placed each item back into our footlocker in the designated space.

"You are to take your small vinyl bag and insert your shaving cream, razor, razor blades, toothpaste, toothbrush container, soap dish, and mouth wash. Then, place your shaving kit on the right side of your tray. Next, place your shower shoes in the lower right side of your footlocker."

"Once you have finished placing all of your items properly in your footlocker, place the tray back in the footlocker." Sgt James then said, "Once you have completed this, stand up." When everyone was standing, Sgt Martinez walked up the left side of Platoon Street checking to ensure each Recruit followed directions. Sgt James walked up the right side checking the other half of the Platoon.

Sgt James told us we would always use the black ink on everything we marked unless the item or article or piece of equipment was black. Then we would use the white indelible Ink for marking things like socks. There was a specific location for your name on each article of clothing or equipment, and every location was shown in the Marine Handbook.

Sgt James had one hut at a time return our footlockers and buckets to our huts and place both the footlockers and buckets under our racks. The person who occupied the lower rack, but his footlocker under his pillow side of his Rack and the person on the upper rack had his footlocker under the opposite side of the lower rack which would put it on the same side as his pillow.

Once all the footlockers were returned to our huts, Sgt James had Sgt Martinez "**Fall-In**" the Platoon-on-Platoon Street. Apparently we took too long to Fall-In, so Sgt James had us "**Lien Two**." He yelled and screamed as we did pushups, Sgt Martinez yelled and screamed as we did pushups, and so we continued to do pushups for the next 30 minutes.

Sgt James had us "**Fall-In**" on the Platoon Street, and again, it took too long for us to get in position to satisfy Sgt James, so he had us "**Lien Two**" once again. We continued to do pushup, "**Down**," "**Sir, Down Sir**," "**Up**," "**Sir, Up Sir**," "**Down**," "**Sir, Down Sir**," "**Up**," "**Sir, Up Sir**."

By the time we finished doing pushups, it was time for evening chow. Our Platoon as well as the other three platoons in our training series were scheduled for evening chow at 1745. Our Platoon was marched over to the 2nd Battalion Mess Hall and we went through the same routine as we did for morning and noon chow. I was starving and was hoping evening chow was better than the meatloaf we had for lunch.

To my surprise, evening chow was a choice between breaded pork chops, or fried chicken, diced potatoes, corn or peas, salad, dinner rolls, apple sauce, milk, iced tea, coffee, water, and chocolate pudding. I will never forget my first evening meal at Boot Camp. Although I wasn't a big fan of the meatloaf we had for lunch, I was surprised at how good the food was that we were being served for dinner.

After Evening chow, the platoon didn't march very well back to the platoon area, so when we were standing in Formation on Platoon Street, Sgt Martinez had us "**Lien Two**." We did pushups for what seemed like an hour, but in reality it was only 30 minutes.

That first day seemed like an eternity, and I don't remember ever doing so many pushups, but I had many more pushups in store for me in the days, weeks and months ahead. Our first day ended with what came to be known as "**Commanders Time**". We went to the "Head" and washed up and brushed our teeth before hitting the Rack.

Lights out at 2200, and as soon as we heard the first notes of Taps being played over the Base loud speaker I hoped our first full day of boot camp was over. Sgt James made his way through every hut and told us no grab ass, no goofing off, no talking and the only time we were to get out of our rack was to go to the Head. If we disobeyed any of the instructions he gave us, he told us we would stand at "**Attention**" on Platoon Street until Reveille.

Reveille would be at 0500 and when we got up we would put on our red PT shorts, yellow sweatshirts, socks and tennis shoes along with our utility cover and "**Fall-In**" on the Platoon Street.

We were all so tired, we were all sleeping as soon as the lights went out and our heads hit the pillows. It was 2200 hrs. (10:00 P.M in civilian time), and after our first full day on the Depot, it felt like two days long. I was looking forward to seven hours of uninterrupted sleep.

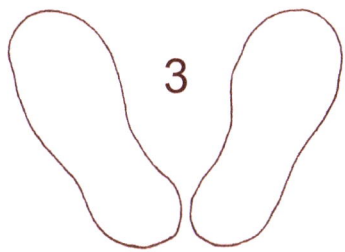

The Nightmare Continues

Exactly at 0500 Reveille was a loud and distinct sound we would hear every morning all through Boot Camp, and as I learned later, it was also heard on every Marine Corps Base everywhere at exactly 0500. At the first note I was awake and immediately out of my Rack as Sgt James and Sgt Martinez were in and out of all four Huts yelling and screaming making sure we were up and out of our Racks, and dressing in our PT gear wearing our utility covers as instructed.

Once dressed, everyone ran out of their Huts to "**Fall-In**" on their designated position on Platoon Street. Once everyone was out of their Huts and in formation, Sgt Martinez had the Platoon count off. So we began with the first person on the Platoon Street yelling, "One Sir," then "Two Sir," continuing down the left hand Rank until we heard, "44 Sir." And then from the rear on the right-hand Rank, "45 Sir," continuing until we heard, "87 Sir."

Sgt Martinez reported to Sgt James, "Platoon 2227 is all present and accounted for." Sgt James answered, "**Very Well**." Then Sgt James said, "When I say, "**Fall Out**," you go to the Head and make a Head Call, then return to your Huts, grab your duster off your Rack and fall back-in on Platoon Street. There is to be no talking and I want you to double time. Do you maggots hear me?" The Platoon replied in unison, **"Sir, Yes Sir."** Sgt James then said, **"Fall Out."** "**Sir, Fall Out, Yes Sir."**

The entire Platoon headed directly to the Head to make a morning Head Call and afterwards returned to our Huts. There was total chaos again as every recruit went into their Hut to get their blanket and then return to Platoon Street. Both our DI's yelled the entire time, from the time we were told to **"Fall Out"** until everyone was back on both sides of Platoon Street at Attention. Each recruit was told to hold their blanket under their left arm.

While the entire platoon was back on Platoon Street at **"Attention"**, Sgt James gave the command, **"About Face."** Some did it properly and others just turned around. Sgt James again observed the Recruits not executing the **"About Face"** properly, and let it be known in an angry tone, "We will have to work on that" and then gave the command to **"Forward March."**

We all marched forward in two single files towards the end of Platoon Street. At the end of our Platoon Street was a walkway that separated all the Quonset Huts from the **"Grinder."**

The **"Grinder"** (The large Parade Ground, known as the "Parade Deck" made out of asphalt that was a half mile long and just over 200 yards wide and known as the "Grinder.") was directly at the end of our Platoon Street.

The MCRD occupies 506 acres of land next to the San Diego Airport. The Parade Deck, or "**Grinder**" is known as Shepherd Memorial Field named after Gen. Samuel Shephard, 20th Commandant of the Marine Corps, who had a very distinguished Marine Corps career. To this day, there is a protocol followed regarding the Parade Deck. No civilians are ever allowed on the parade deck. No Marine is allowed on the parade deck out of uniform.

Our Platoon arrived at the "**Grinder**" in two ranks, Sgt James had each of us pair up with another recruit and had us lay our blankets on the "Grinder." One for a recruit to kneel on and one under the other recruit to sit on. We began with sit-ups, with one recruit doing the sit-ups and the other recruit holding down his feet. After five minutes we would switch positions, with the recruit doing sit-ups now holding the feet of the other recruit. Since we had an odd number, Sgt Martinez held the feet of the odd recruit as he did sit-ups.

After sit-ups, we all did push-ups together, using the blanket to put our hands on. We did push-ups by the numbers as a four count exercise, down was always one and up was the two count, down was a three count and up kept track of the number of push-ups we did. Normally we were given a number to exercise. As an example the DI in charge would say, "25 push-ups, cadence count, ready exercise."

We would then say, "1,2,3, one Sir, and then 1,2,3, two Sir, followed by 1,2,3, three Sir, and we would continue until we counted to 25." After 25 push-ups, we would stop and come to "**Attention**" unless while counting the DI would stop us and make us start over, which happened many times.

We also did jumping jacks and they were also a four count exercise and counted as, 1,2,3 one Sir, 1,2,3, two Sir, 1,2,3,three Sir, and so forth and normally was counted up to 25 repetitions. We then did bends and thrusts.

Bends and thrusts were also a four-count exercise, starting in a standing position, squat down bending your knees placing your hands on the deck then, kick your feet out into a push-up position keeping your back straight. Quickly reverse the motion to return to the starting position. That's one rep. This exercise is counted as, 1,2,3, one Sir, 1,2,3, two Sir, 1,2,3, three Sir, and continue until the repetition number is met and was normally 25 repetitions.

This ordeal of doing PT was repeated every morning the entire time at boot camp. Seven days a week regardless of the weather. After morning PT, we returned to our platoon area, we would remove our PT shorts, our yellow sweatshirts, and only wearing our boxer shorts, put on our shower shoes, take our shaving kit, a towel and a wash cloth and were directed to the Head at the opposite end of the Platoon Street.

Each Platoon had their own Head which included 24 toilets, 12 urinals, 24 sinks with mirrors and 30 shower heads. We would then make a morning head call, shave, shower and return to our Hut, put on a clean t-shirt, a pair of socks, utility trousers, yellow sweatshirt, tennis shoes, utility cover and then make our Racks. We'd place our wet towels on the end of our Racks with the wash cloth on top of the towel and then "**Fall-In**" on Platoon Street.

That second morning, because we were the newest recruits on station, we were first to go to morning chow. Our Platoon was 2227 and assigned to FOX Company. There were three additional platoons in FOX Company, all new recruits and the four platoons made up a Training Series. The other Platoons were 2225, 2226 and 2228. All four platoons have the exact identical training schedule the entire time of Boot Camp. We will compete with each Platoon for streamers and honors as well as for the Best Platoon during Boot Camp.

Our Platoon followed the same routine going to morning chow as we had done the day before. When we arrived at the 2nd Battalion Mess Hall, all four platoons in our series waited for morning chow. Each day we rotated as to what platoon would go first. Each platoon would line up in two single file lines and stand "asshole to belly button" as it was called, and follow one another into the chow hall. Each platoon would sit where their DI would assign them. We very seldom sat at the same tables depending on whether we were first, second, third or fourth in line to eat.

While we waited for our turn to enter the Mess Hall for chow whether it was morning, noon or night, we would study our Red Notebooks and Gunny Wolfmule made it clear we had just two weeks to memorize our 11 General Orders. The Red Notebooks held much information that we needed to learn during our time at MCRD. The 11 General Orders were the most important to know as they would apply to us every day the entire time in the Marine Corps.

The Command structure of our Platoon was GySgt Wolfmule as our Platoon Commander, Sgt James was the Senior Drill Instructor and Sgt Martinez was the Junior Drill Instructor. Each day, one or more of them would be on Duty, depending on what the Training Day looked like. One of them or more than one would always be on Duty at night and would sleep in the Duty Hut. For the next eleven weeks, I would come to know each of them intimately.

On our second day at MCRD, we stood in line to enter the Mess Hall. Something we didn't pay much attention to on day one, as there was no need to, but there was a mirror on both sides of the mess hall entrance just before you entered. We hadn't been taught the proper way to salute yet, but on day four of Boot Camp we would have a class on saluting.

The Tradition was when you reached the mirror before entering the Mess Hall, you would either turn half right or half left to face the mirror depending on which line you were in, standing at "**Attention**", face the mirror and render a hand salute looking at yourself making sure you rendered the salute properly and were to say, "**Good Morning, Sir**," or "**Good Afternoon Sir**," or "**Good Evening Sir**," depending on which meal you were attending, then enter the Mess Hall. You would then remove your cover before entering the Mess Hall and stick the brim behind your back into your trousers. This was repeated at every meal three times a day, every day at Boot Camp.

After morning chow, we were marched back to our Platoon area and "**Fell-In**" on Platoon Street. The Platoon Street is where we would "**Fall-In**" at least 8 times a day, so it was important we knew where we were to stand. When everyone was at attention, the DI's would keep us at Attention for about ten minutes, sometimes more, and if they wanted to mess with our heads they would have us do push-ups for ten additional minutes or more, depending on who was on Duty and what kind of day we were having.

While standing on the Platoon Street on Day two and after our usual stint of doing push-ups, Sgt James had the Duty during the day and disclosed that we still needed additional gear to be issued, so after attempting some "Close Order Drill," we were to be marched over to another warehouse behind the Administration building. We actually were going to be marched across the "**Grinder**," in broad daylight our second day on the Depot.

We were in a Platoon formation of four Squads attempting to march. After assigning four Recruits to be In-Charge of each Hut, Sgt James had the same four Recruits he chose to line up in Platoon Formation as Squad Leaders. I was the 1st Squad Leader, Pvt Havranek was 2nd Squad Leader, Pvt Gagnon was 3rd Squad Leader and Pvt Wilson was 4th Squad Leader. I have to admit, as we attempted to march, we looked pretty sloppy while we were marched across the "**Grinder**." We were passed by other Platoons marching in Formation, some with rifles and other Platoons without.

We were dressed in our yellow sweatshirts, utility trousers and tennis shoes. The Platoons that passed us by were dressed in starched utilities, spit shined boots and looked like Marines. We looked like a group of clowns, dressed like the recruits that we were.

Once our Platoon arrived on the other side of the "**Grinder**," Sgt James had us "**Halt**." Sgt James had the platoon face half left and "**Lien Two**," and we did push-ups for ten minutes. As we were doing push-ups, he told us we resembled a heard of cows and we were embarrassing him. It wasn't hard to see why we were an embarrassment to Sgt James. That day, Sgt James was really upset with us, because of how badly we marched, so push-ups continued for another 20 minutes. When Sgt James thought we had had enough, he had us "**Fall-In**" Platoon Formation, and as we were standing at **Attention**, he gave us the Command of "**Right Face**," then "**Platoon, Forward, March**."

We continued marching toward the warehouse looking like the heard of cows we were told we looked like. Trying to stay in step with the cadence being called out by Sgt James. Our journey to the warehouse took us by the yellow footprints which was a reminder of our first moments arriving at MCRD and the beginning of things to come. We were halted outside a warehouse that had a blue line from where we were halted that ran into the warehouse.

Sgt James gave us instructions to **"Fall-Out"** by Squad beginning with the 4th Squad on the right and to follow the blue line into the warehouse in single file. Sgt Martinez was on the other side of our formation yelling at recruits to shut their mouths and stand at **"Attention"** until it was their turn to move.

As the 1st Squad Leader, I tried very hard not to make any mistakes and to listen and make sure I followed every command perfectly. I followed the blue line into the warehouse and once inside, I followed the recruit in front of me. We were told by a large Sgt to stay on the line and when I got to the first counter, to face inwards towards the clerk and sidestep to the right as we received our gear.

The first thing I was issued was a white cotton laundry bag that I opened, and the clerk dropped in a roll of deodorant, a container of lip balm, a small vinyl pouch containing finger nail clippers and a small file. As I sidestepped to the next clerk, he gave me a green book with the title "Guide Book for Marines" then deposited six cotton handkerchiefs and a package in a plastic bag that turned out to be a raincoat. Next I got a sewing kit, a package of 12 clothes pins, a can of black Kiwi Shoe polish, a small brush used to apply polish on boots and shoes, and a shoe shinning brush.

All the items we were issued had a purpose, and the Marine Corps paid special attention to details. If we were issued something, we would need to use it, and they would show us how to use it properly. There would be other items we would need before our training was completed, but they would be issued when the time was right.

After the last items we were to be issued were placed in our laundry bag, we fell back in Formation, and we were marched back to our Platoon Street. Sgt James had us "**Fall-Out**" and return to our Quonset Huts where we marked our names on the cotton laundry bag, on the bottom right corner. We were to put our names on each clothes pin, our shoe brush, on each handkerchief, in the collar of our raincoat and on the inside of the green "Guide Book for Marines."

Sgt James had us put our stamp kit back in our footlocker, and then hang the laundry bag on the right side of the bunk where we would place our dirty laundry. All the other items issued were placed on the inside tray of our footlocker, except for our raincoat which was refolded and placed on top of our sea bag and the handkerchiefs were placed on top of our skivvies. I was surprised that during the 45 minutes we were in our huts putting away our latest gear and marking our names it was fairly quiet, but nothing lasts forever.

It is important to note that whatever was wrong with any of the four Huts, the Private in charge of the Hut paid for it with either punches in the gut or push-ups. The guilty recruit causing the issue was always dealt with decisively and made an example of. Gunny Sgt Wolfmule or Sgt James inspected each Hut daily paying special attention to how our racks were made. Gunny Sgt Wolfmule never seemed to be happy with our efforts. Racks not made properly were torn up and push-ups were always his solution.

We spent the rest of the afternoon on the parade deck being taught how to march, understanding formations and close order drill. We worked on trying to look like a platoon. Our Platoon as well as the other Platoons in our Training Series had a long way to go to look like the other platoons that had been at the depot longer than us. It was frustrating to the DI's, that some people had two left feet and just were slow learners, but just as frustrating to me, as I got it, and it wasn't really that difficult. But the whole Platoon paid the price with push-ups for the screwups just the same.

The DI's would stop us after every mistake and would tune up the recruit who messed up. The yelling continued and when too many mistakes were made, the whole platoon was punished by having us face half right and "**Lean Two**" in the push up position, and then do up downs for 10 to 15 minutes. Having mass punishment kept all of us on our toes and made the screw ups stand out in the crowd. If you were a constant screw up, there were other ways to deal with you.

We left the parade deck in time for evening chow. For some reason, evening chow that day was delicious. I don't know if the food was really that good or if I was just really hungry. The same routine, stand in line, get a tray, follow the line through the chow line, get to the table, stand at attention, sit when told to, eat fast, get out, back to Platoon Street. After chow that evening, we went back to the parade deck and practiced "**Close Order Drill**." We continued to work on "**Close Order Drill**" until it started to get dark and then returned to our Huts for Commanders Time until it was time to hit the Rack. Taps at 2200.

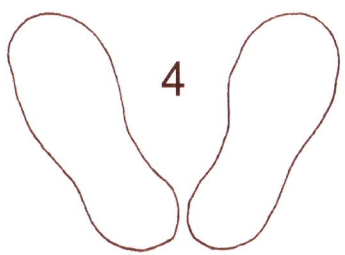

Lots To Learn

The morning of day three was like the morning before. Reveille at 0500, head call, extra blanket, "**Fall-In**" on Platoon Street, march to "**Grinder**", PT, back to Platoon area, morning hygiene, shit, shower and shave, make your rack, field day the Hut, and field day the Head. We were still dressed in our yellow sweatshirts and tennis shoes. Before marching to chow on day three, with the entire platoon standing tall on Platoon Street, Gunny Sgt Wolfmule had the Duty on Day three and ordered the four recruits in charge of the huts to move into the middle of Platoon Street.

Privates Havranek, Gagnon and Wilson and I moved to the middle of Platoon Street and Gunny had the four of us do push-ups. We were responsible to make sure our individual Huts were ready for inspection daily, and the recruits in our Huts performed as directed. When the recruit failed, it was because we failed to show them how to do it the right way. Gunny Sgt Wolfmule assigned the four of us not only in charge of our Huts, but the four of us were also Squad Leaders. It was our responsibility to ensure our Squads were squared away as well as the Huts.

After morning chow, our platoon along with the entire series of new recruits from FOX Company, were marched over to sick bay. The four platoons in FOX Company were at sick bay to receive our first set of shots and to have another physical. Each Platoon utilizes the same training schedule, and each Marine recruit has to complete the same training to graduate.

The little red notebooks we were issued our first night contained much information we needed to know, as well as information we needed to memorize. The 11 general orders we needed to know and memorize word for word, no exceptions. There was other information of importance in the Red Notebook such as how to salute, the position of attention, other movements such as right and left face, about face, Chain of Command, military alignment, how to wear uniforms, etc. We were told that any time we were in formation and told "**At Ease**," we were to pull out our Red Notebooks and study."

When Fox Company arrived at sickbay, we lined up by platoon to get our shots and receive our physical. Platoon, 2227 was the third platoon in line to receive our shots so we studied our Red Notebooks until it was our turn to enter Sick Bay. We were again lined up in single file and ordered to take off our yellow sweatshirt. We tied them around our waists and the single file line moved forward where a Corpsman took our blood.

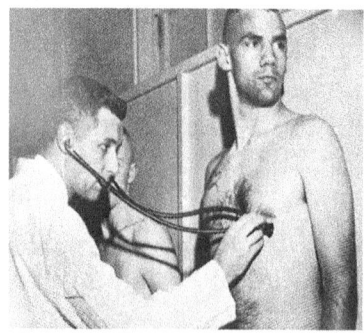 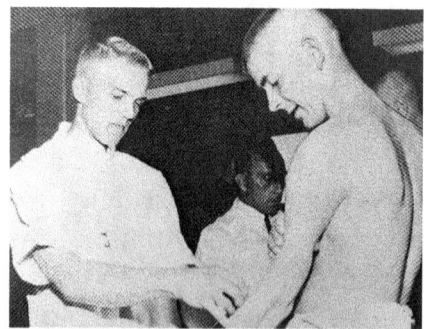

We then moved into another line, where there were two corpsmen with some sort of gun in their hands. Once I got to where both corpsmen were standing, they each took one arm and with their guns gave me a shot in both arms at the same time.

After getting our blood taken and receiving our shots, we were marched in by squad where a Doctor listened to our heart, then to receive a chest X-Ray, followed by having our blood pressure taken then our reflexes checked. A corpsman checked our eyes, had us read an eye chart and after that we had our ears checked. Another Corpsman filled out a

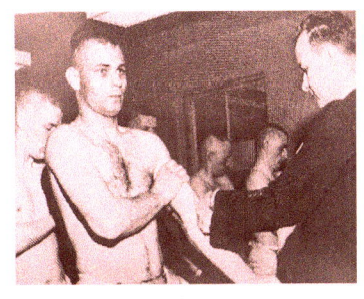

chart on each Recruit which consisted of our height, weight, and any discernable marks such as birth marks, scars, or deformities. Then we had our feet checked.

By the time everyone in our Platoon had finished up with our shots and our physicals at Sick Bay, it was time for noon chow. We had put our sweatshirts back on and "**Fell-In**" formation. Our Platoon followed Platoon 2226 to noon chow, and as we waited in line, I studied my 11 General Orders.

Once we finished noon chow, we were marched back to the Platoon Street and told to "**Fall-Out**", get our tooth brushes, then go to the Head to brush our teeth really well. Afterwards, the Platoon was marched to the Dentist to have our teeth checked. Again, all four Platoons were going through the same training schedule, and this afternoon all four Platoons in our Series were scheduled to get our teeth checked.

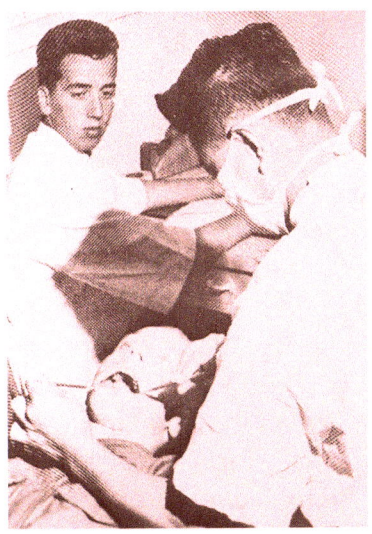

We each had our teeth cleaned, X-Rays taken, and determinations made if a Recruit needed any dental work done, fillings, extractions etc. When we were finished at the dentist, we then marched to the admin. building where we were issued a set of Dog Tags with our military service number which consisted of a seven-digit number that identified who you were. Every record of you from this day forward would have your service number on it as well as your name.

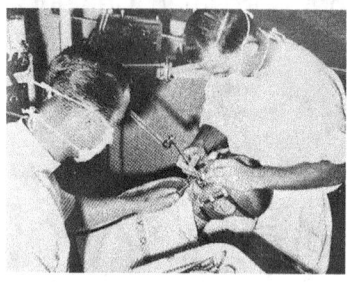

A set of dog tags were two oval, metal disks with your last name, first and middle initials, service number, USMC, religion and blood type. The reason you were issued two dog tags was for identification purposes. Each disk had a hole at one end to insert a long chain and the second tag was put on another chain and both were attached to the first chain to wear at all times around our necks. They were never to be taken off.

The reasons for dog tags was for everyday identification purposes plus, if ever in combat, and you were wounded and unconscious, blood type was important to know. If killed and you had to be left in the field, one of the tags would be placed in between your front teeth and then your jaw would be kicked or slammed shut, so when you were found the dog tag in your jaw would identify you. This was to ensure we would have no more Unknown Soldiers. This became the practice after WWI.

We were marched back to the Platoon Street by Sgt James. Sgt Martinez assumed the Duty for the rest of the evening. We were standing on Platoon Street reading our Red Notebooks when it was time to go to evening chow. We followed the same procedure going through the chow line as we had done the last two days. When the evening chow was finished, we returned to Platoon Street.

Sgt Martinez had us **"Fall-In"** and we spent about an hour and a half on the **"Grinder"** in Close Order Drill, then returned to the Platoon Street for Commander's Time and then Lights Out.

On the morning of day four of boot camp, after we finished PT, morning Head Call, shave, shower, making our racks, clean-up of the Huts, the Head and the Platoon area, we were told to change out of our yellow sweatshirts and put on a green utility shirt and to tuck it in properly. We would be taught proper Military Alignment. Day four was the first day we started wearing our green utility shirts instead of the yellow sweatshirts, and from that day forward, we only wore the yellow sweatshirt for morning PT, free time or special training events.

As we stood on Platoon Street in our Utility Shirts instead of the yellow sweatshirt, we may not look like Marines, but not wearing the yellow sweatshirts made us look much better and we did not perceive ourselves as clowns. We were still wearing white tennis shoes, but now we felt better about ourselves. We stood a little taller this morning as we marched to morning chow. We now had our Red Notebooks in our left hand utility shirt pocket instead of in our trousers.

After morning chow, we were marched over to a classroom and instructed on how to properly salute, when to salute, and who to salute. The proper way to salute as explained in the Marine Corps Manual was printed in our red notebooks, and explained to raise the right hand smartly until the tip of the forefingers touched the lower part of the headgear or forehead above and slightly to the right of the right eye.

- Extend and join the thumb and fingers
- Turn the palm slightly until you can see it out of your right eye
- The upper arm is parallel to the ground
- The elbow is slightly in front of the body

- Incline the forearm at a 45-degree angle
- Hand and wrist in a straight line
- Complete the salute by dropping your arm to your side
- Drop the arm in one sharp, clean motion
- Always salute from the position of Attention
- Never salute when uncovered or indoors, unless on Duty.

We practiced by the numbers while in the classroom with each other. We paired up and rendered salutes to each other as "**Good Morning, Sir**." We continued to practice until it was time to "**Fall-Out**" and get ready for our next class.

We were marched to another building in a single file line. We went in and had our first picture taken with our new recruit haircut. Our new recruit pictures would be used on our military ID card. Marine ID cards were green with the Marine Corps emblem in the top left corner and your picture in the middle. Your Military Service Number, your name, last, first and middle initial and your rank of Pvt A spot for your signature filled the rest of the ID card. The ID card would be laminated and handed out at a later date.

When we finished getting our pictures taken, we were marched to noon chow. As we stood in formation, we read our Red Notebooks and waited for our turn to get in line for chow. Now we were wearing utility shirts, utility trousers and had on a green, Marine, utility cover. When we stopped in front of the mirror at the entrance of the Mess Hall, it looked more impressive to salute the image in the mirror in front of me. As I saluted I said, "**Good Afternoon Sir**," and cut away my salute sharply.

At every meal, as we stood in line, we were covered with our green, Marine, utility cover. After saluting the mirror, as we entered the Mess Hall, we would always remove our cover. Whenever we removed our cover either to go to chow or enter a classroom for instruction, we would tuck our utility cover in the middle of our back inside the waist band.

For lunch on day four we were served Salsbury Steak with cooked carrots, mashed potatoes and gravy, green beans, bread, dinner rolls, peach cobbler for dessert, the usual iced tea, milk, water, coffee. Lunch was delicious. I was amazed how hungry I was at lunch, and we really hadn't done any physical training as of yet.

After noon chow, we "**Fell-In**" Platoon Formation and marched to a building behind the Admin Building. We filed in by squad in single file and upon entering the classroom we sat six recruits to a table and were given an aptitude test. This test was to determine if you had other skills the Marine Corps could use, besides being a "**Grunt**" (***Rifleman***).

After taking our aptitude test, we were marched back to our Platoon area for one hour of close order drill. After we tried to march for one hour, we were then marched over to another classroom and sat through a class on personal hygiene to ensure each recruit understood the importance of keeping clean so not to cause infectious diseases being as all Recruits live and train in such close quarters.

Once our hygiene class was finished we were marched back to our Platoon area before being marched to evening chow. After evening chow we found ourselves back on the "**Grinder**" being taught how to close order drill and then returning to our Platoon area for evening Commanders Time and then hitting the rack. Taps at 2200. I looked forward to taps every night, because after a complete day beginning at 0500, there was no down time. When lights went out there was no more yelling, and we could get seven hours of uninterrupted quiet time. Or so we thought.

On day five after morning chow, we were marched over to another warehouse where we were fitted for and issued two pairs of boots. Both pairs of boots were tied together by the boot laces and we were told to hang both pairs around our neck. We then marched back to the Platoon Street and were shown how and where to put our name on the inside of each pair of boots.

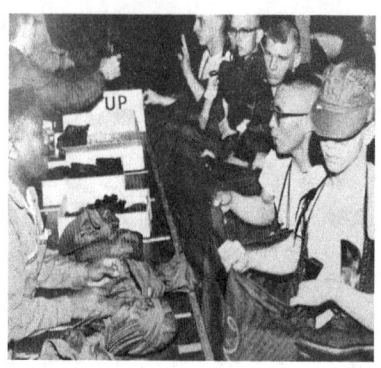

Gunny Wolfmule had the Duty on Wednesday, day five and had us go into our Huts, take out our marking kits and stamp our names on the inside of each pair of boots as we were shown. Once the entire platoon had their name in both pairs of boots, we were told to take off our tennis shoes and put one pair of boots on our feet and the other pair of boots under our rack. Then place our tennis shoes in our footlocker.

Our extra pair of boots were to be next to our footlockers facing outward under our racks, and afterwards, we were told to **"Fall-Out"** on the Platoon Street. We then marched onto the **"Grinder"** for close order drill. All of a sudden, it was different marching in boots rather than tennis shoes. For some reason as we marched we actually marched better than any time before. Gunny had a distinct cadence different from both Sgt James and Sgt Martinez.

Although we always seemed to march better while Sgt James was in-charge, now that we were in boots, we seemed to march just as well with Gunny Wolfmule. Gunny put us through our paces for almost an hour and finally had us stop, and commanded, **"Face Half Left,"** **"Lien Two,"** and had us do at least 50 pushups because we still marched like cattle instead of Marines.

When it was time for our platoons to go to noon chow, we were marched over to the 2nd Battalion Mess Hall. Again we waited for our turn to go into chow, so we took out our Red Notebooks and studied. I was getting close to memorizing the first six General Orders in just four days and I was going to make sure I had them all memorized as soon as possible and when asked, I would be able to spew them out loud and proud.

As we split into our two lines, I couldn't wait to get in front of the mirror and pop a "High ball," *(A High Ball was slang for a sharp, snappy salute)* and say, "**Good Afternoon Sir**." I was getting pretty good at my facing movements as well, and although I still didn't come close to looking like a Marine I was beginning to feel like one.

After we finished with noon chow, Gunny marched us over to the armory where we were to be issued an M-14 rifle. The Armorer took a new M14 out of the rifle rack and handed it to me along with a cartridge belt, a bayonet and a first aid pouch.

He asked me my name and my Service number, so I told him my name was "Rilley, T.S." and looked on my dog tags and gave him my assigned seven-digit Service Number. He told me I should memorize my Service Number as soon as possible as well as memorize my rifle number, because I will be asked to repeat it many times over the next 11 weeks. The Platoon went through the Armory one Squad at a time in single file, and once everyone was issued his rifle, Gunny marched the Platoon back to our Platoon Street while we were at "Right Shoulder Arms."

First time marching with a rifle, and Gunny only spent about ten minutes showing us how to get to "Right Shoulder Arms" so we could make it back to the Platoon Street with our rifles. Sgt James was waiting on the Platoon Street to take over the Platoon from Gunny Wolfmule.

Gunny had marched us right up the Platoon Street and gave us the Order "**Platoon, Halt**." He then had us "**Order Arms,**" and "**Left Face.**" As the Platoon was facing him, he was saluted by Sgt James who took command of the Platoon. Sgt James then had us **"Fall-Out,"** to our Huts and he showed how to attach our M-14 rifle to our rack and lock it with a pad lock, as well as attach our utility belt and bayonet to the end of our rack 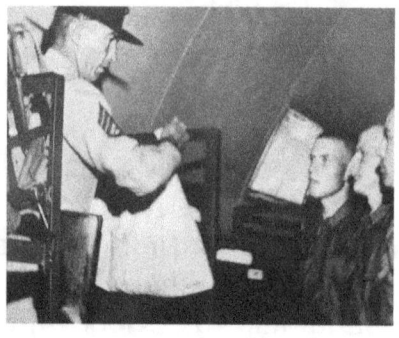 centered between our towels and our laundry bags.

Once finished with our rifles, the platoon was marched over to a classroom across the drill field for a class on Marine Corps history. The History class was very interesting, beginning with the forming of the Corps in 1775 at Tun Tavern. The Corps was now celebrating its 191st year of existence. The instructor was a Staff Sgt who made the information he taught us very interesting, you almost felt like you were there as history was being made.

Class lasted for just over an hour, and after the class ended, we **"Fell-In"** a Platoon Formation and marched back on the drill field for more close order drill practice before being returned to our Platoon area and finishing that day's training before going to evening chow.

As we were eating evening chow, I was wondering what was going on back at home. I missed spending time with my best buddy, Zane and his girlfriend Susan as well as some great times with a girl I had dated named Linda. We had shared a great summer together. I wondered what they all were doing.

I had enjoyed being part of my brother and my sister's weddings the early part of summer and visiting with aunts, uncles and cousins as well as my mom and dad. I hadn't received any mail yet, but I haven't sent any either, so until I write, I won't be getting any. We are kept pretty busy, and except for the time just before hitting the rack, there isn't much time to think about home.

It seemed that the first week we had been at MCRD, we'd put two weeks of training into one. Although we looked better in utility shirts rather than our yellow sweatshirts, we still looked like Boots. We still marched like Boots. We still acted and performed as Boots.

Sgt James had us get our rifles and cartridge belts and "**Fall-In**" on Platoon Street. When the entire Platoon was standing at "**Attention**" on the Platoon Street, Sgt James tried to teach us the **Manual At Arms** with our new M14 rifles. He went by the numbers to show us the position of "**Attention**" with our rifles He took my rifle out of my hands and went through the Manual At Arms for all of us to see and had us attempt to follow his movements for the next hour before having us lock our rifles back on our racks.

I looked forward to Commanders Time, which meant we would be hitting the rack to get some sleep. I was tired from being on my feet almost all day for the last six days, and the only time we had the opportunity to sit was meals and while in the classroom. We have 11 weeks left of Boot Camp, and I know whatever we have gone through so far was nothing compared to what was still in front of us.

Friday, Day 7, began just like the six days before it. Reveille at 0500, PT, hygiene, consisting of head call, shave, shower, clean-up of our huts, the area around our huts, and then our next training day would start. Once on the Platoon Street, Sgt Martinez reported to Sgt James that all Recruits were "Present and Accounted for." It felt different to be wearing boots and a full uniform instead of our yellow sweatshirts and tennis shoes. Sgt Martinez marched us to morning chow and afterwards back to our Platoon Area.

As we stood on the Platoon Street studying our Red Notebooks, both Sgt Martinez and Sgt James inspected each Recruit to make sure we understood the proper uniform alignment. Two or three Recruits were recipients of being punched in the stomach by Sgt James for infractions I was not witness to. I just heard the punches and the Recruit grunting with each blow he took to his solar plexus.

The proper military alignment of wearing our uniform was the utility shirt being tucked in, and the front seem of the shirt was lined up with the front seem of the trousers. The right edge of the belt buckle was in line with both the seams of the shirt and the trousers making a complete straight line from the top of the shirt to the crotch of the trousers.

There is no exception on how the military alignment works for every recruit or Marine on every Marine uniform. However, a Recruit never unbuttons his top button on his collar or blouse his trousers until reaching and passing certain requirements in Boot Camp. We had a long way to go before we unbuttoned our shirts or bloused our trousers. Next we had to learn to spit shine our Boots.

After we were checked on how to properly align the utility uniform, Sgt James marched the Platoon over to the wash racks. The wash racks were located next to the Heads where we showered and used the toilet facilities. The wash racks were also where we will spend time weekly doing our laundry. Adjacent to the head and next to the wash racks were the wash tubs, and behind the wash tubs, there were twelve clothes lines where we would hang our laundry to dry after doing our laundry.

We stopped in front of the wash tubs, and Sgt James had 1st Squad put the stopper in the bottom of the wash tubs and turn on the water until the water level in the wash tub was approximately eight to ten inches deep. Then he ordered 1st Squad to stand in the wash tubs for 15 minutes moving our legs up and down making sure the boots were totally wet inside and out.

Each recruit in 1st Squad marched in the wash tubs until told to get out, and then "**Fall-In**" formation with wet boots while the next Squad climbed up and submerged their boots until they were completely wet inside and out. After all four Squads took their turn, and every recruit had his turn at standing in the wash tubs, the entire Platoon was standing in Formation with wet boots. For the rest of the day, we marched in our wet boots.

We wore them to chow, we wore them on the Parade Ground, we wore them to class, and we wore them to evening chow. We marched in our boots all day until they were dry. This process was known as "walking our boots dry" so as the leather dried, they form fit to our feet. This process also was the cause of many recruits getting blisters either on their heels or somewhere on their foot.

The DI's inspected our feet daily and issued band aids and foot powder where necessary, other than that, we just had our feet checked every night. From that day on, these would be our everyday boots. The other pair of boots stayed under our racks and would be designated as inspection boots, but never worn as work boots. We never got the second pair wet, and just kept them spit shinned under our Rack for inspection or special occasions.

One of the things the DI on duty did each day of Boot Camp was to march us to the **Grinder** where there was a senior platoon or a seasoned platoon, marching in formation so we could see how Marines march, and to show us how far we have to go to look like Marines. To watch a platoon of Marines in formation marching totally in step, exactly spaced, moving as one in a platoon formation instead of 70 or 80 recruits as an unorganized mob or a heard of cows was a sight to behold. Watching these platoons march each day was meant to make us feel inept. Would we ever be that good? Would we ever become Marines?

The first week of Boot Camp was coming to an end and we had experienced so much in that first week. We were continually called civilian pukes, a piece of shit, a maggot or other insulting, humiliating names and we still had 11 more weeks of things yet to learn. I began to question myself as to whether I would have what it would take to make the grade and become a Marine. I survived week one, and I promised myself I would take it one day at a time and give it my best.

We learned some new vocabulary by listening to our DI's, and also learned there is a difference in how you would answer a question or respond to a statement. Even though you always start your response with a "Sir" and end it with a "Sir", when you answer to direction, "You would say "**Sir, Aye Aye Sir**." When you acknowledge a question, you answer, "**Sir, Yes Sir**,".

We were taught why the Marines were a Department of the Navy, and we used Navy vernacular to describe things. Doors were "hatches," floors were "decks," walls were "bulkheads," meals were "Chow," mopping the floor was "Swabbing the deck", bathrooms were called "Heads," "Cleaning our barracks was "Field Day," etc., etc., etc.,

But Marines also had a vocabulary of their own, a house mouse was a small recruit who was like a valet to the DI's, a person always screwing up was a "Shit Bird," a "Fat Body" was an overweight recruit, a Sailor was referred to as a "Squid," the "Grinder" was the Drill Field, Asshole to Belly Button" was getting close to the man in front of you, "Devil Dog" was a slang name for a Marine, etc., etc., etc.

Saturday which was day eight ended our first week of Boot Camp. We went through the same morning routine as we had the 7 days before, and after morning chow we attended a class on the Chain of Command, Rank Structure for not only the Marine Corps, but for the Navy as well.

The rest of the day was spent doing Close Order Drill, practicing the Manual at Arms with our Rifles, and for the second time, we actually tried marching with our rifles. The DI's weren't patient people, so we did plenty of push-ups Saturday before our day finally ended.

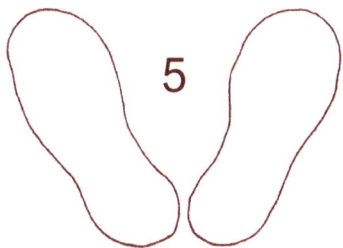

Guidon and Right Guide

Week two began on a Sunday, and as usual, Reveille was at 0500. We followed our normal morning routine by getting our blankets and doing morning PT on the Grinder. However, after morning hygiene and making our racks, we "**Fell-In**" on Platoon Street in our Utilities and boots. Instead of morning clean-up or being marched to morning chow with our Platoon, we were given a choice to attend the Sunday Church Service of our choice.

Gunny Wolfmule informed us that while we are in Boot Camp, the Marine Corps gives its members the opportunity to worship as they choose no matter what their denomination. Each Religion or denomination forms up on the "**Grinder**," goes to Sunday morning chow together and holds services independent of each other. When their Service finishes, the recruits return to their Platoons.

There were formations for Catholics, Lutherans, Protestants, Mormons, Jews, Baptists, Methodists, and non-denominational. All Recruits while attending Boot Camp are given their choice and are never interfered with on Sunday mornings. Whichever DI is on Duty Sunday Mornings dismisses the Recruits to "**Fall-In**" with their choice of Service.

Those who choose not to attend Sunday Services remain with the Platoon and after going to chow Sunday morning, have Commanders Time until 1100 on the Platoon Street. Also, those choosing not to attend Sunday Services are responsible for morning clean-up of the Huts, Field Day the Heads and the Platoon Area. When they finished, they could enjoy Commander Time, shining their boots, read the Sunday paper or write letters home. As Boot Camp continued, there were other tasks they would be allowed to take care of.

A typical Sunday Commanders Time would be after returning from morning chow and morning clean-up, to take our buckets and sit on them on the Platoon Street. The Recruit had free time to do what he wished from the time clean-up was finished until 1100 on Sunday morning. As the recruits began returning from their chosen Service, they were allowed to join-in and take part in Commanders Time. It was funny how the atmosphere changed on Sunday mornings.

At 1100 on Sunday mornings after Commanders Time ended, the DI on Duty followed the Training Plan of the Day which could include Close Order Drill, Manual at Arms, lessons on shining our boots, or special classes away from our Platoon Area in classrooms or lectures on specific top-ics. We normally ate noon chow between 1130 and 1230, depending on the Mess Hall schedule and we enjoyed evening chow around 1730.

Every Sunday Evening we would have a detailed Hygiene Inspection when our feet, our hands, our ears, and each recruits ability to function physically were checked. We would normally stand on our footlockers for this Inspection which would be administered by either the Gunny and one other DI or by both DI's.

Monday morning of week two began with Reveille at 0500, head call, formation on platoon street for PT, shit, shower and shave, and then morning clean up before going to chow. The first week we had done a lot of Administrative tasks and learned how to do things the Marine Corps Way. We had been taught a lot so far, and week two was spent reviewing what we had already learned.

We now had morning Inspections of our Huts every day. The DI's checked the way we made up our Racks. Also, how we cleaned up the Head and our Platoon area. The consequences of not passing daily inspections and following the instructions and orders given by the DI's and our Platoon Commander would determine how many push-ups we did daily.

The Training Schedule for week two included Close Order Drill to and from morning chow. We attended at least one classroom lecture every morning and sometimes two. After afternoon chow on Monday, Sgt James had us get our rifles and cartridge belts and "**Fall-In**" on Platoon Street. We spent two hours practicing the Manual at Arms before attempting Close Order Drill with our Rifles.

After Evening Chow on Monday, as the Platoon was in formation on the Platoon Street studying their Red Notebooks, Gunny Wolfmule had the Platoon put their notebooks away and come to Attention. Gunny Wolfmule was carrying a Red Flag which was referred to as the "**Platoon Guidon**". A red flag with the gold numbers 2227 and trimmed in gold and was attached to an 8-foot pole.

Each Platoon that goes through Boot Camp is issued a Platoon Guidon which identifies their Platoon. Our Platoon was designated as Platoon 2227, assigned to Fox Company, 2nd Battalion, Recruit Training Regiment, MCRD, San Diego, CA.

MCRD had three Training Battalions assigned to the Recruit Training Regiment. The 1st Battalion, 2nd Battalion, and 3rd Battalion. Each Battalion has four Companies with each Company in each Battalion designated by the letters of the alphabet, i.e. A,B,C,D is the 1st Battalion, Alpha, Bravo, Charlie and Delta Companies. The 2nd Battalion E, F, G, H are designated for Echo, Fox, George and Hotel Companies, and the 3rd Battalion letters are I, J, K, L are for India, Juno, Kilo and Lima Companies.

Each Company in each Battalion has four Platoons, and each Platoon in that Company is designated with the number relating to that Battalion i.e. 1st Battalion, Company Platoons begin with the number "1", i.e. 1025, 1126, 1227, 1456 etc. 2nd Battalion, Company Platoons begin with the number "2", i.e. 2075, 2137, 2227, 2458 etc. and 3rd Battalion, Company Platoons begin with the number "3", i.e. 3025, 3145, 3317, 3512 etc.

Each Platoon in each training series regardless of Battalion, are in different phases of their training, but all Platoons in each Company are going through the exact same training schedule and hold the same classes or training exercises.

The Guidon became not only something to identify which Platoon is in which Battalion but becomes a symbol of honor and pride for your Platoon. It identifies who we are, because we will compete between Platoons in our series for certain honors and recognitions. Wherever the Platoon goes, the Guidon goes with us for everyone to see. The next decision to be made by our Platoon Commander, Gunny Sgt Wolfmule, was who would carry our Platoon Guidon.

Someone has to carry the Guidon, and whoever it would be would be known as the Platoon "**Right Guide**." According to Marine Corps Guidelines the choice of choosing the recruit to carry the Platoon Guidon is based on a combination of factors including demonstrated leadership qualities, strong work ethic, exceptional drill performance, high level of discipline and a positive attitude. Essentially, the recruit who best exemplifies the desired traits of a Marine and represents his platoon with pride and honor.

Gunny Sgt Wolfmule made the decision to designate me as the Platoon "**Right Guide**." I had been one of the original four Squad Leaders since the first day of training, and apparently my performance to date had stood out enough for Gunny and our Platoon DI's to choose me. Gunny must have thought I possessed the essential traits and characteristics to earn the right to carry our Platoon's Guidon!

To be viewed as a stand out recruit in his Platoon, made my chest stick out and improved my self-esteem and self-confidence, and I decided I would work to continue to be a stand-out recruit every day and continue to gain our DI's trust. Although I had been picked to carry the Guidon, I could lose the privilege just as quick if I didn't continue to perform to our Drill Instructors expectations.

Now that I was picked to be the Platoon "**Right Guide**," Gunny Wolfmule and the other DI's had to pick my replace-ment as Squad Leader. Gunny picked Pvt Surma to replace me as 1st Squad Leader. There was no guarantee that I could keep the honor as "**Right Guide**" or that Squad Leaders could keep their positions as Squad Leaders. If you screwed up, you could be replaced in a heartbeat. For example, Pvt Wilson was replaced in week four and Pvt Gagnon was replaced in week six but was reinstated in week eight.

I proved myself as a Leader, and once I became the "**Right Guide**" and carried the Platoon Guidon for Platoon 2227, I kept the honor of being the "**Right Guide**" for our Platoon from the end of week 1 until we graduated from boot camp. As the right guide, I always marched at the head of the platoon and carried our platoon Guidon with pride and honor wherever our platoon went!

Whenever the Platoon went anywhere, the Guidon went with us, however, when I wasn't carrying the Guidon, it would be placed in the flag stand just outside the DI Duty hut.

It would stay in the flag stand overnight whenever we were in the Platoon area, or in the morning while we were doing PT or morning Hygiene or clean-up. But whenever we were to "**Fall-In**" to be part of the daily training schedule, I took the Guidon out of the stand and held it by my side.

The only other exception to my not carrying the Guidon was when we were Learning the Manual at Arms or being Inspected with Rifles. Also, other than the Rifle Range, no matter what the training or where we went, I never carried a rifle except for rifle classes and our final Uniform Inspection on Week 11.

On Tuesday morning after morning chow, we were marched again to Sick Bay to receive another round of shots. We fell into single file by Squads and took off our utility shirts and tied them around our waist and went through the line with Corpsmen on each side taking an arm to give us our shots. We put our utility shirts back on and **"Fell-In"** Platoon Formation, and then were marched to a class on Marine Corps History and Traditions.

After classes we were marched to noon chow and we studied our Red Notebooks while we waited to get into chow. I carried our Platoon Guidon and would place it in a flag stand provided outside the Mess Hall for all Platoon Guidons.

On Tuesday when we came out of the Mess Hall, I had experienced one of the worst days of Boot Camp. After being given the privilege of being chosen the Platoon "Right Guide" and allowed to carry the Platoon Guidon, when I came out of the Mess Hall to retrieve our Platoon Guidon, it was gone. It was not in the flag stand and Gunny Wolfmule was furious.

I looked around to see if one of our DI's might have taken it or if a joke was being played, but instead, Gunny was livid and when I couldn't find the Guidon, he punched me in the gut not just once, but two times, for not knowing where our Platoon Guidon was. Just as he was getting ready to punch me again, the DI from Platoon 2207 brought our Guidon back to the Mess Hall and placed it in the flag stand.

It seemed that his "Right Guide" took the wrong Guidon after chow and left their Platoon Guidon in the flag stand. The other DI looked at Gunny Wolfmule and apologized as he returned our Guidon to the flag stand and then took his. His Platoon number was 2207, and apparently his Right Guide took ours without looking to make sure he took the right Guidon. 2207 looked pretty close to 2227. After the other DI apologized, he just left.

Gunny Wolfmule just looked at me, but never apologized to me for punching me in the gut. But he did tell me, that in the future I better not ever lose or take the wrong Guidon. My stomach was kind of sore where he punched me, but I was glad we didn't lose our Guidon, and although Gunny never apologized, I believe he felt bad and treated me differently the rest of my time at MCRD.

Once back in formation, Gunny marched the Platoon over to the Admin. Office where we were to pick up our new Military ID Cards. We were instructed to put them in our left breast pocket, and we were to carry it at all times while wearing utilities.

After receiving our Military ID Cards we were marched over to a class on the Military Code of Conduct. On the way, Gunny didn't like the way we were trying to march. So, he halted the platoon right in the street, had us face half right and "**Lien Two**" and we did pushups on the street for 15 minutes before getting back in formation and continued our march to the class room. When I did pushups while in formation, I would lay our Guidon on my shoulder, so the flag lay on my back and not on the ground as we did pushups.

Another lesson learned that you didn't want to forget is there were times recruits would fall asleep our doze off while we were in a classroom. It was made perfectly clear that if you felt sleepy, you were to stand up to stay awake. You didn't need permission, you just stood up. If you were caught falling asleep while in a class, you were dealt with harshly by the Instructor and the DI on Duty. Plus, you missed out on the information being taught, and when given a test, if you didn't score high on that subject, you were punished severely again.

That day after our class was over, Gunny marched us back to the Grinder, where we practiced Close Order Drill and facing movements. Although only in Boot Camp for less than two weeks, we were as bad as the DI's said we were at Close Order Drill. After evening chow we spent another two hours on the Drill Field before returning to our Huts for Commanders Time.

On Wednesday morning after morning chow we were told to get our rifles and "**Fall-In**" on Platoon Street. Sgt James told me to get my Rifle as well and when I reported to the Platoon Street, Sgt James told me to sling my Rifle and put it over my shoulder onto my back so I could still carry the Guidon.

The Platoon was marched to another classroom, and the reason Sgt James had me bring my rifle was this class was on the M-14, learning it's nomenclature and how to take it apart, strip it down and clean it. The class lasted two hours, and after class we made a detour and stopped back on the Grinder. We spent the rest of the morning doing Close Order Drill.

While we marched the rest of the morning on the Grinder, I had my M-14 over my back and carried the Platoon Guidon. It was getting close to noon chow. Sgt James marched us back to our Huts so we could return our rifles and lock them to our racks. We then "**Fell-In**" for noon chow.

After noon chow we returned to our Huts and were told to get our Marine Corps Guide Books. We were then marched to another classroom and spent the next hour and a half learning about the .45 Caliber pistol.

The nomenclature of a .45 was in our Marine Corps Guide Books to study later on our own time. However, the Instructor passed out a .45 pistol to be shared by every four Marines at each table so we could actually touch it, hold it, break it down and learn how to clean it.

Outside each classroom there were at least four flag stands to put the Guidon in during classes. However, the first thing I did after leaving any classroom or the mess hall after eating chow was to grab the Platoon Guidon and make sure it was Platoon 2227. I never wanted to go through getting punched by Gunny Wolfmule ever again.

It was important to note that during each phase of training, our times for going to chow would change. The newest platoons on the Depot would eat at the early or first chow times. The longer you were on the Depot, the times would become later until you were the oldest platoons on the Depot and then you would have the last chow times.

Thursday morning after morning chow, we were told to change back into our red PT shorts, yellow sweatshirts, and tennis shoes. Apparently, in the second week of Boot Camp, each Platoon in a Series would participate in a scheduled and scored PT Test. This Test had a minimum score a Recruit had to achieve to stay in that Platoon and continue his Training.

Next to the obstacle course there were a number of athletic fields. There were two Baseball Fields, a Football Field, a Track Field and other space meant for sporting or physical activities. All four Platoons in Fox Company were marched over to the large Track Field where our initial PT Test was to be administered.

Besides finding out which of our Recruits were not qualified to continue training at that time, we were competing between platoons to see how many sit-ups we could do in two minutes, how many pushups in two minutes, how fast we could run 100 yards, how many pullups we could do, as well as how many bends and thrusts in two minutes.

Each recruit would have to pass a physical fitness test in order to graduate from boot camp. There would be two or three practice tests along the way. This was the first. Those Recruits who didn't meet the minimum score were sent to one of three different places.

The "**Fat Farm**" was where overweight Recruits who were given a chance to make the grade, but didn't score high enough to stay with the Platoon went. The "**Motivation**" Platoon was where Recruits who weren't motivated, lazy or not committed, who just couldn't score the minimum physical standards required to stay in the Platoon and the DI's felt needed extra motivation to succeed.

The third category was individuals who failed to meet the minimum requirements due to an injury, or a temporary physical handicap that caused them to fail. Platoon 2227 lost four more Recruits from our Ranks after testing on that day, bringing our total Platoon Strength to 83. We had two Recruits go to the "**Fat Farm**," one Recruit go to "**Motivation**" and one of our Recruits had a bad ankle injury which sent him to "**Sick Bay**."

All four Recruits would be given the chance to return to training once they were physically fit or able to meet the Marine requirements, but they would be re-assigned to a different Platoon and would not rejoin Platoon 2227. It was possible our Platoon could pick up other Recruits that were dropped by their Platoon during different phases of training so they could continue and graduate from Boot Camp.

Friday morning Reveille at 0500, morning PT, morning hygiene, shit, shower and shave. One of the things that we did every Friday morning was strip our bunks and turn in our sheets and pillowcase. Sgt James picked two of the smallest Recruits in each Hut and referred to them as "**House Mice**." These Recruits were the ones who collected our linen every Friday, ran errands for the Gunny and the DI's, made up the DI's racks in the DI Duty hut, kept it clean, swept the floors, etc. The same "House Mouse" recruits were responsible for passing out two sheets and a clean pillowcase every Friday after we finished the noon chow.

Whenever one of the DI's would yell out "**House Mouse**," the whole Platoon would repeat, "Sir, House Mouse to the Duty Hut, Sir." The House Mice would all make their way to the Duty Hut and take care of whatever the DI's needed done. After the second week, the DI's decided they only needed four House Mice not eight, so they took the four smallest Recruits, one from each Hut. No one messed with the House Mouse.

Since we were only at the end of our 2nd week of training, it was very unlikely that we would pick up any new Recruits any time soon. But, on Friday we lost another Recruit, because his father had died from a heart attack. So the Recruit was quickly issued a complete Dress Marine Corps Uniform and went home on Emergency Leave for two weeks. When he returns he would join a different Platoon just finishing up their second week of training, to finish his Boot training. Our total Platoon strength was now at 82.

After we returned from morning chow on Friday of week two, we were taught how to do our laundry. Sgt Martinez had us collect our PT gear which consisted of our yellow sweatshirt, red PT shorts, two pair of skivvies, two white t-shirts, two pair of black socks, one utility blouse and one pair of utility trousers, our towel and wash cloth. Our laundry bags were hung on the opposite side of the end of the rack from our towel and wash cloth.

To do our Laundry, we would get our laundry bag, wisk, scrub brush and clothes pins in our buckets. Then stand on Platoon Street and wait for our next command. Sgt James marched us over to the wash rack to do our laundry. We filled a wash tub with hot water and then dumped all of our dirty whites into the wash tub.

When all the white laundry was soaked in the water, we would take them out and scrub

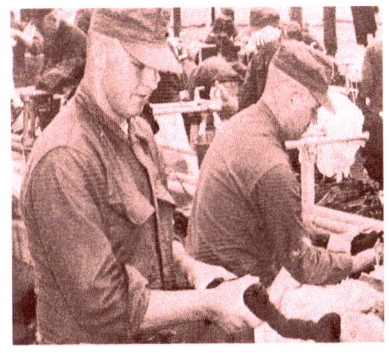

them with the scrub brush and put the whites in our bucket. We would repeat the same thing with the dark clothes. Then we drained the wash tub of dirty water and refilled with fresh clean hot water.

Then rinsed each article of clothing starting with the whites. After they were all

rinsed, you would ring the water out of each article, then hang everything on the clothes line.

After everything was hung up to dry, the DI on Duty would pick two Recruits to sit on their buckets and guard the clothes line. We would go about the rest of that mornings training and return before going to noon chow and take down our laundry and return it to our Huts. We would fold our clothes and place everything in our footlockers. God help the person if you tried to steal someone else's clothing. The House Mice would pick up clean linen from the Duty Hut and pass it out to the Huts before we would go to noon chow. After noon chow we would return to our Huts and make-up our Racks.

Another first for Friday of week two after evening chow, was the Platoons first mail call. The DI's would mess with us in the evenings after chow and after being in boot camp for two weeks it was nice to finally receive news from home. When we arrived at MCRD, other than our initial phone call, we were allowed to send five postcards home with our mailing address on it. The only other time we had time to write home was on Sunday during Commanders time for those who chose not to attend Church Services.

Mail call for those who received mail at the end of week two was held after evening chow on the Platoon Street. If you had mail, the DI would call your name and you would go to the head of the formation on Platoon Street just outside the DI duty hut. There the DI would hold your mail in his hand, and you would have to slap it with your hands and hope you never touched the DI's fingers. If your hands hit or even touched the DI's fingers, you had hell to pay in the form of bends and thrusts or pushups. I received a letter from my mother at the end of week two.

Those who received mail had a chance to read their mail while Mail Call was going on. Once Mail Call was terminated those with mail were told to put their mail in their pocket until Commanders Time. Sgt Martinez had the Duty and decided we could get in another hour of Close Order Drill before the sun went down. So, we "**Fell-In**" Platoon Formation and Sgt Martines put us through our paces. He did have us stop once and "Lien Two," and we performed at least 50 push-ups before continuing Drill.

The sun was beginning to go down by the time we returned to Platoon Street. Sgt Martinez dismissed the Platoon and began Commanders Time. He had us make a Head Call, brush our teeth and get ready for evening lights out.

Saturday morning Reveille at 0500, same routine as every other morning. PT, hygiene, shave, shower, make our Racks, clean our Huts, clean the Head and the Platoon Area then "**Fall-In**" on the Platoon Street. I made a count of all the Recruits and waited for Sgt Martinez to come out of the Duty Hut. I Stood in front of Sgt Martinez and Reported, "Sir, All Recruits from Platoon 2227 Present and Accounted for, Sir."

He replied, "Very Well. Have the Platoon "**Fall-In**" for morning chow." I answered, "**Sir, Aye Aye Sir.**" As the "**Right Guide**," the DI's would give me a command, and I would carry out their Orders. I became almost like another DI, only in the sense that I repeated their wishes to the Platoon and the Platoon obeyed just like they heard it from the DI. I relayed the DI's wishes to the Squad Leaders as well.

I was given a great responsibility by Gunny Wolfmule, and it was important that I didn't abuse or mistreat his trust by letting my position go to my head. I made it a point to meet with the four Squad Leaders every morning and every evening. I would pass on instructions from Gunny Wolfmule and the other DI's and make sure Recruits were squared away.

It was suggested that since we had four Hut's and four Squads, that we move each Squad to their own Hut and put the Squad Leaders in charge of their Squads and their Huts,

which made it easier to hold Recruits accountable. Plus, we could use competition between Squads to motivate the Recruits as well.

Gunny liked our suggestion, and we spent the rest of Saturday after we finished noon chow moving gear, so each Hut was occupied by one Squad. 1st Squad in the first Hut, 2nd Squad in the second Hut and so on. I stayed in the first hut. Each Squad was responsible for keeping their Hut clean, floors swept and the rocks outside their Hut raked and orderly.

There was a Wall locker in each Hut that held cleaning materials like brooms, rags, mops, rakes, buckets, sponges, etc. Each Hut had four Recruits who were responsible to clean the head, which included the toilets, showers, sinks, mirrors, floors, pipes etc. Each Hut had recruits responsible to sweep the deck, swab the deck, dust the racks and the window ledges. Each Squad Leader was responsible for their Hut.

After Evening chow, Sgt James had the Platoon "**Fall-Out**" on the Grinder for Close Order Drill. We drilled until dusk and then made our way back to the Platoon Street and "**Fell-Out**" for evening hygiene and Commanders Time. Lights out at 2200 hours with Taps and another night of seven hours sleep.

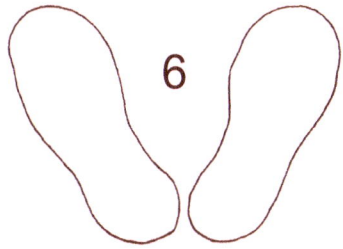

Push-ups, Push-ups, Push-ups

Sunday morning of week three wasn't as chaotic as mornings past. Reveille at 0500 as usual, head call, PT, morning hygiene, then "**Fall-Out**" for Church Services for those who choose to attend. All the denominations held their own Formation on the Grinder and then marched to morning chow. The Recruits who chose not to attend Church Services "**Fell-In**" on Platoon Street and we waited for our turn for Sunday morning chow.

After our Platoon returned from morning chow, the Platoon held morning clean-up and Field Day of our Huts before taking our buckets to the Platoon Street for Sunday Commanders Time. On Sundays, the DI's would bring six Sunday San Diego Newspapers to pass around for the Recruits to read. I took the morning time to clean my M14 rifle and to shine my two pair of boots.

Recruits who attended Church Services continued to return to the Platoon Street. Commanders Time lasted until 1100 at which time we were told to put our writing, gear, rifles, boot shining gear, newspapers, or anything else being worked on away and "**Fall-In**" on the Platoon Street.

Sgt James marched us to noon chow by way of the Grinder. We split into two single file ranks just after 1200 and as usual, I placed our Guidon in the flag stand and stood in line waiting my turn to Salute the mirror and enjoy lunch. After noon chow, we were marched back to the Platoon Street. We were told to get our Rifles, cartridge belts with bayonet and first aid pouch and "**Fall-In**" Platoon Formation.

Sgt James marched the Platoon onto the Grinder and after giving the command to "**Halt**," had us "**Order Arms**," then a "**Left Face**." The entire Platoon was now in a Platoon Formation in Line. The Platoon was facing Sgt James with the Squad Leaders to the right and four columns of 20 Recruits in line facing Sgt James as well. The Right Guide was to the right of the 1st Squad Leader.

Since we had our rifles, the entire Platoon was standing at "**Attention**" with their rifles to their right side. Sgt James explained how they were to hold their rifle while in the position of "**Attention**." The right hand shaped in a "V" with fingers and thumb grasping the sides of the stock. Rifle butt placed on the ground with the toe of the butt in line with the toe of the right shoe.

Sgt James told us that we will learn how to "**Open Ranks**." Sgt James explained to us what "**Open Ranks**," was going to look like and what each Recruit was supposed to do when given the command to execute. He also explained that every command we will be given while in Boot Camp will have two parts. The first part is called the "**preparatory**" command followed by the "**execution**" command.

The preparatory command gets you prepared to make a movement, and the execution command is to actually execute the movement. The new Formation is going to be "**Open Ranks**." The preparatory command will be "**Open Ranks**," and the execution command will be "**March**." When I give you this command, the 1st Squad will take two steps forward starting with the left foot and then stop.

The 2nd Squad will take one step forward starting with the left foot and then stop. The 3rd Squad will not move and remain stationary, and the 4th Squad will take one step backwards starting with the left foot and then stop. On my Command, Platoon, "**Open Ranks**, **March**." The Platoon attempted to execute this command. Although it wasn't perfect, all four Squads followed instructions well.

The next thing you will do upon "**Opening Ranks**," is automatically go to "**Dress Right, Dress**." Keep that position until you hear, the next command, "**Ready, Two**." At which time you will "**Stand at Attention**." The last thing that is done is the command of "**Cover**."

The Command of "**Cover**," means to stand directly behind the man in front of you so there is a straight-line side to side and front to rear. To "**Close Ranks**," the 1st Squad stands still, the 2nd Squad takes one step, the 3rd Squad takes two steps and the 4th Squad takes three steps all of which are with the left foot first. All commands, and movements are made with the Left foot first always.

Sgt James had us practice "**Open and Close Ranks**," for the next two hours. Other than not doing it exactly as one yet, we were at least doing it right. Now everyone just had to remember how to do it every time we were ordered to do so. It was getting close to evening chow, so Sgt James marched us back to the Platoon Street and had us put up our rifles and cartridge belts and get ready for chow.

The march to evening chow for some reason felt pretty good. We had a good afternoon on the Grinder and it seemed like we had not only learned something new, but gained a little confidence. So far, unless we screw up somehow, this was the first day since being on the Depot that we haven't been told to "**Lien Two**."

We studied our Red Notebooks while we waited our turn for chow. As usual, once we split into two single file lines, I placed the Guidon in the flag stand and fell in for chow. As I stood in front of the mirror giving my evening salute, I thought I saw someone else in the mirror. A more confident, more knowledgeable, more experienced Recruit with a look of accomplishment.

As we filed into the chow hall, there were two stacks of metal trays and we each grabbed one and held it in front of our chest standing at attention, looking straight ahead, no talking and made our way through the chow line.

talking and made our way through the chow line.

Sunday evening chow was fantastic, roasted chicken, mashed potatoes, gravy, stuffing, corn, green beans, corn bread, lemon pie or lemon Jello for dessert, iced tea, milk, water, and coffee. The chow line moved fairly quickly, and Sgt James led us to our seating tables, and we stood at attention until the entire Platoon was standing at their tables. He then gave the command, "**Seats**," and in unison the Platoon answered "**Sir, Seats, Aye Aye Sir.**"

We hit our seats with one big thud, all 81 butts at the same time, and then began eating. There was to be no talking

while we ate. You could ask for salt or pepper, or hot sauce, but no conversations were allowed during chow. When our 20 minutes were up, Sgt James came over and told us to get up and get out and "**Fall-In**" outside the Mess Hall.

I had the Platoon "**Fall-In**" as I retrieved the Guide-On. Once in formation we automatically went to "**Dress Right Dress**," Falling-In off the 1st Squad Leader. I put my left arm up to meet the right shoulder of Pvt Surma to keep my distance and aligned myself with the 1st Squad. Since we learned to "**Dress Right**" automatically every time we "**Fall-In**," there was no command to "**Ready Two**," it just happens once the Recruit is aligned and then "**Cover Down**" from the man in the 1st Squad.

By the time Sgt James joined the Platoon, we were standing in Platoon Formation waiting for Sgt James to give us our next Command. He gave the command to "**Right Face**," and then marched us to the Grinder before taking us back to the Platoon Street. Sgt James wanted to have us practice "**Open Ranks**," again, and that's what we did. We actually performed it two times, and afterwards he marched us back to the Platoon Street.

Sgt James had the Duty Sunday night. We got ready for Commanders Time and brushed our teeth and got ready for sack time. Sgt James held a Hygiene Inspection and then gave us 45 minutes to write letters home.

Monday morning began as usual, Reveille at 0500, morning headcount, Head Call, PT, morning hygiene, clean-up of huts and surrounding areas, Field Day the Head, and then morning chow. When we returned to the Platoon Street after morning chow, Gunny Wolfmule and Sgt Martinez took over the Duty from Sgt James.

One of the unique aspects of our Platoon Street was that we shared it with another Platoon from our training series. Our Platoon area ended with an imaginary line outside the DI Duty Hut so the area on the other side of that imaginary line belonged to Platoon 2225.

When Platoon 2225 Falls-Out on Platoon Street they also utilize the other end of our Platoon Street and their DI's have the Duty Hut next to our Platoon Duty Hut that houses the DI's. An Identifying aspect which separates our two Duty Huts, is our Platoon Guidon is Posted in front of our Duty Hut and the Guidon for Platoon 2225 is Posted in front of their Duty Hut.

We have Gunny Wolfmule as our Platoon Commander, and Platoon 2225 has Staff Sargeant Richards (SSgt) as their Platoon Commander. Each morning as Platoon 2227 **"Falls-In"** on the Platoon Street, Platoon 2225 also Falls-In on their Platoon Street. At times, SSgt Richards will say "Good Morning Pvt Rilley," to me when he comes out on his Platoon Street which causes me a problem.

By Policy, no Recruit is allowed to talk to any other Drill Instructor or Platoon Commander from a different Platoon at any time unless given permission from their own DI or Platoon Commander. So when I am standing on the Platoon Street each morning and SSgt Richards says "Good Morning" to me, I am not allowed to answer him back. However, if I don't answer him back, I am being disrespectful to a Non-

Commissioned Officer and subject to discipline. What a conundrum.

On Monday morning, SSgt Richards made it a point to say "Good Morning" to me at least three times, and as instructed, I ignored his greetings and just stood at Attention waiting for Gunny Wolfmule to come out of the Duty Hut and take charge of our Platoon.

While I waited SSgt Richards kept talking to me in a very nice friendly way asking me how I was, and if I slept well, etc. When Gunny Wolfmule came onto the Platoon Street, he witnessed SSgt Richards talking to me, and became furious. He walked up to me and told me I was not to talk to any other DI or Platoon Commander from another Platoon, and I believe he was getting ready to hit me again in the solar plex.

I was about to answer Gunny that I hadn't spoken to SSgt Richards when SSgt Richards came to my rescue and said, "Good morning GySgt Wolfmule. I have attempted to get Pvt Rilley to talk to me with no results. I guess you have told Pvt Rilley to ignore my morning greeting." I untightened my stomach muscles. SSgt Richards had a southern accent and was probably from someplace like Alabama, Mississippi, Kentucky, Georgia or someplace like that.

Gunny relaxed and said, "Good morning SSgt Richards. Are you trying to get my "Right Guide" in trouble by talking to him and getting him to talk to you?" SSgt Richards answered, "I am sorry if I infringed on any Platoon policies Gunny, I was just being friendly and wished Pvt Rilley a "Good Morning," not wanting to cause any trouble or issues.

Gunny looked at me and said, "Pvt Rilley, you were right not to acknowledge SSgt Richards greeting, however, from this moment on, since we share the Platoon Street with SSgt Richards Platoon, if he greets you in the morning, you may answer him without repercussions. We must be polite to our neighbor's. Do you understand me?" I answered, "Sir, Yes Sir."

SSgt Richards said, "Thank you Gunny, I promise not to abuse or misuse your trust or policies." Gunny answered, "I believe you SSgt and hold you to that." He then turned to the Platoon and Commanded, "**Fall-In Platoon Formation**."

The Platoon "**Fell-In**" on the 1st Squad Leader to the right facing the Duty Hut and the rest of the Platoon Fell-In on him and spaced and aligned themselves in a proper "Platoon In Line Formation". Gunny then commanded, "**Platoon, Right Face**." Followed by "**Forward, March**."

Gunny marched the Platoon to a classroom across the Grinder on Marine Corps History. The subject being taught in our morning class was the Marine Corps involvement in the Spanish-American War in 1898 and then the Boxer Rebellion against the Chinese in 1900. Class lasted for one hour and a half and afterwards, we were marched over to Sick Bay again to receive our second round of Shots.

Our Training Series of four Platoons consisted of 320 new Recruits. We were run through Sick Bay in a single File line. Two Corpsmen with what was some kind of a gun, took hold of each recruits arms, wiped each arm with alcohol then pulled the trigger injecting whatever drug it was we were scheduled to receive.

Guns were used instead of needles to save time and the cost of using traditional needles. However, there was only one draw- back in using guns. While receiving your shot, if the recruit moved at any time as the gun was shot, it would rip the skin. It happened because some recruits would jump and move if both guns didn't go off at the same time. Luckily, both guns went off at the same time when I received my shots, but some recruits weren't as lucky.

Once the Platoon received our second round of shots, it was time for the noon chow. Gunny marched us across the Grinder on our way to the 2nd Battalion Mess Hall. Gunny had us study our Red Notebooks while we again waited for our turn to go into noon chow. When it was time to form into two single file lines, I placed the Platoon Guidon in the flag stand outside the Mess Hall and got into line for chow and saluted as I passed the mirror outside the Mess Hall door.

After noon chow, Gunny marched us back to our Platoon Street. Upon arriving at our Platoon area, we were told to get your rifle and cartridge belt and "**Fall-In**" for Close Order Drill. We were marched out onto the Grinder somewhere close to the middle. Gunny had each Squad form a square on the Grinder with each Squad forming one side of the square.

There were 20 Recruit's in each squad and when the entire Platoon was in position, each recruit was one arms' length apart and was aligned perfectly in four straight lines making up the square. The entire Platoon other than myself were at "Attention" under arms. I stood at Attention in front of the line of the 1st Squad holding the Platoon Guidon. Gunny stood in the middle of the square formation and gave commands for the Manual at Arms.

There are 15 counts to the Marine Corps Manual at Arms. What that means is you go from Order Arms to Port Arms, to Right Shoulder Arms, to Left Shoulder Arms, to Present Arms, to Port Arms, to Order Arms. It takes 15 counts for all of the counts. The Manual at Arms can be performed standing at Attention or while marching. There are a few changes if performed while marching, but the movements are always the same.

Each Movement in the Manual at Arms needs to be practiced individually so we become proficient with each movement. We had to know how to perform the Manual at Arms while standing still, at Attention, before we will be able to perform it while marching.

There are different positions of the Manual at Arms that are used at different times while on Duty or at ceremonies.

Besides the positions of the Manual at Arms, there are also other positions that can be performed with a rifle. They are, but are not limited to; Inspection Arms, Rest, Parade Rest, Trail Arms, Sling Arms, Rifle Salutes, Fixing and unfixing Bayonets. Each are used at different times and are taught at different segments of trainings.

As we were lined up in the Platoon Square Formation with Gunny in the middle, we began to run through only the Manual at Arms. With the Platoon at "**Attention**" and rifle at their right side, the right hand shaped in a "V" with fingers and thumb grasping the sides of the stock. Rifle butt placed on the ground with the toe of the butt in line at the toe of the right shoe.

The Gunny gave the command, "**Platoon, Port, Arms**." Port Arms is bringing the rifle from the Order Arms Position diagonally across your body with the right hand. The left hand grasps the rifle at the balance below the bayonet stub with fingers and thumb. The barrel is at an angle that bisects the juncture of the neck and shoulder. The heal of the butt is on line with the right hip. The rifle is held at a height that allows the right forearm to be horizontal when the small of the stock is grasped with the right hand. The distance of the rifle from the body is four inches from the belt.

The Gunny then gave the command, "**Order Arms**." From Port Arms to Order Arms, the right hand is moved to re-grasp the upper part of the hand guard without moving the rifle. The left hand is removed from the balance and the rifle is lowered to the right side with the right hand until the butt is three inches from the ground. The left hand is placed immediately below the bayonet stud, fingers and thumb extended to steady and hold the barrel vertically. Then the left hand is cut sharply to the side while the rifle is lowered gently to the ground and returned to the position of Attention.

The next Command was, "**Right Shoulder Arms**." The first movement is the same as going to Port Arms, with the right elbow held down without strain. Then the rifle is re-grasped at the butt with the right hand, the heel of the butt between the first two fingers, and the thumb and fingers closed around the heel with the thumb and forefinger touching. The rifle is placed on the right shoulder with the grasp of the right hand unchanged. The left hand is moved from the balance to the small of the stock where it is used to guide the rifle to the shoulder. The thumb and fingers are extended and the joint of the left forefinger touches the rear of the receiver. The right elbow is horizontal to the ground and then the left hand is cut sharply back to its position by the side, as at Attention.

The next command from the Gunny was, "**Order Arms**." The rifle is pulled quickly toward the body with the right hand. As the rifle clears the shoulder, the right hand smartly twists the stock 90 degrees in a clockwise direction causing the rifle to be guided diagonally across the body. The right hand is moved up to grasp the upper part of the hand guard. The rifle is at Port Arms and is returned to Order Arms from Port Arms position to stand at Attention.

We then were ordered to "**Left Shoulder Arms**." The first movement is the same as going to Port Arms, with the right elbow held down without strain. The rifle is placed on the left shoulder with the right hand from the small of the stock and at the same time the heel of the stock of the rifle is driven smartly and audibly into the palm of the left hand as the right arm comes across the body. The butt is grasped with the left hand and the right hand is cut smartly to the side as in the position of attention.

Gunny next commanded "**Order Arms**." To Order Arms from Left Shoulder Arms, the right hand grasps the small of the stock and pulls the rifle from the left shoulder and the left hand grasps the rifle at the balance below the bayonet stub with fingers and thumb. The rifle is at Port Arms, and then follow by bringing the rifle from Port Arms to Order Arms.

The last movement in the Manual at Arms is, "**Present Arms.**" To execute "**Present Arms**" from "**Order Arms**," is a two-count movement. On the first count, the rifle is raised and carried to the center of the body. It is held vertically approximately 4 inches from the body with the barrel to the rear. The right elbow is down. The rifle and sling are grasped at the balance with the left hand. The left forearm is horizontal and the elbow is against your side. On the second count, the right-hand re-grasps the rifle at the small of the stock.

The next Command from Gunny was "**Order Arms**." To Order Arms from Present Arms, the rifle is grasped at the upper part of the hand guard with the right hand with the right elbow kept down and against your side. The rifle is lowered to the ground with the right hand until the butt is three inches from the ground. The left hand is placed immediately below the bayonet stud to steady the rifle and hold the barrel vertically, then the left hand is cut sharply to your left side while the rile is lowered gently to the ground, and the position of Attention is assumed.

All movements are made from the position of Attention to their finality other than performed while marching. When doing the Manual at Arms as one command, with all 15 movements, the Manual of Arms begins from the position of

Attention, and from there, all movements, are executed from the position of Port Arms. The same is true when returning to Order Arms, minor movements to Port Arms and then to the position of Attention.

We continued to execute the Manual at Arms for the next two hours. On one occasion, Gunny had us lay our weapons on the ground and had us "**Lien Two**." Once the entire Platoon was in a "**Lien Two**," position, Gunny gave the command, "**25 pushups, cadence count, ready, exercise**." We then began to count off, 1,2,3 one Sir, 1,2,3, two Sir, 1,2,3 three Sir and so on until we got to 25. When doing 25 pushups at cadence counts, you actually do 50 pushups.

After we finished doing our 25 pushups, Gunny had us grab our rifles and assume the position of "**Attention**," and align each Squad. We were again in a perfect square with each Squad of 20 Recruits forming each line. We then began to practice the Manual at Arms again. The other punishment Gunny would give us when we had our rifles, was to hold our rifles straight out in front of us until told to go back to "**Attention**." God help you if you let your arms and your rifle down before being told to do so. We continued until 1600, then the Gunny had us "**Fall-In**" our regular Platoon Formation.

Gunny Wolfmule wasn't as efficient in getting our platoon to march in Close Order Drill as Sgt James on the Drill Field. Sgt James had a different cadence then Gunny or Sgt Martinez. We seemed to be more relaxed and more in step with his cadence than the other two. Besides, Gunny scared the Hell out of us most of the time when he had the Duty. It seemed like his favorite words to say were "**Lien To**," plus he liked to hit the Recruits in the solar plex.

With Sgt James, Close Order Drill became very interesting, with commands and movements that tested us in many ways even though we were only in our third week of training. He would introduce new movements like, "**Right Oblique**," and "**Left Oblique**." Flanking movements, both

'**Left and Right Flank**," and how to change direction to the rear as we marched, "**Platoon to the Rear, March.**" We were attempting to get better, but it seemed certain individuals had no rhythm, no coordination, two left feet and couldn't follow instructions very well. All of these shortcomings cost us hundreds of pushups daily.

As Gunny was marching us back to the Platoon Area we passed a Platoon from the 1st Battalion that was Graduating on Friday, so Gunny had us "**Halt**," "**Order Arms**," and then execute a "**Left Face**," He then gave us the command to "**At Ease**." We stayed in that position for the next 15 minutes watching the 1st Battalion, Platoon 1153 perform Close Order Drill on the Grinder.

Gunny stood next to me while Platoon 1153 went through their paces of Close Order Drill while looking like they have been in the Corps for years. Gunny told me to pay attention to their Guidon. I noticed that there were at least 4 streamers under their Spindle of their Guidon. Gunny also told me Platoon 1153 was the Honor Platoon of their Training Series and won the Close Order Drill Competition and the Gold Streamer that sits upon their Guidon.

As I stood there watching Platoon 1153 go through their paces, I was surprised that Gunny talked to me as casually as he did about what we were watching. I was as scared as I got when Gunny was around. I seemed to relax just a little even though he stayed next to me the entire time we watched Platoon 1153 perform for us. That was one surprising memory I never forgot.

Week 3 of Boot Camp consisted of Head Calls, clean-up, formations, PT, extra pushups, classes, close order drill, chow three times a day, getting shots at sick bay, and the biggest surprise during week 3 came on Friday after we stripped our racks when returning from morning chow. We were told we would participate in our first Payday since joining the Marines.

On Friday, 30 September at 1000 hours we would form up to receive our first Pay Day. In the Marine Corps, you get paid every two weeks, on the 15th and the 30th of each month. You never received a Pay Check, you were always paid in cash. Gunny Wolfmule took charge of the Platoon on Friday and marched us to meet the Disbursing Officer.

Disbursing would set up a couple of tables, inside the 2nd Battalion, FOX Company Office, and each Platoon would file through, one squad at a time, to get paid. Platoon 2225 went through the Disbursing Line first and our Platoon waited our turn. As you go through the Pay line, the first person you meet is the Disbursing Clerk. He would ask for your name, service number, and you would have to show your ID Card.

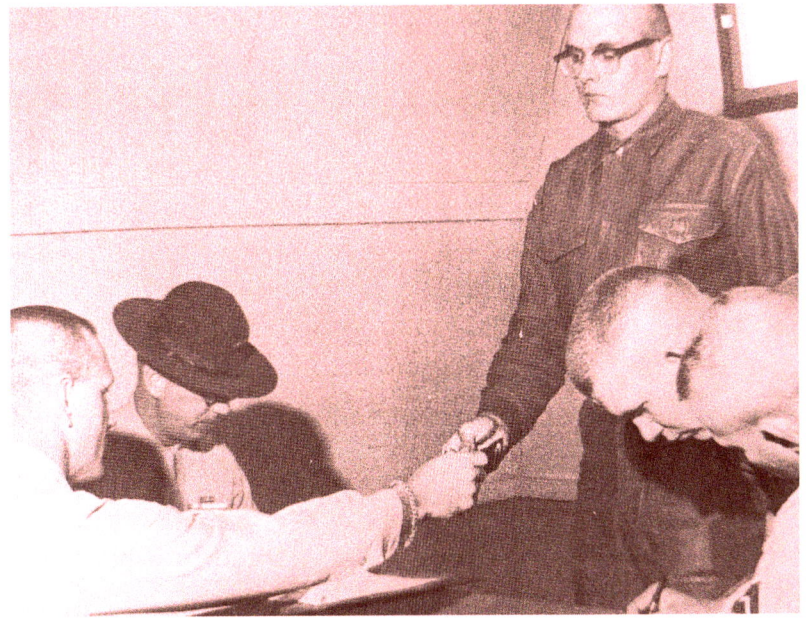

Once your name was found, you would sidestep to the right and the Disbursing Clerk would tell the Disbursing Officer how much you were to be paid. The Disbursing Officer would count out your Pay while you watched and then he would have you sign your name on the Pay Log.

Besides signing for my Pay, the Disbursing Officer had me sign a W-2 Form acknowledging that Taxes were withheld. I claimed zero dependents.

Since we were all Privates attending Boot camp, we all received the exact same amount of Pay. The Gross monthly Pay for a Marine Corps Private in Boot Camp in 1966 was $90.00 per month, and after deducting Federal Income Tax we would receive $41.00 per Pay Day while we were Privates.

Once we received our Pay, at the end of the Disbursing Table, there was a bucket which was designated as the DI Training Fund, and it was suggested that each recruit donate $2.00 of their pay towards the Fund. The way the Fund was described to me I was more than happy to donate my $2.00.

That first Pay Day was The first Pay Day on the 30th of September. We all received $57.00 instead of $41.00, because we didn't get paid on the 15th of September, which is the normal Pay Day. Our first day of Boot Camp was on the 9th and our Training Schedule didn't allow us to get paid on the 15th. So instead of 15 days, we were paid for 21 days.

Those who had wallets put their money in their wallets. Those that didn't have a wallet put their pay in their left breast pocket with their ID card until we could return to our huts where we could lock it up in our footlockers.

Our Pay would remain the same all the way through Boot Camp and would continue at $41.00 per pay period. The only way to earn more income while in the Marines was to get promoted to a higher Rank. The next Rank after Private is Private First Class. There was a chance that six or seven Recruits in our Platoon could be promoted to Private First Class (PFC) at the end of Boot Camp. Those not promoted out of Boot Camp could be eligible for promotion after nine months in the Corps.

After our Platoon received our Pay, Gunny marched us over to the PX for the first time. Once in Formation outside of the PX, Gunny told us what we would be allowed to buy and what we were not allowed to buy. He made it clear that if we

purchased anything we were not enti-
tled to, we would pay the consequences
of which would be to have our purchase
confiscated and lose the privilege to go
to the PX for a month.

The only items we would be allowed
to purchase at the PX while in Boot
Camp, were cigarettes, a cigarette case,
a lighter, Kiwi Shoe Polish, Brasso for
shinning our brass belt buckles, liquid
starch, a wallet, writing paper, envelopes,
stamps, and a writing pen. We were not
allowed to purchase anything else at this time, and especially
no Gedunk. *(gum, candy, snacks or food of any kind).*

The funny thing about buying cigarettes was that so
far in Boot Camp we had never been given permission to
smoke. The only way we would be allowed to smoke would
be when, or if, either Gunny Wolfmule or either DI would
Light the "Smoking Lamp." Unless the "Smoking Lamp" has
been lit, don't even think about smoking or ever get caught
smoking without permission.

While we were at the PX Gunny had one Squad at a
time enter and make their purchases. As the Right Guide, I
went in with the 1st Squad and there was a Flag stand outside
the door to place our Platoon Guidon. I purchased a can of
Brasso, a tablet of writing paper, a box of envelopes, a page
of 10 stamps, and a Pen. My purchase cost me $5.25.

After I paid for my purchases, I picked up the Platoon
Guide-On and returned to our formation to wait for the next
three Squads to make their purchases. When everyone was
finished and were back in formation, Sgt Martinez relieved
Gunny Wolfmule and marched us back to our Platoon area.

As Sgt Martinez marched us back to the Platoon area,
he didn't like the way we were marching so, he stopped the
Platoon in the middle of the street and had us "**Lien To**." We
had to do 25 pushups to cadence count. When we did pushups

to the cadence count, it went exactly like Gunny would do it, **"25 Pushups, Cadence Count, Ready exercise."**

We would then count off "1,2,3, 1 Sir, 1,2,3, 2 Sir, 1,2,3, 3 Sir, 1,2,3, 4 Sir" and so forth until we hit 25. If we didn't do our pushups together while counting, he would say, "Whoa mob, get it together. Let's start over. "25 Pushups, Cadence Count, Ready **Exercise**." We would begin again, "1,2,3, 1 Sir, 1,2,3, 2 Sir, 1,2,3, 3 Sir" and hopefully stay together until we hit 25 uninterrupted.

There were times we would get up to 15 or even 20 and have to start over again. Sometimes we would start over again four or five times. It depended on the mood of who was punishing us, or how pissed off they were at us that day. Of course if recruits weren't doing the Pushups correctly, or weren't keeping in cadence, we were made to start over. If recruits knees were on the deck we would start over. There were times in the first couple of weeks that we did so many pushups, we were too weak to do anymore.

The main idea in the first couple of weeks of Boot Camp was to break us down physically and mentally. After that was accomplished, their goal was to build us back up again, but to their specifications both mentally and physically. So far up through week three, they were accomplishing their intended purpose.

We spent Saturday morning in the **"Platoon Box Formation"** doing the **"Manual at Arms,"** and after the noon chow, we spent the rest of the afternoon just doing "Close Order Drill." The other change at the end of week three, was after evening Chow, Gunny Wolfmule lit the *"Smoking Lamp"* for the first time since Boot Camp began. Also, Commanders Time became longer in the evenings before hitting the rack. We were given time to write letters or perform other personal things.

The first *"Smoking Lamp"* was given after evening chow when we returned to the Platoon Street. Gunny Wolfmule told the Platoon that if you have cigarettes, you were to go into your hut and retrieve them. Then he said, "The *"Smoking*

Lamp" is lit for one cigarette. Those who smoke light-um up. Those not smoking return to your Hut and shine your Inspection Boots until the "*Smoking Lamp*" is out."

He then dismissed the Platoon and at least 35 guys came back on Platoon Street and lit up a cigarette. As they smoked, Gunny walked up and down the Platoon Street and observed those smoking while the rest of us shined our boots. The "*Smoking Lamp*" was lit for only 15 minutes and when the Recruit finished his cigarette, he was to field strip his cigarette butt and those who didn't do it properly, were told to "**Lien To**" and Gunny had them do at least 25 pushups.

If you smoke, you need to know how to field strip your cigarette butt when you are finished. Non-filtered cigarettes have a small butt left, and the proper way to field strip it is to pinch the lit end between your finger and thumb letting the ash and tobacco drop to the ground. The tobacco is biodegradable and the ash dissolves. Roll the remaining paper between your hands, rolling your hands back and forth until the remaining butt falls apart and any remaining tobacco that's left is just like dust. The paper that's left is balled up into a small piece of paper that you put in your pocket for disposal in the trash.

Filtered cigarettes are field stripped the same way, except the filter does not get rolled between your hands, just pinch the lit end and roll between thumb and finger and let the remaining tobacco fall to the ground and then put the filter and any paper left in your pocket to dispose of in the trash.

You smoke only one cigarette unless you are told the "*Smoking Lamp*" is lit either for a stated period of time or in a certain space where smoking is allowed. To be honest, when the "*Smoking Lamp*" was lit the non-smokers had some other task to perform or were put on a work detail, so many non-smokers became smokers within the first week of having the "*Smoking Lamp*" turned on. I was one of the non-smokers who became a smoker.

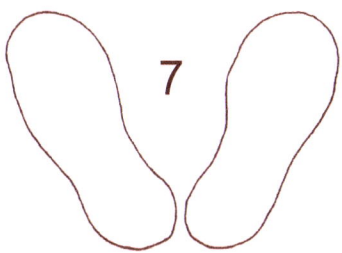

The Obstacle Course

On Sunday morning, those who chose to, were allowed to attend Church Services, and Sunday morning after chow was reserved for Commanders Time, also for writing letters, shining boots, reading the Marine Corps manual and at times, rifle cleaning, or other personal choices. The *"Smoking Lamp"* was lit on Sundays during Commanders Time which meant if you stayed back with the Platoon, after morning chow, you could smoke as much as you liked until 1100.

So on Sunday of Week 4, some of the Recruits who normally attended Church Services decided not to attend after they found out the *"Smoking Lamp"* was lit all morning. I took time during Commanders Time to write to my mother, my buddy Zane, and to the girl I had been dating before the Marines, named Linda. After Commanders Time on Sunday ended and everyone had returned from Church Services, we went to noon chow and then training began again in earnest.

Sunday afternoons were normally spent on the Grinder with our rifles and cartridge belts doing Close Order Drill. This Sunday Sgt Martinez and Sgt James had the Platoon **"Fall-In"** Platoon Formation in Line and after having us **"Open Ranks,"** showed us how to **"Stack Arms."** The first movement when ordered to **"Stack Arms,"** has each Squad to count off by three starting with the Squad Leader. The number two man of each set of three is designated as the "**Stackman.**"

The next command is, "**Prepare Slings**." The Stackman places the butt of their rifle on their right hip and cradle it in the crook of their right arm. The individual then adjusts the sling keeper to form a four-inch loop (a palm's width within the loop) next to the upper sling swivel. As soon as the Stackman has prepared the loop, he returns to "**Order Arms**." After all Stackmen are at "**Order Arms**," the command "**Stack Arms**" is given.

The Stackman places his rifle directly in front of and centered on his body with the sling facing to the front. The heel of the rifle butt is on the ground on line with the toes of the Stackman. The Stackman grasps the rifle by the hand guard with his left hand. The first two fingers of the left hand hold the inner part of the loop against the rifle and grasps the outer part of the loop and holds it open for the insertion rifles from #1 and #3. All individuals hold their rifles vertical at all times.

After the Stackman has his rifle in position, the individuals on the right and the left, raise and rotate their rifles, sling up to a horizontal position across their body. Individual to the left and the right hold the rifle at the small of the stock and the other hand, palm downward over the sling. As soon as both individuals have their rifles ready to sling, they each take one step towards the Stackman and insert the muzzle of their rifles into the loop held by the Stackman until the bayonet stud protrudes past the far end of the loop.

When both rifles have been inserted into the loop, the individuals swing the butts of their rifles outward and down to the ground until the stack is tight with the rifle butts on line and approximately two feet from the base line. After any necessary adjustments have been made, all three individuals come back to the position of attention.

Once the entire Platoon had their rifles stacked, Sgt James put the Platoon "At Ease," and lit the "*Smoking*

Lamp." Not everyone smoked, but those that had cigarettes lit them up and enjoyed their 15 minute smoke while the rest of us just relaxed while they smoked.

When the *"Smoking Lamp"* was turned off, Sgt James brought us back to **"Attention,"** and discussed how and why **"Stack Arms"** are used.

Sgt James then had us reverse the process of unstacking our Arms. The Command of unstacking arms is called **"Taking Arms."** Upon the command of **"Taking Arms,"** have the individuals on the right and the left grasp their rifle and bring it horizontally across their bodies with the sling up and then removed them from the loop returning to the position of **"Order Arms."** The Stackman then takes his rifle and placing it on his right hip, adjusts the sling removing the loop and return to **"Order Arms."**

We actually went through the same procedure of **"Stacking Arms,"** a total of three times. Sgt James and Sgt

Martinez were confident that we had a general idea and were satisfied to have us **"Close Ranks,"** and had us march with our rifles doing **"Close Order Drill,"** and the Marching **"Manual at Arms."**

We were marched back to our Platoon Area Huts to return our Rifles and cartridge belts back on our racks then **"Fall-In,"** on Platoon Street for evening chow. Sgt James had the evening Duty and marched us to evening chow. We were told to read our Red Notebooks again while we waited our turn to get in line for evening chow. I placed our Platoon Guidon in the flag stand outside the Mess Hall and took my place in front of the Platoon. I took my Red Notebook out of my pocket and studied my 11 General Orders.

When our time came to go through the chow line, we were treated to a pot roast, mashed potatoes, broiled fish, brown rice, vegetables, dinner rolls and all the fixings, with Lemon pie for dessert and the usual milk, iced tea, coffee and water to drink. After evening chow, we were returned to our Platoon area to clean-up, enjoy Commanders Time, brush our teeth, get ready for lights out and couldn't wait until Taps. I was tired and looked forward to getting some sleep.

There were no changes from our morning routine through week four. Reveille still at 0500, head call, PT, shit, shower, shave, field day and morning chow. We began to start looking like Marines although we were far from it. We still had our top button on our utility shirt buttoned and had not yet been given permission to blouse our trousers. This indicated we were still Boots in the beginning of training. Appearance at this stage wasn't as important as the knowledge we were gaining every day.

We continued classes on the M-14 rifle as well as classes on the .45 caliber pistol. We attended classes on the history of former Marines who won Medals of Honor and Marine battles as far back as the Revolutionary War. We learned what everything on our uniforms meant, the Eagle,

Globe and Anchor, the Quatrefoil on Officers Covers, the Blood Stripe on NCO Trousers, Rank and Insignias.

We practiced the 15 count Manual At Arms with our M-14 Rifles. We marched with rifles and many hours were spent on the parade deck honing our skills while in a platoon formation, staying in step and finding a comfort level listening to the DI's cadence as we marched. We learned not to bounce as we marched 30 inches to a step, 120 steps per minute, arms-length front to rear, covering down behind the Marine in front and staying aligned to the Marine to your right or left.

We were finally starting to get it. We still didn't look as good as the senior platoons on the depot, but we were coming along. The Platoon began bonding with each other and we were learning how to perform for Gunny Wolfmule as well as both Sgt James and Sgt Martinez. Believe it or not, our Platoon began to take on the personality of each of our DI's when they were on Duty, but each one treated the Platoon differently, so it was like the Platoon had a split personality.

Gunny could be ruthless, or he could be a big teddy bear. When he was ruthless, he was unbearable to be around, but when he was mild and meek, he would light the "*Smoking Lamp*" and compliment us on our progress. His hot button was showing off our Guidon as he marched his Platoon around the Depot.

If we screwed up while marching he had no mercy on us and no matter where it was, he would have us "**Lien To**" and we'd do pushups until his anger subsided. The other thing Gunny was famous for, was if you pissed him off in any way, he would have you stand at Attention in front of him, then he would look to his right, then he would look to his left, and then when he was sure there were no Officer's around, he would punch you in your solar plexus. The reason he looked to make sure there were no Officers around was if he got caught hitting a recruit, he would be in trouble.

Sgt James was a perfectionist when it came to Close Order Drill. He had a special cadence compared to Gunny Wolfmule or Sgt Martinez. We performed Close Order Drill much better while marching to Sgt James cadence than for Gunny or Sgt Martinez. Sgt James was also a masochist when not on the Grinder. He liked to torture recruits who screwed up when he disciplined them and his favorite penalty was either grabbing or hitting the recruit in the nuts. He had a good side if he liked you, if you were a screw up, he had a sinister way of seeking you out for punishment.

Sgt Martinez was mostly meek and mild compared to the Gunny or Sgt James. His discipline was always pushups or bends and thrusts. I never witnessed him hitting any recruit like Gunny or Sgt James, he didn't yell very loud, but he could make his point just the same. His cadence with Close

Order Drill wasn't as smooth as Sgt James, but he had more patience than either Gunny or Sgt James.

Wednesday of week 4 after morning clean-up and before going to morning chow, Gunny had the Duty and after Inspecting the 4th Squad Hut, Gunny had Pvt Wilson the Squad Leader in the sand pit next to the Duty Hut doing "**Bends and Thrusts**." Before we "**Fell-In**" for morning chow, Gunny re-placed Pvt Williams as Squad Leader and replaced him with Pvt Hesch.

After morning chow on Wednesday, we got our first glimpse of the Obstacle Course. Gunny marched us to the Obstacle Course so we could get a taste of what was to come. He had us double time in

formation around the Track Field, had us climb over an 8 foot wall, walk over a field of uneven stumps, climb a rope and swing across a ditch full of water, and climb up to a platform and walk hand over hand across a rope 20 feet off the ground.

I thought that first time through the Obstacle Course was kind of fun, and it was something I could look forward to doing again. However, there were a number of Obstacles we didn't attempt that first day, but they looked like they would be a challenge when we finally got around to attempting them.

We had been here four weeks now, so we were getting into a disciplined routine and getting used to certain inconveniences. No matter what we were put through, it was apparent nothing they did was going to kill us. One thing was certain, everyone looked forward to lights out. Once the light was turned off, we felt safe in our racks and when we heard Taps, it was OK to close our eyes.

On Friday of week four we changed the linen on our racks, and after morning chow, we spent the rest of the morning attending classes. The first class was on the Chain of Command, responsibility and discipline when it comes to standing Watch. The OOD, Sgt of the Guard, CPL of the Guard, the how and why there are 11 general orders, and how

to report from our assigned post or report a violation while on duty. The second class was on Uniforms and Equipment.

After noon chow we returned to our Huts and got our rifles and cartridge belts and spent the afternoon working on close order drill with rifles and reviewing the Manual at Arms while marching. After evening chow we remade our racks and drilled for about an hour before holding mail call. After the *"Smoking Lamp"* was lit we spent the rest of the evening on Commanders Time.

Saturday was a regular training day, and we attended classes all morning and after we had noon chow because Sgt James had the Duty, we spent the entire afternoon on the Grinder. Of all the training we had experienced since arriving at Boot Camp, Close Order Drill was where we spent most of our time. After four weeks, it seemed we were getting better while marching, and I suppose everything had a time frame. I believe we were on schedule. We had been taught the basics, now it was time for more complicated movements. We actually spent most of the day doing **"Column Right"** and **"Column Left"** while marching with our rifles.

Sgt James' emphasis was to have each of our 81 Recruits have the heel of their boot hit the ground all at the same time which made a certain sound that was distinct and when one person out of 81 wasn't in sync, you could hear it. Twice we were "Halted" and told to **"Lien Two."** Both times we executed more than 50 push-ups and Sgt James called out those Recruits that caused us to **"Lien Two,"** making sure each Squad Leader knew they had work to do to motivate and square away a few members of their Squads.

Once back at the Platoon area, Gunny made time to explain to me that as the **"Right Guide,"** from time to time, I would be given instructions from the Platoon Commander and the two DI's to pass on to the Squad Leaders now that we were getting into the crucial part of training. If they wanted to stay Squad Leaders, they better shape up the shit birds in their Squads. As the Platoon Leaders, we were encouraged to motivate, and help Recruits with their individual shortcomings.

I would meet with the Squad Leaders every morning and every evening for five minutes to pass on both positive and negative comments from the Gunny or the DI's. Based 118 on our success in solving the issues that were brought to our attention, the Squad leaders and I were either punished our rewarded.

The punishments for Squad Leaders included being punched in the gut, or trips to the "sand box", or being replaced like already happened to Pvt Wilson. Punishments were not just limited to Squad Leaders. Mass punishment was the order of the day whenever anyone messed up whether it was on the Drill Field, in a classroom, during clean-up, or on the obstacle course. We were getting pretty good at doing pushups and after being broken down physically, we were being rebuilt every day.

Our reward for positive performance whether on the Grinder passing Inspections, or not screwing up, was a possible extra *"Smoking Lamp"* being lit. Other rewards came in the form of extra time during Commander's Time to write letters or to read the mail we received. After four weeks, we were now settled into a normal routine and the training schedule was becoming more intense.

Sunday morning of week five began as usual. PT on the Grinder, morning hygiene, and then we made sure all our racks were made before those Recruits who chose to attend Church Services were dismissed to "**Fall-In**" with their denomination. Those who chose to stay with the Platoon, "**Fell-In**" for morning chow and afterwards conducted clean-up of our Huts, our Platoon area and places of responsibility.

After Sunday Commanders Time, Sgt Martinez had the Duty and had us "**Fall-In**" for noon chow. Afterwards we spent the majority of the day on the Grinder. Although we performed better when Sgt James was marching the Platoon, Sgt Martinez ran us through our paces, marching with our rifles. We spent all day reviewing every Drill movement we had been taught except "**Stack Arms**."

Monday morning of week 5 routine continued as all the weeks before us, 0500 reveille, PT, morning hygiene, field day, chow. After we returned from morning chow, while standing on Platoon Street, SSgt Richards leaned over from his Platoon and said, "Good morning Pvt Rilley." I answered, "Sir, Good Morning Sir." He then asked, "How are you this morning Pvt Rilley?" Before I could answer, Gunny came out of the Duty Hut and said, "Good Morning SSgt Richards haven't you got something better to do than harass my Recruits?" SSgt Richards answered, "Just saying good morning to Pvt Rilley Gunny, not being disrespectful." Gunny said, **"Carry-On SSgt"** He answered, **"Aye Aye, Gunny."**

Gunny shot me a look but then said, **"Report Pvt"** I answered, "Sir, 81 Recruits present Sir." He answered, **"Very Well."** Sgt James was also on Duty this morning and today we were going to begin less classroom and more physical training, starting on the obstacle course. Sgt James and

Gunny both marched us over to the area where the track field and the obstacle course were.

The first thing we did whenever we went to the Obstacle Course was to run in Platoon Formation around the track field. After our run, there was a flag stand at the entrance to the obstacle course and Gunny told me to Post our Guidon and we began our physical training by Squad. I always trained with the 1st Squad, so we were led to the area where we got into three lines and had to climb a rope with no knots that was 30 feet high to get to the top. When you got to the top, you swung yourself over to one of three ladders that took you to a platform 20 feet below. Once at the bottom, you were on a platform six feet off the ground. To get to the other side, you had to walk 25 feet on a log to get across to the other side. Once on the other side of the log crossing, you had to climb another 25 foot log wall with the logs 20 feet across and four feet between logs. The top seven feet had a wall built onto the logs which you had to climb and cross over to a rope and hand-over- hand make your way 25 feet to the ground at a 45-degree angle

The obstacle course was also referred to as the "Confidence Course," because some of the obstacles were pretty scary and it built your confidence to overcome them. Some of the Recruits were scared of heights, and needed to be coaxed to attempt them. Although some Recruits had to be pushed and persuaded to attempt certain obstacles, everyone had to get over, under and through every obstacle on the course.

During week three, Gunny had given us a taste of some of the obstacles, but today we'd be engaged in overcoming more challenging obstacles in front of us. The Obstacles we were encountering today were scary and until actually traversing each one, our confidence would increase.

In the Marines, we at times travel by ship and are trained to hit the beach. To descend from the ship, Landing Nets are

used like ladders to get over the side and onto landing crafts, so we had a Landing Net Ladder to practice on. There was a platform 30 feet high and on both sides of the platform, a landing net ladder was set up. The net was 20 feet wide made out of rope and the steps were spaced in 12 inch squares. We would line up at the base and three at a time would climb to the tower, go across to the other side and climb down the other side.

There were two scary obstacles yet to come. One you needed help to conquer because it was a tower with 4 floors, and you had to work in teams to get from one floor to the next. The tower was 35 feet high, with four large poles at each corner that held the structure up. The first level was four feet off the ground, and you could manage to scale that by yourself. The second floor was six feet higher, and you needed to work as a team to get to the second floor. The third floor was eight feet higher, and you definitely needed help from both above and below to get to that level.

The ceiling on the third floor was another seven feet high with a cutout in the middle of the floor, but you didn't need to get onto the fourth floor. There were two ropes attached on the poles that held the floors up and it was 25 feet to the ground. The ropes were attached to another platform that was 40 feet away from the tower that you had to go hand over hand to get to the bottom. You would have to reach out and grab the rope and either swing your feet onto the rope and shimmy down or go hand over hand until you reach the bottom.

Of all the obstacles we had encountered that day, the last one was absolutely the hardest and the scariest. We had one Recruit fall while climbing over the wall and missing the rope to get to the ground and broke his arm. He would be dropped from our Platoon and after he healed he would join another Platoon to Graduate Boot Camp.

There were other obstacles we encountered, like the rope crossing, which was 15 feet off the ground and 20 feet across and we had to go hand over hand and cross the 20 feet. As an added attraction, there was a three foot deep water ditch below if you decided to fall off. There was also a 20 foot Monkey Bar crossing, and a pull up bar.

One of the Platoon's favorite exercises on the obstacle course was the Log Roll. There were two versions, a 14-foot log which weighed approximately 300 pounds and a 16-foot log that weighed 400 pounds. Eight men to a log would hold them over their heads and do up downs, then pass them across to eight other men and then pass them back. We did sit-ups with them; we stood and threw them in the air and caught them.

This was the time when Squad Leaders paid special attention to those not carrying their own weight or not giving 100%.

There were other training exercises we would experience before we finished Boot Camp, but not during week five. We spent all morning at the Obstacle Course then enjoyed a great lunch at noon Chow. Sgt Martinez had us "**Fall-In**," after noon chow, and right there in formation outside the Mess Hall, he lit the *"Smoking Lamp."* That was a big surprise, and doing so endeared Sgt Martinez to the smokers of our Platoon.

After Sgt Martinez had us Field Strip our cigarettes, we were marched back to our Platoon Street and told to switch out of our utility shirts and put on our yellow sweatshirts, get our rifles and cartridge belts. Gunny Wolfmule met Sgt Martinez as we "**Fell Back In**" on Platoon Street and then we were marched back toward the Obstacle Course.

There was a large field next to the football field with a platform about four feet off the ground and about eight feet by eight feet square. Sgt Martinez marched the Platoon until we were centered on the platform and had us "**Halt**." Gunny was standing on the platform holding an M14 rifle. Sgt Martinez had us "**Open Ranks**," and then had us "**Dress Right Dress**." We then doubled our distance between each recruit.

Sgt Martinez had each Recruit pick up his rifle and touch it to the recruits left shoulder giving each Squad twice as much space between each recruit. We were now spread out front to rear and twice as much as usual left to right. Sgt Martinez then turned to Gunny Wolfmule and said, "All yours Gunny."

Gunny told us to hold our rifle out in front of us, right hand on the small of the stock and the left hand on the front of the hand guard, sling up. He told us to follow his every move. With our arms straight out we began to exercise with our rifles. We spread our feet shoulder length and began what was known as Physical Drill Under Arms.

We held our rifles over our head and lifted our rifles up and down to a cadence count. We held our rifles in front of us and push out and in to a cadence count. We side stepped to the right and then to the left. We bent at the waist and did up downs to cadence count. We continued Physical Drill Under Arms for an hour before Gunny had us take the bayonet with scabbard off of our cartridge belts and then Fix Bayonets onto the front of our M14 rifles. This took a few minutes, because some recruits had to undo their cartridge belts to get the scabbard off the belt.

Once everyone had their Bayonets attached to their rifles, the Gunny brought the Formation to "**Attention**," and then the next Command was "**Port Arms**." The entire Platoon as well as Gunny went to "**Port Arms**." Gunny instructed us that all Commands begin and end at "**Port Arms**."

"There are many positions, and you will learn and practice all of them. They are Guard, Whirl, Jab, Thrust, Parry, Smash, Slash and Butt Stroke. Some positions like Thrust has a Long Thrust and a Short Thrust, same with Jabs, Short Jabs and Long Jabs. Butt Strokes can be Vertical Butt Stroke or Horizontal Butt Stroke."

BAYONET COURSE

Gunny demonstrated how each movement was executed. The Platoon did each movement by the number, as the Gunny told us what the movement would be and then gave the Command to execute it. We practiced Bayonet Training all the rest of the afternoon. Before we left the training area, Gunny lit the "*Smoking Lamp*."

When the "Smoking Lamp" was out, Sgt Martinez marched us back to the Platoon Street where we made a Head Call, changed back into our utility shirts, put our rifles and cartridge belts back on our racks and got ready for evening chow.

We marched to evening chow and afterwards we attended a class on The Code of Conduct. When we returned to the Platoon area, we enjoyed a leisurely evening with having the "*Smoking Lamp*" lit and mail Call, cleaning our rifles then

shining our boots during Commanders Time and at 2200, lights out and TAPS.

While I lay in my rack before I fell asleep, I was thinking of home and how much I missed taking showers with my girlfriend Linda and drinking beer with my buddy Zane and his girlfriend Susan. A cold beer would taste good right about now. I fell asleep and before I knew it, Reveille.

Tuesday morning after our usual routine and morning chow, we were marched again to Sick Bay to get our last series of shots. Afterwards, Sgt Martinez marched us to another class on Marine Corps History. After class we spent an hour or so on the Grinder and then headed for noon chow. We actually spent the entire afternoon on the Grinder going through Close Order Drill, evening chow, Commanders Time and Lights Out. Tuesday went by pretty fast without much incident.

Wednesday morning started like every other morning since arriving at Marine Corp Recruit Depot. Reveille, PT, morning hygiene, clean-up, morning chow and this morning after chow we returned to our Huts and we told to put on our red PT shorts and yellow sweatshirt, socks and tennis shoes along with our utility cover. Sgt James had the Duty and had us **"Fall Out"** on the Platoon Street and marched the Platoon over to the other side of the 1st Battalion Mess Hall where we moved into a building that held a swimming pool.

Today we were going to find out who could swim and who couldn't and be taught how to drown proof. The first thing we did was take off our yellow sweatshirts, put our

socks inside our tennis shoes and wrap our tennis shoes and covers inside the yellow sweatshirt and place them on a shelf.

The Swim Instructors took over the Platoon and asked by a show of hands who did not know how to swim. There were six or seven recruits who raised their hands. They were moved to the end of the pool. The instructor then ordered the rest of our Platoon to form ten lines and to stand at the deep end of the pool.

The next thing to figure out was whether you were a floater or a sinker. Everyone floats but not everyone floats the same because of the way their body is structured. The human body is slightly less dense than water. People who float have a higher percentage of body fat. People who sink have higher bone density or more muscle mass.

Muscular or thin people have a tendency to sink, people with high body fat content are more likely to float. The average human body has 3 – 4 pounds of positive buoyancy in fresh water. In sea water everyone is much less dense and will float easier.

Drownproofing is a survival technique that involves floating vertically in water while keeping the head submerged and the lungs filled with air. In order to do Drownproofing properly, you must stay calm – using breath control. Float in a relaxed posture and raise your head to breathe approximately every 10 to 15 seconds.

This process was continued until all Recruits were identified. It was amazing to see we had more floaters than sinkers. Two Instructors took charge of the Floaters and two Instructors took charge of the sinkers. The rest of the morning, the Recruits were taught how to stay calm and use breath control, to float in a relaxed vertical posture and to raise their head to breathe and then submerge their head and float again repeating the process until they could do it for 45 minutes.

We continued to drown proof until 1130 and then got out of the pool, dressed and returned to our Platoon area to change clothes and get ready for noon chow. Our time for noon chow this day was 1250 so we had plenty of time to get dressed and get to noon chow.

After noon chow, we attended a class on Code of Conduct. We were given stories on the History of Prisoners of War from WW II, how the troops who were captured, how they were treated by the Germans, the Japanese and how some prisoners cracked, and others were executed. The class ended on stories of Prisoners of War during the Korean War. How they were treated and the attempt to brainwash them and how others were tortured.

After our first class we then attended a class on our 11 General Orders. Part of the class was to ask for volunteers to stand and recite our General Orders from memory. I volunteered four separate times to recite the Orders, but was only called on once, although I promised never to volunteer.

Thursday after our normal morning routine, and after morning chow, we spent the entire day at the Obstacle Course, attacking the challenging Obstacles that challenged us. Then after noon chow we returned to the Obstacle Course area, where we participated in the Endurance Course and Log Drill.

The Endurance Course consisted of the Rope Walk which was a platform 15 feet off the ground 20 yards long with six ropes which you had to go hand over hand the 20 yards to cross. The Monkey Bar Run was 12 feet off the ground and had 20 rungs from start to finish, using hand to hand to complete.

One of the biggest challenges is the Log Drill with logs that weighed 300 to 400 pounds. There were 6 of each size Log set up for this Physical Fitness Challenge. The Log required six to eight Recruits to carry each Log. The exercises consisted of Bicep curls, Overhead presses, Shoulder to shoulder passes, Side benders, Log squats and throwing the log back and forth.

The last exercise we performed before finishing the Endurance Course was the three-mile run. For this we moved to the Track Field which was a quarter mile oval track. Instead of running it individually, our Platoon ran it in Platoon Formation staying in step and at times calling cadence. The time necessary to complete the three miles was 12 laps in 28 minutes or less.

After finishing the Endurance Course, we were spent as it had been a full day. Obstacle course in the morning and tackling the Endurance Course in the afternoon. I am sure we will all sleep well tonight. We made our way to evening chow and although we had a full training day, after evening chow we still spent another two hours practicing Close Order Drill on the Grinder.

After securing our rifles to our racks and hanging up our cartridge belts, the Platoon was back on the Platoon Street to hear Sgt James explain what we could expect on Friday. We were to strip our Linen, do our laundry, enjoy another Pay Day and if we didn't screw up, make another trip to the PX. He then lit the *"Smoking Lamp."* Those who do not smoke were dismissed to begin Commanders Time while the rest of the smokers enjoyed our evening smoke.

The 15th of October was on a Saturday, so we got paid on Friday the 14th. After morning chow and stripping our Racks, Sgt James had the Platoon get our dirty clothes, our buckets, our bottle of Wisk, our scrub brush, and marched the Platoon over to the wash racks to wash our clothes. Then we hung them on the clothes lines. He also had to pick two Recruits to guard our laundry while we went to get paid.

Sgt James picked Recruits Pvt Evanoff and Pvt Bowman to sit on their buckets and guard our laundry. He told them he would have them relieved to get paid. We marched back to our Platoon area to put our Wisk and scrub brush back in our footlocker and return our buckets under our rack. We then "**Fell-In**" and were marched to the area where the Disbursing Officer would give us our Pay.

When we reached the area outside of the 2nd Battalion Headquarters Hut, Platoon 2228 was getting paid. Sgt James had our Platoon "**Fall-In**" by Squad behind Platoon 2228 while they finished getting paid and then followed them through the Pay Line. Again, we would give our name, show our ID Card, then receive our Pay of $41.00 in Cash, and then place $2.00 in the DI Fund bucket. After the first two Recruits were paid, Sgt James had them go and relieve Pvt Evanoff and Pvt Bowman from the wash racks so they could get paid.

Once the entire Platoon had received their Pay, we were then marched over to the PX. Upon arriving at the PX, we had to wait again until Platoon 2228 finished up their shopping before Sgt James let us enter the PX, one Squad at a time. We stood at Rest and were told to read our Red Notebooks until it was time to enter the PX. I never read my Red Book while I was holding the Platoon Guidon.

Once the last Recruit from Platoon 2228 finished shopping and left the PX, Sgt James brought our Platoon to "**Attention**" and instructed the entire Platoon that upon entering the PX, besides purchasing the items we needed, we were also instructed to purchase two sets of blousing garters, as well as a small bottle of liquid starch and a small paint brush to apply the starch to our covers.

I then placed the Guidon in the Flag stand, before I entered the PX with the 1st Squad. I had begun smoking in earnest in week four, with the other Recruits, when the

"*Smoking Lamp*" was lit. I never bought cigarettes that first time at the PX, I was bumming cigarettes from other Recruits when the "*Smoking Lamp*" was lit to avoid work details. Those that smoked got at least one or two cigarette breaks a day, and those who didn't smoke normally had some kind of work detail to do instead.

I bought 2 packs of Pall Malls because they were longer and lasted longer than Lucky Strikes or Camels. I only needed to buy one pack, but I bought an extra pack so I could give back to the guys who I had borrowed smokes from the first couple of weeks we were allowed to smoke.

Besides buying a couple packs of cigarettes, I bought another can of Kiwi shoe polish, another package of razor blades, and another lip balm. I also bought a Zippo lighter, a can of lighter fluid, and a package of flints. As instructed, I purchased two sets of blousing garters, a small bottle of starch and a small paint brush to apply the starch.

All my purchases totaled up to $23.47 with the most expensive item being my new lighter. The clerk put my purchases in a bag and I made my way out of the PX and retrieved the Platoon Guidon and got back in formation as the rest of the Platoon made their way through the PX to make their purchases.

Once everyone had finished their shopping and returned to our Platoon Formation, Sgt James had us take a set of blousing garters and taught us how to blouse our trousers. We placed a blousing garter around each leg above our boots and tucked our trouser into the garter so no trouser leg was below the top of our boots.

Then, Sgt James brought the entire Platoon to "**Attention**," and had us unbutton our top button on our utility shirt. Although our utilities were wrinkled, having our top button unbuttoned, trousers bloused and our boots shined made us look closer to Marines than anything we had done since arriving on the Depot.

You couldn't imagine the difference it made in the attitude of our Platoon now that we were standing at **"Attention"** with our trousers bloused, our top buttons unbuttoned, and with a slight grin on our faces. Our shoulders were back we all felt closer to being Marines than ever before.

Sgt James marched us back to our Platoon Area to return our purchases to our Huts and put them in our footlockers. He then marched us over to the wash racks to take our laundry off the line. Once we took our laundry off the clothes line and folded it, we returned it to our Huts where we were given 15 minutes to return our clothes to our footlockers.

Once all our laundry was secured into our footlockers, Sgt James marched us to noon chow. When we arrived at the Mess Hall, due to getting paid and going to the PX, there was a back-up waiting to get into chow. Sgt James had us take out our Red Notebooks while we waited for our turn to go into chow.

When our turn finally came, we marched in two single files one to the right and one to the left, making our way in front of each mirror at the entrance to the Mess Hall. Each recruit stopped facing the mirror and saluted and for the first time with our top button unbuttoned and because we now felt more like Marines, although still a long way to go, that salute had more snap and each movement seemed more-crisp as we entered noon chow.

After we finished eating, Sgt James lit the *"Smoking Lamp"* before marching us back to the Platoon Street to unlock our rifles and put on our cartridge belts. We then spent the afternoon on the Grinder doing Close Order Drill.

Here we were, marching on the Grinder with our top buttons unbuttoned, our trousers bloused and even though we had Sgt James calling cadence, it seemed like the Platoon was strutting to his cadence and we felt like we were more than just Recruits.

We drilled on the Grinder until it was time for evening chow. Practice makes perfect, and if Sgt James had his way, we would be the best in our training series and he was determined to win the Close Order Drill Streamer. We returned to the Platoon Area, entered our Huts and returned our rifles and cartridge belts to our Racks. Sgt James had us make a Head Call and then return to the Platoon Street for evening chow.

Now that we have been at MCRD for five weeks, Mail Call was held regularly on Monday, Wednesday and Fridays after evening chow. I had received letters from my mother, my sister Karen and my best friend Zane on Wednesday.

When I left for Boot Camp, I had been dating a girl by the name of Linda and I thought we had a pretty good relationship. I hadn't received any mail from Linda since arriving at MCRD, and in Zane's letter, he explained to me why. Linda was the type of person who didn't like to be alone, and Zane told me she had gone back to dating her old boyfriend.

I was disappointed in the news about Linda, but there was really nothing I could do about it being 3,000 miles away and to be honest, I didn't need the distraction. I wrote back to Zane and thanked him for the information, but told him Linda was going to do what she was going to do and I couldn't do anything about it. I told him to say hello to his parents and his girlfriend Susan.

My sister told me she was pregnant and told me she wanted me to visit her and her husband in Iowa once I had leave. Since we were kept so busy every day, I didn't have much time to be home sick and the only time I had to think of home was once we hit the rack when lights went out after evening TAPS.

Saturday after our normal routine, we spent the entire day at the Obstacle Course. After taking our normal run around the track field, I posted the Platoon Guidon in the Flag Stand and Sgt Martinez had us run by Squad to jump the eight-foot wall and then fall in at the base at the log climb. This obstacle was 10 feet wide, 30 feet high and started off with an angled row of four logs spaced three feet apart. Next

were a row of logs we were to climb over that were three feet apart straight up that we had to climb, get to the top, go over the top log and climb back down. The top of the row of logs was 30 feet high.

The next obstacle after the log climb was the rope swing over a ditch of water. The ditch was 10 feet across and had 4 ropes to swing over. You would take a running leap and grab the rope and swing yourself to the other side. If you failed, you got wet. If you got wet, you stood off to the side and did bends and thrusts.

After that we were led over to a pit which had two sets of four knotted ropes that were 30 feet to the top. The object was to climb the rope by putting your feet on the knots and pull yourself up to the top, touching the cross bar that the ropes were attached to and then come back down the rope using the knots as you descended. Each Squad lined up behind a rope and we raced to see which squad got to the top and finished the fastest.

Another obstacle was the rope bridge. There were two Platforms about 40 yards apart. Between them were four sets of rope bridges which consisted of three ropes each.

One rope was a step down and you were to walk on that rope to the other side by holding onto two other ropes that were approximately five feet above the lower rope and were used to hold onto. It was tricky because you didn't want to get the bottom rope swinging. You placed one foot in front and slid the back foot to meet the front foot and held on to balance yourself with the two top ropes.

Next there were two walls, one was six feet high and was inverted which meant it was slanted towards you as you tried to climb it. The second wall was eight feet high. You had to jump up to catch the top of the wall or got help from one of  the other recruits in order to scale the wall.

We broke for noon chow at 1230 and afterwards Sgt Martinez lit the "*Smoking Lamp*" and then we made a Head Call before marching back to the Obstacle Course. We made our usual run around the track field in Platoon Formation

 and after setting the Platoon Guidon in the Flag Stand, we set to work on Teamwork by heading right to the Log Drill.

After the Log Drill, we again went over to the large tower and continued to exercise team work to complete that Obstacle. However, while on the tower, we had another mishap and had one of our recruits fall from the top floor as he was ascending down the rope and broke his ankle. That along with another recruit who fell and hurt himself earlier during the week left our Platoon at 79.

After dealing with a recruit falling and breaking his ankle, the last Obstacle we attempted on Saturday was the Monkey Bar, hand over hand exercise. We were getting tired, so once the last recruit finished on the bars, I grabbed the Platoon Guidon and we "Fell In" Platoon Formation and were marched over to make a Head Call.

We cleaned up from our day at the Obstacle Course and got ready for evening chow. For some reason, evening chow on Saturday was amazing! We were served ribeye steaks, potatoes, green beans, salad, onion soup, Dutch apple pie, iced tea, milk, coffee and water. Man what a treat.

After evening chow we spent the next two hours on the Grinder and then when we returned to our Huts, Sgt James had us take showers and clean up from the day's activity on the Obstacle Course. After showers Sgt James lit the "*Smoking Lamp*," and those that smoked, stood on the Platoon Street in our skivvies and shower shoes enjoying our cigarette.

While enjoying having the "*Smoking Lamp*" lit, Gunny called me aside. He informed me that normally during Week 6 the entire Training Series which includes Platoons 2225, 2226, 2227, and 2228, are to assume the Mess Duties in the 2nd Battalion Mess Hall. However, since there only needs to be three Platoons for Mess Duty, our Platoon will not be needed. Instead, we will be assigned to Maintenance Duty for the week.

Gunny had explained to me how Maintenance Duty was going to work for the upcoming week. He said that after morning chow, on Monday morning, the Platoon will be marched over to the Maintenance Building located behind the warehouses that stores all the necessary equipment and supplies for the Depot. We will Report at 0800 and the Platoon will be assigned to Clean-up Details and distributed throughout the MCRD.

Maintenance and Clean-up Details would be cutting grass, raking leaves, trimming trees and shrubs, sweeping sidewalks, washing windows, painting curbs and other places that needed paint. We would report Monday morning and work on the Maintenance Detail through Friday.

I took a deep breath and smiled to myself because we wouldn't have to peel potatoes, wash dishes and serve the other Recruits their food for the next week. Mess Duty began on Sunday morning at 0300 and doesn't end until the next Saturday after evening chow. Gunny told me to inform the Squad Leaders that we wouldn't be doing Mess Duty but, if the Platoon screws up in any way, he will ask to exchange places with one of the other Platoons.

I thanked the Gunny for the information and assured him we would not disappoint him in any way and looked forward to performing the Maintenance the best it had ever been done. He told me I could have another cigarette if I chose, but I told him one was enough and left to meet with the Squad Leaders.

I had the four Squad Leaders meet me on the Platoon Street and I informed them of the conversation I just had with Gunny Wolfmule. I told them how lucky we were to miss doing Mess Duty and to be assigned to Maintenance instead. I also informed them that if we screwed up any time tonight or tomorrow, the decision for us to do Maintenance could be reversed. So, make sure everyone is squared away and don't give the DI's any reason to reverse our good fortune.

After we all agreed to make sure not to screw up in any way, we returned to our Hut to stand a Hygiene Inspection. We stood on our footlockers and both Sgt James and Gunny Wolfmule checked our feet, between our toes, our hands, finger nails and made sure there were no other injuries from our day on the Obstacle Course.

After lights out, I waited for that magic sound of TAPS, knowing I would get a good night's sleep. We had now spent five full weeks at Boot Camp. We had been broken down physically and built back up. We had learned Marine Corps History and surprisingly, we looked pretty good on the Grinder doing Close Order Drill. We were almost half way through Boot Camp and I thought the worst was behind us.

We missed a bullet by not having to do Mess Duty. Being assigned Maintenance Duty would be almost like a reward. I was determined since we were lucky enough to get assigned Maintenance instead of Mess that we would do the best job possible.

Life was settling down daily and we were more comfortable with the daily routine. We still had a few episodes with some recruits screwing up, or just not listening and that caused a couple incidents of mass punishment. I believe even if we were perfect, the DI's would make up an excuse to punish us just to remind us we were in Boot Camp.

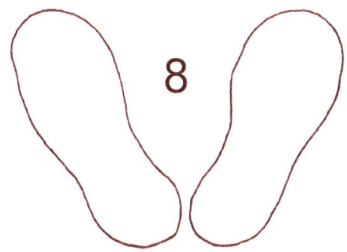

Maintenance Week

Sunday of week 6 was different than the past 5 weeks, as Platoons 2225, 2226 and 2228 had to get up early and report to the 2ⁿᵈ Battalion Mess Hall by 0300. Platoon 2227 had Reveille as usual on Sunday morning at 0500, then PT, hygiene, making our racks and then Fall-Out for Church Services. Those not going to Church Services would "**Fall-In**" for morning chow and afterwards would have clean-up duties of the Huts, the Head and Platoon Area before starting Commanders Time.

When we returned from morning chow and as clean-up was being performed, Gunny Wolfmule had me Report to the Duty Hut. When I got to the entrance to the Duty Hut I knocked on the wood frame of the door. Gunny yelled out, "Who's knocking on my Pine?" I responded loudly, "**Sir, Pvt Rilley Reporting as Ordered, Sir**." He told me to enter. I went into the Duty Hut and squared myself in the middle of his desk.

He asked me if I had talked to the Squad Leaders regarding doing Maintenance this week? I told Gunny that I told the Squad Leaders we were not going to be assigned to Mess Duty and would be doing Maintenance instead for the week.

Gunny asked how they received the news they weren't going on Mess Duty. I told Gunny that all four Squad Leaders were committed to making sure that our Platoon did the best job on Maintenance that could be done and will leave those we do maintenance for impressed with Platoon 2227. Gunny smiled and told me to go enjoy Commanders Time. I said, **"Sir, Aye Aye Sir,"** and left the Duty Hut.

As I left the Duty Hut, Pvt Havranek and Pvt Gagnon stopped me and asked what was up. I lit a cigarette and explained to both my Squad Leaders that Gunny was curious as to how the Squad Leaders were reacting to not having to do Mess Duty but instead Maintenance. I told him we were excited to do a great job and to make Gunny and the D I's proud of us.

Gagnon said this was our chance for the Platoon to stand out in the mind of Gunny, Sgt James and Sgt Martinez and maybe help us going forward in motivating the Platoon to want to exceed expectations. Havranek mentioned that we still have three or four Recruits that are on the side of "shit bird" status and we needed to tighten them up before they interfere with our progress.

Gagnon suggested we have a talk with those individuals and if we can't get their attention and square them away, we'd either have a blanket party or figure out a way to get them out of the Platoon. Three out of the four "shit birds" didn't go to Church Services so we decided to have a conversation with the three that were participating in Commanders Time. I suggested to Havranek that he include the two other Squad Leaders with him and Gagnon.

During Commanders time, it was decided that two Squad Leaders would take the Recruits we identified as a problem, one at a time, into one of the Huts and have a serious conversation. They'd get their attention and put the fear of God into them so they would change their ways and get with the program.

Sgt James arrived at 0930 to relieve Gunny of the Duty. When the Gunny was leaving, he called me over to talk to me before he left. He wanted to know what was going on, because he observed Squad Leaders taking Recruits into one of the Huts. I told him we identified four Recruits that were a drag on the Platoon and needed Motivation. The Squad Leaders are trying to square them away and get them motivated and with the program. We can't have a few hurt the entire Platoon.

Gunny was impressed but told me to be careful of anything physical. I was impressed that Gunny was so intuitive as to what we were trying to accomplish. Gunny said he would be back in the morning before we left for Maintenance and told me to keep up the good job. I said, "**Sir, Aye Aye Sir**."

Sgt James called me to the Duty Hut. All those on the Platoon Street yelled out, "Sir, Right Guide to the Duty Hut, Sir." I reported to the Duty Hut and pounded on the door Frame. Sgt James yelled, "Who's pounding on my hatch," I answered, "**Sir, Private Rilley reporting as Ordered Sir**." He said, "Get in here." I went into the Duty Hut and stood directly centered on his desk and reported," "**Sir, Pvt Rilley Reporting as Ordered Sir**." He said, "Stand easy Pvt."

He began by telling me how lucky the Platoon was to get the Maintenance Duty instead of Mess Duty. He continued, "When Commanders Time is over, have the Platoon in Utilities and boots "**Fall-In**" on Platoon Formation for noon chow. After chow we'd be running the C.M.C. Physical Readiness Course because while on Maintenance for a whole week, we wouldn't be getting any Physical Fitness training other than morning PT."

I answered, "**Sir, Aye Aye Sir**." and made an "**About Face**," then a "**Left Face**," and left the Duty Hut. I met with all four Squad Leaders and relayed what I was told by Sgt James. I asked them if they had talked to all four "Shit birds," and was told they had only talked to three because one still hadn't returned from Church Services yet. I wanted to know the results of their conversations with the three they had talked to.

Havranek told me we should see a positive change in all three they had talked to and they were told the consequences would not be pretty. Gagnon said the fourth Recruit they hadn't talked to yet was in his Squad and he would take care of it as soon as he returned. I thanked them and asked that we make sure we have a good training this afternoon so we can have a quiet evening for Commanders Time.

When the fourth Recruit returned from Church Services, Pvt Gagnon and Pvt Hesch took him into their Hut and had their little talk with him. When they returned to the Platoon Street, Pvt Gagnon gave me a thumbs up letting me know he thinks his conversation hit home. Now that all Recruits had returned from Church Services and before Commander's Time ended, I was satisfied all four Squad Leaders were on the same page. I decided to meet with Pvt Havranek, Pvt Gagnon, Pvt Hesch, and Pvt Surma, and gave them a pep talk to remind them how important it was to motivate each of the recruits in their Squads.

Commanders Time ended, and Sgt James had us "**Fall-In**" for noon chow. On our way to the Mess Hall, we made our way to the Grinder to spend an hour doing Close Order Drill before it was our time for chow. Again we waited in Platoon Formation outside the Mess Hall reading our Red Notebooks until it was time to "**Fall-In**" two single file lines. As we stood in front of the mirror, Sgt James watched each Recruit Salute and make the salutation of, "**Good Afternoon Sir**," as we saluted.

After we finished chow and "**Fell-In**," Sgt James lit the "*Smoking Lamp*." Sgt James seemed to be in a good mood and all was well in San Diego, California. When the "*Smoking Lamp*," was turned off, we were marched back to our Huts on the Platoon Street to get our rifles and cartridge belts.

We were then marched over to the field next to the Obstacle Course.

There were two buildings located just outside the Obstacle Course separating the track field and sports fields from the Obstacle Course. The Platoon was "**Halted,**" just outside the main building. Sgt James had each Squad go into the building on the left where we were issued a back pack that contained about 40 pounds of weight, a helmet, and a canteen to add to our cartridge belt. After leaving the building we were to fill our canteens at the six water taps next to the building before Falling back in Platoon Formation.

Before we graduate from Boot Camp we will have to complete the C.M.C. Physical Fitness Test. We will have to complete the test both individually as well as a Platoon. Each Recruit Carries his rifle, a 40 pound pack, helmet, boots, cartridge belt with bayonet, canteen and first aid pouch. The test consists of running 25 yards and jumping a six foot ditch. There is a stair step you have to step up and down 30 times in a specific time. We climbed a knotted rope 30 feet up and down and completed a "**Fireman's Carry,**" which is run 50 yards, pick up a wounded Marine and carry him back 50 yards in a specific time. Finally, a three-mile run with full gear in under 28 minutes.

We spent the entire afternoon running through the C.M.C. test and ended by running the 3-mile run in Platoon Formation. By the time we were finished with the afternoon training, we were exhausted. We turned in the helmet, pack and other gear we were issued and were marched back to Platoon Street. We locked our rifles back on our racks and hung up our cartridge belt, and "**Fell-In**" for evening chow.

Although we had a pretty good lunch, I was starved. I don't remember any day in Boot Camp when I was any hungrier than I was that day for evening chow. While we waited for our turn to enter the chow line, we took out our Red Notebooks and studied. Before we fell-out into two single file lines, I heard my stomach growl, and I couldn't wait to get my tray filled so I could eat.

For Sunday evening chow they were serving breaded pork chops with fried potatoes, corn, green beans, salad, bread, Jello, iced tea, milk, coffee and water. The servers on the chow line were from Platoon 2225, and I thought about the training we had gone through Sunday afternoon. I smiled and thought how lucky we were not to be on Mess Duty. We were here to do Physical training, not wash dishes, or peel potatoes, although that's part of the training and what some guys will do the whole time they are in the Corps.

After evening chow we were marched back to Platoon Street where Sgt James lit the *"Smoking Lamp,"* and for those who didn't smoke, they were released to their Huts to study their Marine Handbooks. Sgt James requested to see all the Squad Leaders in the Duty Hut. Those standing on Platoon Street smoking yelled, **"Sir, Squad Leaders to the Duty Hut Sir."** I field stripped my cigarette and beat feet to the Duty Hut. Pvt Havranek was first in line and pounded on the door frame of the Duty Hut.

Sgt James asked who was knocking on his hatch? All the Squad Leaders answered together, **"Sir, Squad Leaders Reporting as Ordered Sir."** He told us to enter. We all squeezed into the Duty Hut and lined up in front of his desk. Pvt Havranek was first, followed by me and the rest of the Squad Leaders. Sgt James had us **"Lien To"** and we squeezed to get down in the push-up position.

He asked us if we were aware of the "Chain of Command." We screwed up because the "Right Guide" should be in line first followed by the Squad Leaders and because Havranek entered first, he had us "Lien To" and we did no less than 50 push-ups.

Once he was done punishing us for not Reporting properly, he wanted to know if there were any Recruits that had any issues or were not totally with the program? He mentioned that Gunny told him we identified a few Recruits that fit that description and that we were dealing with it.

I spoke up and said, "Sir, we have identified four Recruits who need to be more motivated, and the Squad Leaders and the Pvt have talked to them individually. We believe we have their attention and got our point across that they needed to step it up and quit being "**shit birds**." Sgt James wanted to know their names.

Pvt Havranek gave the four names, Pvt Dupree, Pvt Evanoff, Pvt Morris and Pvt Ray. Sgt James then asked, "How have you decided to handle these four and what will be the consequences if they don't improve or get motivated." I spoke up again, and answered, "Sir, if they continue to be "**shit birds**," and affect the performance of the Platoon, a blanket party would be solution number one, and if that doesn't get the job done, finding a way to remove them from the Platoon would be next, Sir."

Sgt James told us to carry on and return to the Platoon. We all answered in unison, "**Sir, Aye Aye Sir,**" and left the Duty Hut. Sgt James stopped me and said "Rilley, have Dupree, Evanoff, Morris and Ray report to the Duty Hut." I answered, "**Sir, Aye Aye Sir**." When I got out of the Duty Hut and onto Platoon Street I yelled out, "**Privates Dupree, Evanoff, Morris and Ray, report to the Duty Hut.**"

The four reported to Sgt James and he had them get into the sand box next to the Duty Hut and begin "**Bends and Thrusts**." The rest of the Platoon continued to stay in their Huts and study their Marine Hand Books. One point should be noted, at no time was anyone ever allowed to sit on their Rack, other than "Lights Out" for Taps. We would sit on our footlockers or on our buckets when in our Huts if we were to study, clean our rifles, shine our boots, fold our clothes or any time other than sleep. Don't ever get caught sitting on your Rack.

The four "**shit birds**" were still in the sand box one hour later when Sgt James had the rest of the Platoon "**Fall-In**" on

Platoon Street. Sgt James had the four stand at "**Attention**" in the sand box and told them that if they didn't get squared away and soon, they would spend a minimum of one hour twice a day in the sand box. He then had them "**Fall-In**," with the rest of the Platoon.

The Platoon spent the next two hours on the Grinder going through Close Order Drill before returning to our Huts for evening hygiene and Commanders Time. Sgt Martinez arrived to assume the evening Duty with Sgt James and they both held our weekly Hygiene Inspection checking our feet, toe nails, between our toes, our hands and finger nails, and made sure there were no injuries that had gone unnoticed. Lights out and Taps at 2200.

Monday morning Reveille at 0500 as usual followed by PT on the Grinder in our Red PT shorts, yellow sweatshirts, socks and tennis shoes. Afterwards, head Call, shave, showers, making our Racks and morning clean-up. Gunny Wolfmule arrived around 0700 and both DI's and the Platoon Commander accompanied us to morning chow.

When we finished morning chow we "**Fell-In**" on the Platoon Street and Gunny lit the "*Smoking Lamp*." Both DI's and Gunny held a short meeting among themselves and then Sgt Martinez took charge of the Platoon and marched us across the Grinder to the Maintenance Building to begin our week of maintenance. As we were crossing the Grinder, Sgt Martinez had the Platoon come to a "**Halt**" and stand at "**Attention**" for morning Colors. The Platoon stood at "**Attention**" while Sgt Martinez Saluted the main, Base Flag, located just off the Grinder outside the Administration Building, with Sgt James and Gunny also Saluting as I dipped the Platoon Guidon which was a designated Salute for the Platoon.

When morning Colors were over, we continued our march over to the maintenance building passing by the yellow footprints that we stood on the first night we arrived at MCRD. The footprints brought back memories of that first night and the nightmare we experienced. For me, those footprints were a reminder of the transition we had made after our first five weeks here at Boot Camp.

When we arrived at the Maintenance Building, we were met by a Staff Sergeant, named Ferguson, who shook Gunny's hand and said good morning to both Sgt James and Sgt Martinez. Gunny called me forward to where he was standing with Staff Sergeant Ferguson. The Gunny introduced me, "This is our Platoon Right Guide, Pvt Rilley, and he will help with assignments for your work details."

Staff Sergeant Ferguson told me I could Post our Guidon just outside the door that enters the Maintenance Office. I answered, "**Sir, Aye Aye Sir**," and Posted our Platoon Guidon. Staff Sergeant Ferguson told me I didn't have to address him as "Sir," and Gunny also told me I was able to talk to all the NCO's in Maintenance because they were not DI's assigned to the Training contingent at MCRD. Talking to them did not violate any Orders or Policies I had been Ordered to obey regarding talking to other DI's or Platoon Commanders.

Staff Sergeant Ferguson gave me a clip board with job assignments and a space to assign a name to each person on that detail. Gunny told me to address the Platoon and assign a Recruit for each job on every work detail and write their name for each assignment. I looked over the job assignments and took the pencil attached with a string and stood in front of the Platoon.

The Platoon was facing forward standing at "**Attention**," and the first thing I did was give the command, "**Platoon, Left Face**." The Platoon executed a perfect "**Left Face**," and were facing me. I then commanded, "**Platoon, At Ease.**" I was standing in front of the Platoon in a position normally held by either the Gunny or a DI and I was in charge of making assignments for work details as listed on the clip board.

The first Job was ten Recruits to cut the grass, rake outside the Admin Office and sweep the sidewalk. I picked nine recruits and one of the Squad Leaders and put their names on the clipboard. The next was for ten Recruits to paint the curbs around the Admin building. I picked nine more recruits and another Squad Leader and placed their names on the clipboard. The next was four Recruits to trim the bushes by the main gate and then pick up trash around the main gate area. I added them to the clipboard.

I looked over what type of jobs were listed and tried to place my Squad Leaders to either be in charge of large Work Details, or to be part of Details that weren't difficult. Next was eight recruits to wash windows in the Admin Building. Next were eight Recruits to cut the grass and rake outside of Sickbay. Staff Sargeant told me that he wanted four small recruits to be assigned to sickbay to mop the floors inside the patient wards. I assigned the four House Mice to that job.

I needed to assign 12 Recruits to the Officers Club. I sent Gagnon with that group. I had to assign 10 Recruits to the Marine Museum to swab the floors, polish the brass and wash the windows. I sent Pvt Havranek with that group. The rest were assigned to a Cpl Barns who had a flatbed truck with a number of brooms, rakes and pick sticks. They would be dropped off at different locations at Cpl Barns discretion.

Once I had all of our Platoon assigned to jobs, they were marched off to complete their tasks. I was to stay at the Maintenance Office as my Duty Station all week and do whatever Staff Sargeant Ferguson asked or ordered me to do. The cool part of my job was that there was a large coffee pot so I could drink as much coffee as I wanted.

We would be doing the same formation and the same procedure each morning based on the maintenance that needed to be done on each day during the week. A benefit I enjoyed every day was the ability to drink coffee and some mornings there would be donuts, or pastries. In the afternoons there was cake, pies or cookies. The other amazing thing I benefited from was the "*Smoking Lamp,*" was lit for me all week long.

To my misfortune, I only had a few cigarettes left in my pack to start the week, and they wouldn't last me all week, so I asked one of the Lance Corporal's who worked in Maintenance if he would buy me a couple packs of Lucky's. He said he would, so I gave him a dollar and he bought me two packs of cigarettes and gave them to me on Tuesday morning.

Each day at around 1130, all the Recruits would be returned to the Maintenance Building to be marched to noon chow. While they waited for the entire Platoon to return, the "*Smoking Lamp*," was lit. When the entire Platoon was in Formation, which ever DI had the Duty, would march us to chow and then back to to the Maintenance Building to finish up the day.

Then, around 1630, all the recruits returned to the Maintenance Building and would "Fall-In" and the "*Smoking Lamp*" would be lit until the entire Platoon was back from their work detail and then marched to evening chow. After evening chow we were marched back to our Platoon Street and the only training we actually had during week six was Close Order Drill in the evenings after chow.

We still held our normal daily routine with PT after Reveille, Head Call and morning hygiene of shaving, showers and making sure our Racks and Hut area were cleaned up. The work details responsible for cleaning the Head or mopping the floors in our Huts stayed the same. Squad Leaders didn't actually clean but were in charge of clean-up. If we failed morning Inspection,

whatever wasn't done properly had that Squad Leader in the sand box, besides having the Platoon "**Lien Two**," and do pushups before marching to the Maintenance Building for our work details.

Mail Call was held on Monday, Wednesday and Friday evenings after chow, and evening Commanders Time was pleasant during our week on Maintenance. When we ate morning, noon or evening chow, we could see that the other three Platoons from our Series were working hard on Mess Duty. We truly missed a bullet, and I reminded each Squad Leader and other Recruits how lucky we were to have Maintenance Duty for the week instead of Mess Duty.

On Wednesday after morning chow and before we were marched over to the Maintenance Building, I met with the Squad Leaders and asked if there was anyone on their Details that needed to be reassigned. Pvt Gagnon who was the 2nd Squad Leader asked that I reassign Pvt Evanoff because not only was he not the most squared away Recruit, but he and Gagnon enlisted together and are from the same town and went to school together, and Gagnon thought he may perform better under a different Squad Leader.

I listened to Pvt Gagnon's request to have Evanoff work in a separate Detail and I also suggested we change him out of 2nd Squad and put him in Pvt Havranek's 1st Squad. Gagnon agreed and thought Havranek may be what saves Evanoff from getting kicked out of our Platoon. I told Gagnon I would make the change in Work Details and discuss the change with either Gunny or Sgt James and make the switch from Squad 2 to Squad 1 happen.

Gagnon thanked me and we ran our idea past Pvt Havranek and he agreed it should work. Then I dismissed them to return to the Platoon Street and waited for Sgt Martinez to march us to the Maintenance Building.

When we arrived at the Maintenance Building, SSgt Ferguson handed me the clipboard with the days assignment requests for Work Details. I assigned Recruits as I thought they would be most effective for the jobs that needed to be done. We still needed to rake certain areas, wash windows, paint curbing, mop floors, clean and shine Brass, sweep floors and sidewalks, etc. and after assigning all our Recruits to Work Details, I waited for the permanent personnel who would deliver them to the locations to get to work.

The situation with Pvt Gagnon and Pvt Evanoff had to be resolved. I have to take this time to explain that Gagnon and Evanoff were one of the biggest coincidences in my entire life. When I was in grade school my family lived in a suburb of Detroit called Wayne, Michigan. I attended St. Mary's Catholic School in Wayne, Michigan from the fourth grade through eighth grade.

During the five years I attended St. Mary's, Pvt Gagnon and Pvt Evanoff also attended St. Mary's, at the same time. We were all in the same grade and I played basketball and football with Gagnon and only basketball with Evanoff. My two older brothers and my sister also attended and graduated from St. Mary's High School, but after they finished High School, my family moved back to the city of Detroit, and that's where I went to High School.

I had not seen or had any contact with Gagnon or Evanoff after I left St. Mary's until the second day of Boot Camp. I hadn't seen or talked to either of them for six years until, I realized they were in the same Platoon as me. We have talked a little on Sundays during Commander's Time regarding how they were, how their family were and some of the people I knew when I went to school with them. Otherwise, we didn't have opportunities to visit about our personal lives.

It is a small world to think that of all the people I should meet in the Marines, it was those two. Both had joined the Marines instead of going into the Army, and I shared with them that I had been Drafted and joined the Marines to get out of the Draft so I wouldn't have to go into the Army. It was a surprise to see both of them and catch up. Pvt Gagnon was a good athlete in school and was squared away as a Recruit and also earned the privilege to be the 2nd Squad Leader.

Evanoff on the other hand was not such a good athlete and was constantly in trouble at school and since being here in our Platoon, he wasn't one of the most squared away Recruits either. I believe because Pvt Gagnon is his Squad Leader, Evanoff might be slacking off because of their friendship or familiarity. I think the change of Squads might help the situation, I just have to find a way to make it happen without creating any problems or issues with either Gunny or Sgt James.

I returned to the Maintenance Office and poured myself a cup of coffee. SSgt Ferguson asked me for a copy of the Work Assignment Sheet and asked me if I wanted a donut. I thanked him for his courtesy, and he showed me a plate of fresh donuts that were on his desk. I sure was going to miss working for SSgt Ferguson after getting back to training.

While I drank coffee and ate donuts I thought deeply about how I should approach Gunny Wolfmule or Sgt James on the subject of switching Pvt Evanoff out of 2nd Squad and moving him to the 1st Squad. I didn't want to leave the impression that Evanoff was a total "**shit bird**," but I would need a reason. Maybe just being honest and telling Gunny the relationship between Gagnon and Evanoff would make sense and he'd agree to split them up.

On Wednesday Sgt Martinez had the Duty so, he took charge of the Platoon and marched us to noon chow to the 2nd Battalion Mess Hall. After we finished noon chow and "**Fell-In**" outside the Mess Hall, Sgt Martinez lit the "*Smoking Lamp.*"

We were returned to the Maintenance Building and SSgt Ferguson handed me a new clipboard and I reassigned the Recruits of Platoon 2227 to their afternoon assignments. Afterwards, I went back inside the building and lit up another cigarette. I was kind of excited that I had the opportunity to be in-charge and didn't have to go on Work Details myself.

We finished up Wednesday and went through the same routine on Thursday. It seemed the Platoon was performing their duties on maintenance with no complaints or issues. In the evenings after chow we spent most of our time on the Grinder going through Close Order Drill. Sgt James was impressed with our progress and now that we had our top button unbuttoned and our trousers bloused, we were looking pretty good, while at Close Order Drill.

Friday was the last day of Maintenance week, and when we arrived at the Maintenance Building, I passed out assignments based on what was listed on the clipboard provided to me by SSgt Furguson. I considered myself really lucky to get the job that I was assigned to, being in the Maintenance Office each day enjoying the special perks of treats, coffee and the "*Smoking Lamp*" all day long. Other than spending our evenings on the Grinder, this was quite a nice break from the normal routine of the first five weeks of Boot Camp, but today was the end of a great week and as of tomorrow we would be getting back to the salt mines.

The last day ended at 1630, and while in formation waiting to be marched to evening chow, SSgt Furguson told Gunny Wolfmule, that his Platoon was the best performing and hardest working Platoon he had assigned to him since being in charge of Maintenance. He told Gunny that Pvt Rilley ran everything like a Swiss movement and was a big help in organizing all the work details. His complement of both the Platoon and the execution of my responsibilities made the Gunny very happy and put a smile on his face.

On the way to evening chow, Gunny shared with us complements that he had never shared before. That seemed to put an extra bounce in our step on our way to chow because Gunny hardly ever gives out compliments. Upon reaching the 2nd Battalion Mess Hall, Gunny had us read or Red Notebooks until it was our time to enjoy evening chow.

The other three Platoons in our Series would be finishing up their full week of Mess Duty and again I was enjoying the fact that we were now done with our Maintenance Assignment and we had the advantage over the other three Platoons because their schedule was to report by 0330 each morning and wouldn't finish up their Mess Duty until well after 1900 each day.

The only saving grace for those three Platoons was they would rotate their assignments so not having to all start each day at 0300, but would stager the assignments and would have to rotate their Duties every three days while our Platoons assignment stayed the same for the entire week. Plus we only pulled Maintenance for 5 days, Monday through Friday while they had Mess Duty from Sunday through Saturday.

It was finally our turn to enter the Mess Hall for evening chow, and Gunny had us put our Red Notebooks away, I placed the Platoon Guidon in the Flag Stand and we "**Fell-In**" the two single file lines and went through the same and normal routine for chow. Afterwards, instead of Gunny allowing us the "*Smoking Lamp*" outside the Mess Hall, he marched us back to our Platoon Area.

When we arrived on the Platoon Street, Gunny lit the "Smoking Lamp," and handled the situation brought to his attention by Sgt Martinez regarding Pvt Gagnon and Pvt Evanoff.

He called Pvt Gagnon to the Duty Hut and relieved Gagnon as 2nd Squad Leader, then had Sgt Martinez have Pvt Havranek supervise Evanoff moving his gear to the 1st Squad Hut. With the confusion going on having Pvt Gagnon relieved and Evanoff moved to 1st Squad, we were all glad when evening Commanders Time ended and Light went out with Taps.

Saturday morning we went through our normal morning routine and after morning chow, we spent all day Saturday on the Grinder. Since we were finishing up our sixth week of training, and with Maintenance behind us, it became important that we were now entering our seventh week of training and it was also going to be our first true Uniform Inspection. We would have one whole day to gain an advantage on the other Platoons as they finish up Mess Duty. We used that day to get ready for our seventh week Inspection.

We needed to learn a new command, "**Inspection Arms**" with our rifles. Although it wasn't that difficult, we needed to work on it to become more proficient with that command. We spent the entire morning and again after noon chow going over "**Falling In**," "**Platoon Formation**", "**Open Ranks**," "**Inspection Arms**," "**Close Ranks**," Commanders Time and Lights Out couldn't come fast enough.

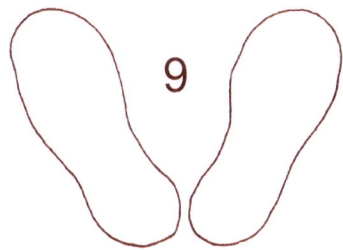

Seventh Week Inspection

Sunday morning was the same as the past six Sundays, Reveille, PT, Head Call, and hygiene. After the Recruits left for Sunday Church Services, Sgt Martinez had the rest of the Platoon "Fall-In" on the Platoon Street and we made our way to morning chow. Afterwards we returned to our Platoon Area and completed morning clean-up and enjoyed Sunday Commanders Time until Gunny arrived around 1100.

Sgt Martinez told us to return our writing gear and buckets back into our Huts and secure, from Commanders Time. As the Platoon was standing in Formation on the Platoon Street, Gunny informed the Platoon that Sgt James would not be with us for the next week as he left early this morning for Emergency Leave. He didn't give us any reason or details, just told us he would be gone until next week.

We went to early noon chow and spent the rest of the afternoon on the Grinder with the Gunny going through the same Drill movements we practiced all day Saturday with Sgt Martinez.

We had practiced getting ready for the 7th week Inspection and I was confident that our Platoon would perform the commands necessary to get use through Inspection. The only thing we needed to work on during the week would be how our uniforms and boots would pass the 7th week Inspection.

After evening chow we spent the evening sitting on the Platoon Street shining our second pair of boots that we would wear for Inspection on Friday. Since we have not yet wore them, the leather wasn't as soft as our everyday boots. Fortunately they had no cuts, scrapes or tears like the ones we'd been wearing every day going through our training. My boots took the polish very well and they were highly spit shined.

Monday morning, as we were standing in platoon formation, a wonderful and surprising thing happened. The Gunny walked up to where I was standing on the Platoon Street and grabbed the Guidon out of my hands and put a Silver Spindle on top of our Platoon Guidon. The Silver Spindle looked wonderful on top of our Guidon and added something special and impressive that highlighted our Guidon. Everywhere we went from now on, I would carry the platoon Guidon with a little more Pride. The only thing missing were the Streamers we would win over the next 5 weeks competing with the other Platoons in our Training Series..

The only person to carry the Platoon Guidon was the Platoon Right Guide. I was given the honor as Platoon Right Guide the end of Week 1 and have not been relieved or removed from that position. I have been the only person to carry our Platoon Guidon to date, and I was bound and determined not to have the privilege of carrying the Guidon taken away from me.

From this point on and for the remainder of Boot Camp, our Platoon would be competing with the other three Platoons in our Training Series for the best Inspections, Close Order Drill, Rifle Range Honors, and PT which would determine the Honor Platoon of our Series. We'd also be awarded Streamers for each of those events to be carried on our Guidon and fly high with pride. There is no Streamer for the 7th Week Uniform Inspection, but the Streamer competition starts with the Rifle range which begins on Week 8. The Rifle Range is a two week training and afterwards, during Week

10 and 11, we will compete for PT, Close Order Drill, and Final Inspection which could earn us the Honor Platoon. Sgt James will be back in time for Close Order Drill competition, so not to worry.

Sgt Martinez and Gunny Wolfmule would take charge of our close order drill sessions for the next week and hopefully we would perform for them as we did for Sgt James. However, Sgt James would be back from his Emergency Leave long before it was important to compete in "Close Order Drill" competition. I don't think we could win Drill Competition without Sgt James to call cadence and lead us for this event. With him on Emergency Leave for the next week, that would mean we would have Gunny and Sgt Martinez on Duty every day.

Sgt Martinez marched us to morning chow, and while we were standing outside the 2nd Battalion Mess Hall, Gunny told me we were going to have a replacement DI to fill in for Sgt James while he was gone on Leave. Gunny told me I would be introduced to him after morning chow when we returned to our Platoon Area.

I had quite the surprise and the second biggest coincidence of my life when the replacement DI for Sgt James came out of the Duty Hut, while we stood on Platoon Street enjoying a cigarette after Gunny lit the "Smoking Lamp." The DI filling in for Sgt James was someone I knew and I hadn't seen since our family moved from Wayne, Michigan back to Detroit over five years ago. A Marine Sargeant by the name of Jerry Porta.

I couldn't believe that I was experiencing another coincidence of such magnitude since arriving at MCRD. It was one thing to meet up with Gagnon and Evanoff and have them be in my platoon for Boot Camp, but to have Sgt Porta be one of my Drill Instructors was really unbelievable because he was from the same town as Gagnon, Evanoff and I. The odds of Sgt James' replacement being Sgt Porta had to be more than one in two million or more.

Jerry Porta went to school with my two older brothers, Jim and Dennis, although he was one year behind my brother Denny. He graduated one year before my sister Karen and also went to St. Mary's Catholic School in Wayne, Michigan. He even asked my sister to his senior prom. My sister turned him down because she already had a date when he asked her. Not to mention he was an underclassman to my older brothers, and had to carry their equipment and shine their football cleats and other underclassman duties while in High School.

Our family lived on 4th Street in Wayne, Michigan, and the Porta family lived eight blocks from us on Chestnut Street. Jerry's Dad was our school Custodian. Jerry also had a younger brother named Mike who was in the same class with Gagnon, Evanoff and I. He also played football with Gagnon and me.

I don't know exactly how Gagnon or Evanoff reacted when Sgt Porta stood in front of the Platoon and was introduced by Gunny Wolfmule, but I swallowed hard and asked myself what other surprises were in store for me. Sgt Porta stood in front of me and asked me if I was from Wayne, Michigan? I answered him that I was. He then asked me if I had two older brothers and a sister, and again I told him, yes. He shook my hand and said, "Nice to see you again, I've heard good things about you."

I said, "Sir, Thank you Sir." I didn't dare start a conversation with him or tell him Gagnon and Evanoff were here as well, as it would be inappropriate to have a personal conversation with a new Drill Instructor. He will find out soon enough and can't punish me for not telling him because I followed my Orders.

Monday, Gunny relieved Sgt Martinez of the Duty and shared the Duty with Sgt Porta, getting him acquainted with our Platoon. We were scheduled for a class on our General Orders and Standing Guard. So after putting out the "Smoking Lamp," Gunny had the Platoon "**Fall-In**" and he marched us to our morning class.

Sometime later, after we finished class, we stopped for a Head Call. Pvt Evanoff took it upon himself to say hello to Sgt Porta while returning from the Head. Sgt Porta went off on Evanoff for his insolence and lack of military courtesy. He had Evanoff stand at "Attention" and chewed him out for at least five minutes and then had him "Lien Two" and begin pushups. I couldn't believe it when I saw Evanoff approach Sgt Porta and just start talking to him.

Gunny was close by, but just stood off to the side while Sgt Porta was dealing with Evanoff. When Sgt Porta finished having Evanoff do pushups, Gunny had him stand at "**Attention**" and then after looking to his right and then his left, punched him in the stomach and then told him… "Return to the Duty Hut and put yourself in the "sand box" and do "bends and thrusts" until I return to the Platoon Area." Evanoff replied, "**Sir, yes Sir**." Gunny told him to double time all the way.

Gunny marched us to the Grinder and had Sgt Porta take charge of Close Order Drill and then he went back to the Platoon Street to deal with Evanoff.

Sgt Porta took charge of the Platoon and put us through our paces to see how proficient we were at Close Order Drill. Porta had a cadence that was similar to Sgt James, but not as smooth. We marched on the Grinder with Sgt Porta until it was time for noon chow.

We waited for our turn for noon chow and once in two single file lines went through the chow line. Although Sgt Porta recognized Gagnon as we drilled on the Grinder, he stood at the front entrance of the mess hall as each Recruit Saluted and that's when he acknowledged Pvt Gagnon. He didn't say anything other than "Good Afternoon, Pvt Gagnon." Gagnon responded, "**Sir, Good afternoon Sir**."

When we were all seated, Sgt Porta gave us the command "**Seats**," and we answered in unison, **"Seats,**

Aye Aye Sir." We all sat down quickly in one movement. He told us we had 20 minutes to enjoy our meal and walked toward the chow line to get his own lunch and sit down with the other Drill Instructors.

When we finished eating noon chow, Sgt Porta had us "**Fall-In**," and marched us back to the Platoon Street. Pvt Evanoff was still in the "sand box" doing "Bends and Thrusts." Sgt Porta asked me what we normally did while standing on Platoon Street waiting for Orders. I told him we normally studied our Red Notebooks. Sgt Porta put the Platoon "**At Ease**," and then told us to study our Red Notebooks. He made his way into the Duty Hut, and I placed the Platoon Guidon in the flag stand outside the Duty Hut.

Gunny told Evanoff to get out of the "sand box" and told the Recruits to "**Fall-Out**," get our rifles and get back in Formation on the Platoon Street. We were headed to a class on the "Proper Care and Use of our M14 rifles for when we get to the Rifle Range next Week. It took less than five minutes for everyone to get our rifle and Fall back in on Platoon Street. Sgt Porta took charge of the Platoon and marched us to our afternoon class.

This was the third class we have had with our M-14 rifles. It was exciting to know that within the next two weeks we would be at the rifle range performing what Marines are known for. We will be firing our rifles at distances of 200, 300 and 500 yards with open iron sights. Every Recruit needs to qualify with their rifle in order to graduate from Boot Camp.

We finished off our Monday training, after class, on the Grinder doing Closs Order Drill. After evening chow we spent an additional two hours on the Grinder, then were dismissed for commanders time and evening hygiene. However, as the rest of the Platoon was attending to evening hygiene and Commanders Time, The Duty Hut called for Pvt Rilley, Pvt Gagnon, and Pvt Evanoff to "Report to the Duty Hut."

I figured it was just a matter of time before Sgt Porta would have myself, Gagnon and Evanoff Report to the Duty

Hut. Gunny was relieved of Duty after evening chow, and Sgt Porta had the Duty that night. When we reached the Duty Hut, I pounded on the door frame and Sgt Porta asked, "Who is knocking on my Pine?" I answered, "**Sir, Pvt Rilley, Pvt Gagnon and Pvt Evanoff Reporting as Ordered Sir.**" We were told to enter, and the three of us lined up in front of the desk where Sgt Porta was sitting. We were standing at "**Attention**," and Sgt Porta told us to "**Stand Easy**."

There was a slight smile on his face and his first question was directed to Gagnon and Evanoff. He asked, "Where is my brother Mike?" Gagnon answered his question by saying, "Sir, the last time this Private saw your brother, he was at home. Mike was not interested in following in your footsteps and decided to try to get into college, Sir." Sgt Porta then said, "Well from what I understand, he isn't in college and you guys were always hanging out together, so why isn't he here with you?" Gagnon said, "Sir, I think he said he wanted to join the Navy, Sir."

That answer didn't seem to be funny to Sgt Porta, so he had Gagnon and Evanoff drop and do pushups. As they were doing up downs, he turned his questions to me. "Pvt Rilley how is your family doing, bring me up to date." I said, "Sir, my brother Jim is married and moved to Wisconsin. My brother Denny is married and lives in Ohio. My sister Karen is married and lives in Iowa, and my mother and father are well, Sir."

"I am glad your family is doing well; we have a lot of history. According to GySgt Wolfmule you have done a very good job since arriving at Boot Camp and congratulations on being the "Right Guide." I have been told you are a very squared away Recruit." I answered, "**Sir, thank you, Sir**." Gagnon and Evanoff were still doing pushups.

He continued, "I understand this Platoon has progressed fairly well in six short weeks, but the real tests are still ahead of you. The next time you write home, tell your family I said hello and they should be proud of you." I answered, "**Sir, Thank you Sir.**" He dismissed me.

When I left the Duty Hut, Gagnon and Evanoff were still doing pushups so, I made my way to my Hut and got ready for evening hygiene and Commander Time. It was almost an hour later when Gagnon and Evanoff reported to their Huts. I have no idea what transpired after I left, but for the rest of the week, I wondered if he ever thought about how he was treated by my two older brothers and his advances rebutted by my sister? During the week he had the DI duties most of the week in Sgt James' absence. He didn't treat me any differently than the other recruits however, he rode Evanoff really hard and put Gagnon through his paces. He expected those two to be more squared away than the rest of the Platoon and he paid close attention to their progress.

Porta was given the scoop on each of us and our individual progress of how we had been doing since boot camp began. As it turned out, he was impressed that I was the Platoon Right Guide and had been in that position since week one. He was disappointed that Pvt Gagnon wasn't one of the Platoons Squad Leaders and told Gunny he thought Gagnon should be a Squad Leader.

Gunny explained to Sgt Porta that Gagnon was a Squad Leader but had been removed because of Evanoff. Gagnon was his Squad Leader, but was unable to get Evanoff squared away, and caused Gagnon some extra punishment. Porta wasn't surprised that Pvt Evanoff wasn't the most squared away recruit in our platoon, Gunny shared with him that the Squad Leaders had a plan to square Evanoff away and Gunny wouldn't be surprised if Gagnon worked his way back to being a Squad Leader.

Tuesday morning after chow, the Platoon was scheduled to get our laundry done. We took our laundry bags, bucket, Wisk and scrub brush and Sgt Porta marched us to the wash racks. After finishing our laundry and hanging our clothes on the clothes line, Sgt Porta picked Evanoff and Pvt Folk to sit on their buckets and guard our laundry while the Platoon went about training.

Sgt Porta marched us over to the Obstacle Course and we spent the rest of the morning being challenged by running the difficult Obstacle Towers. The Towers took teamwork and Sgt Porta wanted to see how we worked together. The Platoon went through all the rotations, and by the time we finished, it was time for noon chow.

When chow was over, Sgt Porta returned us to the wash racks to collect our laundry and then to our Huts to fold and put our clothing away. Gunny told me to pass the word to bring the clean pair of utilities we had just washed, which included the blouse and the trousers, and "**Fall In**" on to the Platoon Street along with five dollars.

We were marched to the Dry Cleaners where we each turned in our utilities to have them starched and pressed. We would pick them up on Thursday and wear Starched Utilities for the first time on Friday for our 7th Week Uniform Inspection. We still needed to learn how to starch our utility covers but that lesson would come later on during the week, and needed to be done by Thursday.

Besides practicing and getting ready for our 7th Week Inspection, our Series had two additional training events that required all four of our Series Platoons to participate in. On **Wednesday** morning after chow, we were returned to the Platoon Street and told once we "**Fell-Out**," we were to go into our Huts, take off our utility shirts and change into our yellow sweatshirts. We should unlock our rifles from our rack, put on our cartridge belts and "**Fall-In**," back on Platoon Street.

All four Platoons from FOX Company were marched over to the Training Field next to the Obstacle Field for Bayonet Training. The entire Company was assembled on the Training Field in a Company Formation. Platoons 2225 was next to Platoon 2226 and Platoon 2227 was directly behind Platoon 2225 and next to us and behind Platoon 2226 was Platoon 2228.

Each Platoon was marched into position, one Platoon at a time and were commanded to "**Open Ranks.**" In front of the Company Formation was a bench which the Instructor stood on as we did Physical Drill Under Arms. There were two Instructors, one on the bench, holding an M14 rifle like all four Platoons, and one with a hand-held Megaphone.

The Instructor with the Megaphone gave the Command for the four Right Guides to Post their Guidons in front of the Platform. The four Right Guides marched up front and placed the Platoon Guidons into the Flag stands and returned to their Platoons.

The Instructor with the Megaphone gave the Commands and the Instructor on the bench next to him would execute all

the Commands given for us to see and emulate. We spread our legs shoulder width, held our rifle above our heads and did twists to the right and the left. We bent and touched our rifles to our boots and then held our rifles out straight in front of us.

We continued to do Physical Drill under Arms for one full hour and then spent the next 15 minutes going through the Manual at Arms. The Instructor then reviewed all the Bayonet positions, On Guard, Thrust, Parry, Slash, Butt Strokes, Long Thrust, Short Thrust, Short Jab, Long Jab and horizontal and vertical Butt Strokes.

When we completed Bayonet Training, Each Platoon was Ordered to "**Close Ranks**," and the Right Guides went to retrieve their Guidons. Bayonets and Scabbards were returned to the cartridge belts and we were marched back to our Platoon Streets to store our rifles and cartridge belts.

After a Head Call, we were marched to noon Chow and waited for our turn to enter the Mess Hall. We studied our Red Notebooks until we were put into single file columns to pass the mirror, Salute and then get our trays and enjoy noon chow.

After we finished noon chow, Sgt Porta had us "**Fall-In**," and lit the "*Smoking Lamp*." We were marched back to our Platoon Area and told to take off our utility shirts and put on our yellow sweatshirts. Now that we had experienced actual Bayonet Training, we were marched back to the Training Field and we were going to get a chance to do it for real using Pugil Sticks.

Pugil sticks are heavily padded wooden poles the same length as an M-14 Rifle and weighed about 20 pounds. Each Marine wore a football helmet with a cage to cover the face, a padded chest protector, and boxing gloves on each hand.

Each Marine was paired up with another Marine of similar weight and height. When the whistle was blown the two recruits charged one another with their Pugil Sticks. The combat consisted of a slash, a lunge, a horizontal butt stroke, or a vertical butt stroke. They did combat until a fatal blow was delivered or they heard a second whistle. The Recruits ceased their battle when the

Instructor believed a fatal blow had been delivered or he wanted the Recruits to continue fighting until he blew the second whistle.

Each Marine engaged the other Marine in combat simulating both attacking and defending a bayonet attack. At times and at the discretion of the Instructor, he may order a two-on-one training to give the recruit a closer combat scenario or to punish a slacker or someone being disrespectful.

Platoon 2227 was paired up with Platoon 2225 and had a very good showing on the Pugil Stick Range. Sgt Porta was impressed with how we performed and supported each other while competing. As we marched back to the Platoon Street to get ready for the evening chow, it was apparent that our platoon was pretty proficient in how we marched in formation. You could almost say that Platoon 2227 strutted more than just marched. Our unit Guidon stood tall, and the Flag fluttered as we marched.

When we returned to Platoon Street, Gunny was interested in knowing how Pugil Stick Training went. Sgt Porta reported to Gunny that his Platoon hit a Home Run and we were by far the best performing Platoon when we were matched up with the other Platoons. Gunny smiled and had the Platoon make a Head Call and clean-up for evening chow.

When everyone returned from cleaning up and getting back in Formation, Gunny told Sgt Porta to march us for evening chow. The procedures were the same as every other evening, and when we arrived at the 2nd Battalion Mess Hall, the other Platoons from FOX Company were already in line to eat. We were the fourth Platoon from FOX Company to go through the chow line but, we were fourth in line. Sgt Porta told us he thought we were the best Platoon in FOX Company.

When we returned from evening chow, Gunny wanted us to run through practice for the 7th Week Inspection one more time to make sure we had "**Inspection Arms**," perfected and he wanted to minimize any mistakes on Friday. We spent two hours after chow rehearsing "**Open Ranks**," and he had Sgt Porta Inspect each Recruit reviewing how we executed "**Inspection Arms**."

We enjoyed a relaxing evening, and I used Commanders Time to answer my sister's letter and write to my mother. Although I still hadn't received a letter from my former girlfriend Linda, I wrote her a short letter telling her I was fine and was thinking about her. Lights out at 2200 and those beautiful notes from Taps signaled I could close my eyes and get some sleep.

Thursday morning routine went by as usual. Sgt Martinez had the Duty and following Inspection of our Huts after morning clean-up, was complimentary of how well the Platoon was doing. He marched us to morning chow and afterwards lit the "*Smoking Lamp*." We were scheduled to attend a class on Guard Duty after chow which included how our 11 General Orders worked with Guard Duty.

It was interesting that over the entire week, we had not heard the Command, "**Lien Two**," by either Gunny, Sgt Martinez or Sgt Porta. Apparently we hadn't screwed up enough lately to warrant doing extra pushups. However, I didn't want to look a gift horse in the mouth, we still had five weeks of Boot Camp remaining.

After noon chow, Sgt Porta marched us over to the base dry cleaners to pick up our starched utilities which we would wear on Friday for our 7th Week Inspection. Training was going by pretty quickly and we knew this Friday would be an important day for our platoon. Now that we were beginning to look like Marines, everything we did from that moment on had us acting like Marines. We marched better, we stood better, we cleaned better, we acted differently, and our attitudes became apparent that the transition Gunny Sgt Wolfmule talked about on day one, was taking place.

After picking up our starched utilities, we marched back to Platoon Street and hung our starched utilities on our Rack. We then got our rifles off our Racks, put on our cartridge belts and spent most of the afternoon on the Grinder doing Close Order Drill and especially practicing "**Open Ranks**," and "**Inspection Arms**."

Before going to evening chow, Sgt Porta and Sgt Martinez showed us how to starch our Utility Covers. We were told to run to the wash racks and get our extra utility covers wet, then we stretched them over our metal grommet to stretch and form our cover. We then poured liquid starch over the cover and used the small brush that we bought at the PX to spread the starch and then set the cover on the foot of our racks to let them dry. In the morning, we would be taught how to form them for wear.

Sgt Porta marched us to evening chow and afterwards outside the Mess Hall, lit the "*Smoking Lamp*," then marched us back to our Platoon area where we spent two hours getting ready for Friday's inspection. We spit shined our boots, we cleaned our rifles and after commanders time we hit the rack.

Friday 7th Week Inspection would be held by 1st LT. Bazis, who was the Commanding Officer of FOX Company, and GySgt Yamaoka's, who was the Series Gunnery Sgt Our Platoon would follow Platoon 2226 to be Inspected which would be around 1015 on the Grinder. So, on Friday morning we woke at Reveille, completed PT, finished our morning routine and dressed in our regular utilities. Sgt Martinez marched us to morning chow and had us take our time. He marched back to our Platoon Area the long way giving us a chance to march and loosen up for Inspection.

Upon returning to the Platoon Street after morning chow, Gunny Sgt Wolfmule lit the "*Smoking Lamp*." When the "*Smoking Lamp*" was turned off, Gunny had us get ready for Friday's inspection. The first thing we did was spend time cleaning our rifles and each Squad Leader inspected their

Squad. We then took our new starched utility covers off our gromets and Sgt Porta showed us how to form them properly. This would be the first time we would wear starched utility covers and starched utilities.

After our Covers were formed, we changed out of our regular utilities and into our starched utilities, bloused our trousers over our spit shined boots. We put on our cartridge belts with bayonet and unlocked our rifles from our racks and fell in on Platoon Street. While we stood on Platoon Street, Sgt Martinez had us pair up and inspect each other to make sure we were squared away and ready for inspection. Squad Leaders double checked each Recruit in their Squad and then we "**Fell-In**," on Platoon Street.

We would be the third Platoon inspected, so we were checked and double-checked. Sgt Porta and Sgt Martinez double checked our boots, re-checked each rifle to make sure they were cleaned properly and checked each uniform to make sure our military alignment was perfect and we had no Irish Pendants anywhere on our uniforms. Sgt Martinez put us at ease, and we waited for Gunny Sgt Wolfmule to address the Platoon before inspection.

Gunny Sgt Wolfmule told us that after seven weeks, we are finally starting to get it. He told us we were the best Platoon in the FOX Company Training Series, and now had the opportunity to go out and show the rest of our Company how good we really were and earn their respect.

When it was our turn to take the Grinder for Inspection, Sgt Martinez marched us from the Platoon Street just off the Grinder where we waited for Gunny Wolfmule to give the Command to "**Fall-in**." We ran to our spot on the Grinder and once in formation and at attention, Gunny Sgt Wolfmule gave us the command to "**Open Ranks**."

We executed his Command perfectly and then automatically the Platoon went to "**Dress Right Dress**," and Gunny went to the 1st Squad and made sure they were perfectly in line, and then the next and to all four, and after aligning all four Squads, he marched back to the front of the formation and facing next to the 1ˢᵗ Squad, he Commanded, "**Ready Two**." Everyone dropped their arms and snapped their heads forward. Then, Gunny ordered "**Cover**," and everyone covered down behind the person in front of them.

Gunny then took his position in front of the Platoon and Reported to LT Bazis, and saluted, "Sir, Platoon 2227, Ready for Inspection." LT Bazis returned his Salute and said, "Very Well, Gunnery Sargeant." LT Bazis then turned and walked to the 1ˢᵗ Squad and stood in front of the first Recruit, which was me. I automatically came to "**Inspection Arms**," and LT Bazis took my rifle out of my arms and began to inspect it.

He looked down the barrel, the receiver, the sights, the

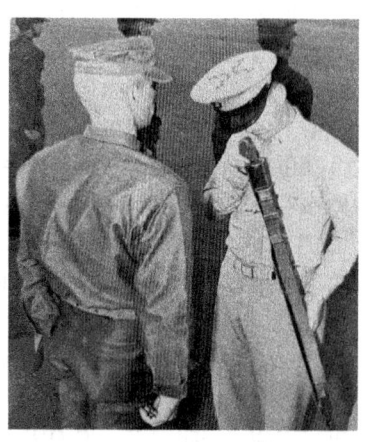

butt plate, then returned the rifle to me. I released the bolt and then went from "**Inspection Arms**," to the position of "Attention." He looked over my uniform, my boots, my haircut and then made a "**Right Face**," took one step and stood in front of the 1ˢᵗ Squad Leader who happened to be Pvt Havranek and repeated his Inspection.

Lt Bazis was followed by GySgt Yamaoka who held a clip board and was marking the name of each Recruit and any infractions committed. GySgt Wolfmule stood next to GySgt Yamaoka and gave him the name of each Recruit. After Inspecting the entire 1ˢᵗ Squad, they walked behind the 1ˢᵗ Squad and checked the length of our trousers, the heel of our boots, the back of our necks and the position of our rifle while at attention.

When the 1st Squad was Inspected, they then repeated the same routine for the 2nd, 3rd, and 4th Squads. After the entire Platoon was Inspected, Gunny stood in front of the Platoon and gave the Command, "**Close Ranks**." 1st Squad stood still, 2nd Squad took one step forward, 3rd Squad took two steps and 4th Squad took three steps forward. Automatically, the Platoon went to "**Dress Right Dress**," and again Gunny marched to the 1st Squad to ensure they were perfectly in line and then did the same with Squads 2,3 and 4. He then marched back even with 1st Squad and Commanded, "**Ready Two**," then "**Cover**."

Gunny returned to the front of the Formation and saluted Lt. Bazis. Lt. Bazis Saluted Gunny Wolfmule and told him to "**Carry On**." Then he and GySgt Yamaoka marched off to Inspect the next Platoon. When they left, Gunny Wolfmule put the platoon at ease, and off to the side of our formation stood Sgt Martinez and Sgt Porta.

Gunny Sgt Wolfmule told us we did one hell of a good job, and he thanked us for the hard work. He thanked me and the four squad leaders and told Sgt Martinez to take us back to the Platoon area and stow our gear and get changed out of our starched utilities and get ready for noon chow. Here we were after seven weeks, wearing starched utilities, our boots spit shined and trousers bloused, shirt collars open, starched utility covers, and almost as squared away as the best platoon on the Depot. Our next challenge was the upcoming rifle range.

We would be leaving for the rifle range on Saturday, when we finished noon chow. Sgt Porta had us do our Laundry again so we would have no dirty clothes before reporting to the Rifle Range. We "Fell-In" with our buckets, wisk, scrub brush, clothes pins, took our towels and wash cloth off our rack and along with our laundry bags, were marched over to the wash racks.

We washed all of our clothes and hung them on the clothes lines and Sgt Porta asked me who he should put on the detail for guarding the laundry. I recommended Pvt Evanoff and Pvt Ray who were both "shit birds," and missing class wouldn't hurt either of them.

After the last item was hung on the line, Sgt Porta had the Platoon make a Head Call and "Fall-In" for the afternoon class on what to expect on the rifle range for the next two weeks. We had many classes on the M 14 rifle, both the operation and care and cleaning, and we would be doing a lot of cleaning of our rifles over the next two weeks.

When the class was over, we returned back and got our laundry and returned everything back to our Hut and folded and put our clothes into our footlockers. We went to evening chow and after being marched back to Platoon Street, Sgt Porta lit the "*Smoking Lamp.*" As the Platoon was enjoying their smoke, Sgt Porta had Pvt Rilley, Pvt Gagnon and Pvt Evanoff report to the Duty Hut.

This was the last day Sgt Porta would be assigned as our Platoon's Drill Instructor and I suppose he wanted to say goodbye to the three of us. When we Reported to the Duty Hut, Sgt Porta had us come in and center ourselves on his desk. Sgt Porta said his goodbyes and told us he was going home on Leave on Monday and would look in on our families when he got home and share with them how each of us was doing and wished us all good luck.

He shook my hand and told me to keep up the good work. He shook Gagnon's hand and said it was nice to see him again, and just told Evanoff he better get his head out of his ass and get squared away. He then had us give him 50 pushups for not getting his brother to join the Marines. After our trip to say goodbye to Sgt Porta, we never saw him again. After leaving the Duty Hut, we went back to our Huts to get ready for lights out.

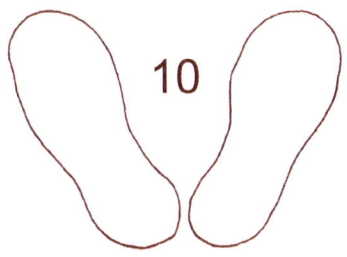

Rifle Range –
Snapping-In at Edson Range

Week eight began on Saturday morning after morning chow. We held a good field day of our Huts, stripped the Racks of linen, took our towels and laundry bags off our Racks and placed them in our footlockers. Gunny had me Report to the Duty Hut to give me my morning instructions for the Platoon.

When he was finished filling me in on what was happening that morning and told me what to do, I said, "Sir, Aye Aye Sir," and left the Duty Hut. I held a short meeting with the Squad Leaders and told them what needed to get done before we left for the rifle range.

The Squad Leaders listened, and I finished my comments by telling the Squad Leaders that so far the Platoon was in good standing with Gunny Wolfmule and I didn't want anyone to screw it up by not paying attention to details. We were at the most important part of Boot Camp, and I wanted the Red Streamer for our Guidon. They all agreed and went to take care of their Squads.

The plan for Saturday morning was to have all the recruits make sure their gear, including their extra pair of boots, were packed in their footlockers. They needed to unlock their rifles from their racks, put on their cartridge belts, bring their footlockers, buckets and rifles and "**Fall-In**" on the Platoon Street. They had 30 minutes to make it happen and I wanted it done in less than 25 minutes.

Without the Gunny or Sgt Martinez having to give any Orders or do any yelling, within 25 minutes, the entire Platoon was standing tall on the Platoon Street with their footlockers in front of them, their buckets on top, and their rifles at "Order Arms." I went to the Duty Hut and banged on the Duty Hut Pine and Gunny asked who was knocking on his Pine. I answered, "Sir Pvt Rilley requesting permission to Report to the Platoon Commander."

Gunny Wolfmule answered, "Enter." I entered the Duty Hut and Reported to the Gunny that Platoon 2227 was in Formation on the Platoon Street, each of the Squad Quonset Huts has had a complete field day, and the Platoon was ready to be transported to Camp Pendleton." He smiled and told me to "Carry On." I returned to the Platoon Street and stood behind my footlocker with my rifle slung on my back and the Platoon Guidon by my side.

Gunny came onto the Platoon Street with Sgt Martinez right behind him. He stood in front of the Platoon and told us to sling our rifles over our backs, pick-up the footlockers and buckets and he marched us over behind the 2nd Battalion Mess Hall where there were eight Cattle Car truck's. (*the cattle car was a wooden trailer attached to a semi tractor, set up with benches that could carry anywhere from 40 to 50 Marines.*) The trucks were to transport all four platoons from Fox Company 2nd Battalion to Camp Pendleton and after we were finished at the rifle range, they would bring us back again.

Each platoon in FOX Company averaged around 80 recruits with two DI's and one platoon commander. There were 2 squads loaded onto each cattle car along with our footlockers, rifles and all our gear. Since I couldn't carry my rifle, my footlocker and my bucket plus carry the Platoon

Guidon, Sgt Martinez took possession of our Guidon until we arrived at Camp Pendleton. The whole series of FOX Company was transported together. The eight Cattle Car truck's caravaned with a Highway Patrol and Military escort to Edson Range, at Camp Pendleton, California.

When we arrived at Edson Range, the cattle car trucks deposited FOX Company to our assigned two-story barracks where we would be billeted while at the range. There were 4 squad bays in each building, two up and two down, that could hold 90 or more recruits on each floor. Each floor of the squad bay was self-contained with a head that had 24 toilets, 24 sinks with mirrors, and an open shower with 36 shower heads. A private room which had 3 beds for our drill instructors and their own private bathroom and showers.

Platoons 2227 and 2228 were assigned to the second floor. The Platoons were separated by a solid brick wall and a stair well between. There were no Bunk Beds, so each individual Rack lined up in four rows, one for each Squad, with twenty plus Racks in each row. Each Rack had a six-inch mattress and one pillow, two blankets, two sheets and one pillow case laying on the mattress.

We carried our footlockers, buckets, and rifles up to our new home for the next two weeks, and Rack assignments were assigned by the squad. 1st Squad was to the left, next to the windows, lined up three feet from the wall, with 2nd and 3rd Squads in the middle of the squad bay back-to-back. The 4th Squad was on the right side of the barracks under the windows. I took the first Rack by the windows with the 1st Squad.

Against the walls under the windows of both sides of the Barracks were Rifle Racks that were shared. The 1st and 2nd Squad were on the left side of the Barracks toward the front of the building. On the other side of the Barracks, the Rifle Racks were shared with 3rd and 4th Squads. There were eight rifles to a Rifle Rack and each rifle was locked with our pad locks. Foot lockers and buckets were placed under each rack.

The first Squad made their Racks with the pillow toward the head of the Rack facing the window with the foot of the Rack facing the aisle between the 1st and 2nd Squad. The 2nd and 3rd Squads were in the middle of the Barracks with the head of their Rack facing each other and the foot of each Rack towards the isle. The 4th Squad was on the other side of the barracks with the head of the Rack under the windows and the foot facing the aisle.

We locked our M-14 in our assigned Rifle Rack, opened our footlockers and put out a towel, wash cloth and laundry bag on the foot of our racks, along with our cartridge belts. We placed our footlockers, buckets and extra boots under our racks as we had in our Quonset Huts. The Platoon Guidon was put in a Flag Stand by the wall, at the top of the stairs, where it was deposited each time we were to occupy our squad bay.

After stowing our gear, Gunny Wolfmule called me to his berthing area and asked me if I had a watch. I told the Gunny that it was mailed back with my clothing and personal items the day we arrived at MCRD. He told me to report to where the Company Commanding Officer and Company Gunny were officed, and I was to make a call home and have my mother send my watch by the fastest means possible to the address the Gunny wrote down on a piece of paper, along with the approval for me to make the call home.

After the Gunny handed me the address, he gave me directions to Headquarters and told me to double time over there, take care of business and beat feet back to the barracks. I answered, "**Aye Aye Gunny**," and took off running and found my way to Headquarters. When I entered the Headquarters building, the Company Gunny asked me what I needed, and I answered, "Sir, Gunny Sgt Wolfmule had the private report to headquarters Sir." and I handed the piece of paper given to me by GySgt Wolfmule to the Company Gunny with the approval to call home from my Platoon Commander. The Company Gunny read the note from Gunny Sgt Wolfmule and led me to where the telephone was located.

I dialed my home phone in Detroit, and luckily my mother answered the phone and was very surprised to hear my voice on the other end. I said hello, and told her this wasn't a social call, and I had no time to talk, but asked her to listen. I asked her to get a pencil and paper and write down the following information. Again she wanted to know why I was calling and what I had done. I said very nicely, go up to Patrick's room with the bunkbeds and on the dresser there is my jewelry box with the Timex watch I got from Zane and his dad as a going away gift. Please put the watch in a box and send the watch by the fastest means possible to this address:

PVT T.S. Rilley
Fox Company, Platoon 2227
Edson Range
Camp Pendleton, CA 90124

She wanted to talk, but I told her although I was fine, I could not talk to her right now but had to return to my barracks at the rifle range as soon as possible. I told her I would write her a letter and explain why I needed her to send me the watch the first chance I got, and I asked her if she understood my request. My mother said she understood. I thanked her, told her to mail it the absolute quickest means possible, and told her I loved her and hung up.

Why Gunny Sgt Wolfmule had me send for my watch he didn't say. He told me once I made the phone call, I was to beat feet back to the barracks and stop for nothing. I double timed back to our barracks as fast as my feet could carry me without stopping for anything. I reported back to Gunny Sgt Wolfmule and reported, "**Sir, mission accomplished, Sir.**" He said, "Good job, Pvt Rilley, report to the squad bay. I answered, "**Sir, Aye Aye Sir.**" When I returned to my bunk, Pvt Havranek told me that Gunny Sgt Wolfmule was going to hold an inspection of the squad bay to ensure bunks were made properly and our gear was stowed properly. I thanked him for sharing with me what Gunny instructed, and told each squad leader to make sure his squad was squared away.

Once everyone had settled in and the squad leaders assured me their squad was squared away, I reported to Gunny that our barracks was ready for Inspection. The Gunny then made his way through the Barracks, and those who didn't make their bunks properly, had their racks torn up to be made again. If towels or wash cloth or laundry bag weren't lined up properly, they were discarded on the floor. Gunny Sgt Wolfmule always held tough inspections.

It didn't matter how perfect we thought the barracks was, the Gunny would always find something that needed correcting. When he had finished his Inspection, he said we had exactly one-half hour to redo everything that was wrong and we would stand Inspection again. If we did not pass this next inspection, we would all be doing bends and thrusts until we couldn't stand. He said, "**Turn Two.**" We all answered loudly, "**Sir, Aye Aye Sir.**"

We began to fix everything that was wrong. Those who's racks were not disturbed, helped those who had their racks torn up to make sure they were made up correctly. The squad leaders made sure everyone in their squad had towels, washcloths and laundry bags placed exactly where they needed to be.

Exactly one-half hour later, Sgt Martinez called the barracks to attention. The entire barracks stood tall on the right side at the foot of their bunks so our towels, laundry bags and cartridge belts could be seen. Gunny Wolfmule walked through the barracks.

As he walked up one side and down the other, not one bunk was torn up and no gigs for any towel or laundry bag out of place. We passed his Inspection although there was no "good job," given, because that was what he expected from us. It was time for noon chow and since we are at a new facility, we didn't know what to expect for meals or how the mess hall was configured. It didn't take us long to find out.

Since all four platoons were staying in the same barracks, there had to be a schedule as to who would eat first, second, third and so on. Gunny Sgt Wolfmule met with the Platoon Commander from the other Platoons, and after he finished talking, it was established that we would eat by platoon each day and rotate accordingly.

For example, Platoon 2225 would eat first on Saturday, 2226 would go first on Sunday, 2227 would go first on Monday and 2228 would go first on Tuesday and then go back in rotation all the way thru rifle range training. So it was, we were to be third for Saturday noon and evening chow.

When we "**Fell-In**" for noon chow, I was excited to see how the food would compare to MCRD. To my surprise, the food was very good, and we did everything the same way we did in San Diego. We "**Fell-In**" in two single file lines, and stood at "**Attention.**" The biggest difference was there was no mirror to salute. Once inside the Mess Hall, we filed in at "Attention" got our trays and silverware, sidestepped through the chow line and stood at our table until told to sit.

The mess hall seemed to be brand new and was laid out differently than the 2nd Battalion Mess Hall back at MCRD. However, the procedure was the same, we still had 20 minutes to eat in silence and we still placed our dirty trays into the drop off area along with our glasses, cups and silverware.

When noon chow was finished, the "*Smoking Lamp*" was lit and after retrieving our rifles and cartridge belts, we "Fell-In" outside the Barracks and we did Close Order Drill with rifles the rest of the afternoon. There was a large open

Drill Field outside our Barracks and besides our Platoon running through Close Order Drill, the other three Platoons were doing the same.

We continued to Drill until it was time to put away our rifles, clean-up and get ready for evening chow. The weather was overcast all afternoon, and it looked like it was going to rain, but it never did. We took our time getting ready for evening chow, because we would have to wait for Platoons 2225 and 2226 to go through the chow line first.

Saturday evening I was surprised that they served a Pot Roast, with cooked carrots, onions, mashed potatoes, gravy, corn or green beans, dinner rolls, milk, water iced tea or coffee and for dessert they served Dutch Apple Pie. Dinner was amazing, and to be honest, it seemed that meal was the best we had received since we began training. After evening chow, we **"Fell-Out,"** on the apron in front of our Barracks and the *"Smoking Lamp"* was lit. Afterwards we had Commander's Time the rest of the evening. We wrote letters, shined boots, read our Marine handbook and cleaned our rifles.

Every evening at 2100, we would have Commander's Time, before we prepared for bed. Either Saturday or Sunday, the DI's would hold hygiene inspection and would check our feet for blister's, toe jam, swollen ankles or feet. Our hands would be checked to make sure they were clean, and fingernails were clean and trimmed. They would check our ears, both inside and out to make sure we were washing properly.

We were government property now, but specifically, property of the United States Marine Corps, and everything the Marine Corps owns must be in good working and healthy order. If a recruit did not follow the hygiene rules he could be dropped from the Platoon. We started with 92 recruits the night we arrived, and after losing five the first night, we began our boot training with 87 recruits. We lost more Recruits for a number of different reasons and were now down to 79 recruits to begin our Rifle Range Training.

We lost a total of eight recruits over the seven weeks of training. Two were sent to the fat farm for not losing enough weight to pass their initial PT test. We lost three to training accidents, two on the obstacle course with broken bones, and one while going through water training when he fell and hit his head and was in the hospital. One went home on emergency leave because his father had died. One recruit was confined to the Brig for trying to go UA (Unauthorized Absence). One was in sick bay with a terrible cold that turned into pneumonia.

Those who were dropped from our platoon would pick up another platoon and resume training where they left off. The recruit in the hospital will be re-evaluated to decide if they are physically fit to return to duty. The two in Motivation Platoon, or the fat farm will lose 30 lbs. before they are allowed back to training. The Marine in the brig will probably be discharged with a bad conduct discharge. He will never be allowed to serve in a government job of any kind.

Before Lights Out on Saturday night, Gunny told us that Sgt James would be at morning Formation. We didn't cheer, but everyone was glad he was returning. Even though it was a new and strange place that we would have to adjust to, it was very easy to fall asleep when we heard Taps and Lights out that first night. The biggest difference being at Edson Range from MCRD was we had to stand fire watch throughout the night in case there was a disturbance or a fire in the barracks. That was regulations.

During Commanders Time, Sgt Martinez, myself and the four Squad Leaders met and established Duty Sections for "Fire Watch." The first night the first Squad had Duty, the second night the 2nd Squad, third night the 3rd Squad and so on and repeating the Duty order until we leave Camp Onofre and return to MCRD.

The "Fire Watch," was set for two-hour watches beginning at 2200 to 2400, 2400 to 0200, 0200 to 0400 and the last watch was from 0400 'til reveille which was at 0500. Each night 4 men from the duty squad were picked to stand watch. There were 18 recruits in each of the first two Squads and 19 recruits in the 3rd and 4th Squads, so no one had more than one night of Duty while at the range.

Whoever had "Fire Watch" duty had a red tag placed on his rack with the time he had the Duty. Since the watch was from the same squad, they were all close together. The watch on Duty would wake up his relief 15 minutes before he went on Duty and there was a log they would sign-In on and they would walk the barracks floor for two hours.

Each recruit while on Duty would wear his boots, utility trousers, yellow sweatshirt, a chrome helmet and carry a flashlight. In the morning, the DI on duty would read and sign off the Duty Log. If the recruit failed to sign the Log, he was in deep shit. Neither the Squad Leaders nor I had to stand "Fire Watch."

Reveille was sounded at 0500 and all four Squad Bays

would wake at the same time. Head call, then PT out front of the barracks just like at MCRD. It was still dark out so we were told to be careful and watch our footing as we moved from the barracks to the grinder to do our morning PT. After PT, shit, shower and shave then field day the barracks before chow. On Sundays just like at MCRD, after morning chow, those going to church services would "**Fall-In**," and march to whatever service they chose. Those not attending Church Services would have Commanders time until 1130.

Sunday morning Commander Time was used mostly to write letters home or re-read mail received during the week. We'd shine boots, clean rifles, read our Marine Corps manual and relax until 1130.

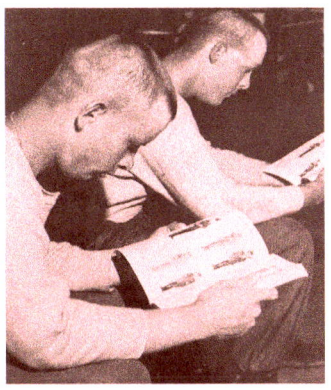

Those choosing Church normally returned to the Barracks by 0930 unless they attended Bible class or lectures.

On Sunday mornings, at 1130 we would get ready for noon chow. After noon chow we would "Fall-Out" with rifles, utility belt, canteen, bayonet and first aid pouch, and practice Close Order Drill most of the day.

Sundays were becoming both predictable and enjoyable days. We would execute Close Order Drill until time for evening chow. We would put our rifles back on the Rifle Racks and hang our cartridge belts at the end of our Rack. After evening chow, we would again get our rifles and cartridge belts and practice Close Order Drill for a couple of hours or until it started to get dark.

Sunday nights we started Commanders Time early, we were given the opportunity to write letters or sit on our footlockers and read letters that we received. Lights out at taps, 2200. Lights on at reveille at 0500 and then morning PT. We would make our Racks before we went to morning chow then returned for barracks clean-up. After the morning barracks inspection, we "**Fell-In**" outside ready for our first day at the range.

Sgt James returned and was at our morning formation with Sgt Martinez. He said he was glad to see us and said he had heard good things about our accomplishments since he was gone. Sgt James informed us what was going to happen while at the rifle range. He informed us that Monday was Pay Day, and we would be paid between 0900 and 1000, and afterwards we would march to the rifle range to FAM, Fire our M14 rifles. Afterwards we would return to our Barracks and clean our rifles.

Sgt James explained that we would be snapping in all week to learn and experience all the proper rifle positions we would be using while at the range, Offhand (standing), Kneeling, Sitting and Prone positions. He also explained we would be assigned a PMI, (Primary Marksmanship Instructor) who will be our Instructor the entire time we are at the Range.

Sgt James told us after we got paid, we would all be issued shooting jackets that we would wear every day while at the rifle range. He then had the platoon sling their rifles and put them over their left shoulder, and that included myself. As the "Right Guide," I carried the platoon Guidon whenever the platoon marched anywhere, and that would also be my responsibility while at the rifle range.

Instead of slinging my rifle over my left shoulder, I would sling my rifle over my head and across my back so I could carry the platoon Guidon as well as my rifle. The entire FOX Company was marched to where the Disbursing Officer set-up the tables so all our Company could get paid.

We went through the Disbursing line by Platoon with Platoon 2225 going first. The other three Platoons stood by while Platoon 2225 was getting paid, and Sgt James put us

"At Ease," and lit the *"Smoking Lamp."* We waited in Platoon Formation since our Platoon was going to be paid third.

The procedure to get paid was the same as at MCRD. Stand in line, give your name, show your ID Card, receive your pay of $41.00 in cash, drop the $2.00 in the DI Fund bucket and move on. After each Platoon was paid, we were to march a little over a mile and a half to the Edson Rifle Range at Camp Pendleton. We were put into two single file columns on both sides of the road as we left our barracks and marched to where the range was located.

Because we were in two single file columns, we did not march in step, instead we did what was called a "Route Step" as our formation was referred to as a forced march. We caught up to Platoons 2225 and 2226 who were also in two single files on both sides of the road, and it was quite a sight as we made our way down the road to the range.

At the bottom of the hill we had just come down, we could see a number of buildings, and a number of bleachers covered with roofs.

When we got close to the range, we got backed up as each Platoon Squad went to one of the buildings where each Recruit was issued a shooting jacket and a shooting glove. Once you received your shooting jacket and shooting glove, we "**Fell-In**" a Platoon Formation. Sgt James had us fold our utility collar under so the collar didn't show and then put on the shooting jacket. The shooting jacket was almost like our utility jacket, and it depended if you were right handed or left handed. The right handed shooters had a thick pad sewed in on the right shoulder and chest area. The left-handed shooter had just the opposite.

There were also pads on both elbows and forearms, there was a pocket on the left front breast on a right-handed shooting jacket and a pocket on the right breast side of a left-handed shooting jacket. If you were right-handed you were issued a left-handed shooting glove and if you were left-handed you were issued a right-handed shooting glove.

Sgt James marched our Platoon over to a set of bleachers where we were assigned to our PMI. (Primary Marksman

Instructor). Each Platoon was assigned a PMI, and our PMI was Sgt Rodriquez. Sgt Rodriquez was a Vietnam Veteran and a rifle Expert. He would be our Instructor for the entire two weeks at the Range. During our first week we would be learning the Snapping-In procedures for learning how to use our slings, get into shooting positions as well as teaching us everything we need to know to qualify with the M-14 rifle.

At the foot of the bleachers was a couple of Flag stands to be used to place the Platoon Guidon during classes or hands on instruction. No matter where we stopped, or what we were doing, I was responsible for our Guidon. When we marched with sling rifles to or from the range, I would sling my M-14 over my back and carry the Guidon. While Snapping-In, shooting on the range, working in the pits, going through the confidence course, going through the chow line, on the Platoon Street or in a classroom, the Guidon would be placed in a flag stand while we trained. While in a platoon formation and moving from one place to another, I would always carry the Guidon.

When we marched without our rifles, I always carried the Guidon. When in platoon formation practicing close order drill, I carried the Guidon without my rifle. The only time I did not carry the Guidon, was Snapping-In, actually firing on line, or doing an actual training function like climbing obstacles, swimming, going through chow, in classrooms, inside the barracks or sleeping, or participating in Final Inspection.

The first week at the range was called Snapping-In. That first morning after getting paid we marched to the range and after getting issued our shooting jackets, and our shooting gloves, we were given the opportunity to FAM Fire our M-14 rifles. We were given five rounds to load into a magazine and then we were placed on the firing line and allowed to fire those five rounds at the target to get the feel of our M-14 rifle.

I had never fired a high-powered rifle before, I had only fired a .22 Rifle while in the boy scouts which was entirely

a different weapon. I never hunted or had anyone in my family hunt and I was never exposed to any high powered weapons. The .22 had no kick, but the M-14 had a huge kick, and gave me a big fat lip because I didn't hold the weapon properly in my shoulder or ride the recoil. Instead, the M-14 kicked back like a smack in the mouth and when I was finished, I was embarrassed as everyone knew by my lip that I did not know how to hold or fire my weapon.

Sgt James walked up to me and told me I looked terrible, but I would learn how to shoot properly and not to be discouraged. When everyone had shot their five rounds, we fell back in and were marched to a closed-in outdoor classroom area to attend classes. Our platoon PMI (Preliminary Marksmanship Instructor) Sgt Rodriquez had just returned from Vietnam and was serious about his job and made sure to instruct us properly on every aspect of the M-14 rifle.

Before we were to shoot again we were taught how to properly get into the four shooting positions. Standing (offhand), kneeling, sitting, and prone (laying on your stomach). In order to have a tight position no matter which position you were in, we needed to learn how to use the sling properly. We needed to learn the proper sling position for all four positions.

The other secret to using the sling is being able to get the flexibility needed to be in a proper firing position. That is what snapping in for a week will teach us, how to be flexible for each position. For example, in the sitting position, you would bend your knees while you were sitting and then bend down until your nose hits the ground. The other example of flexibility would be to take your left hand, put your right arm under your left elbow and with your right hand grab your left wrist. We practiced this at least three hours a day. The rest of the time was spent in the open classroom, on bleachers,  learning about "site picture" and "triangulation" and "holding and squeezing." BRASS was the magic word we were taught to remember. "Breathe, relax, aim, slack, squeeze."

Every day we were instructed and studied "Site picture, target alignment, windage and elevation." All of these things were reviewed every day, all week long. In the Marine Corps you are a rifleman first, last and always. Every Marine goes through the exact same training. The same boot camp, the same yellow footprints, the same exact training whether enlisted or officer. Every Marine is an 0311 Marine, a rifleman. If you can't qualify with your rifle, you cannot make it in the Marine Corps.

If you do not qualify with your rifle during Boot Camp they will either set you back with another Platoon until you learn, or send you home. If you go home, you go home in disgrace. To qualify with your rifle, you must earn either marksman, sharpshooter or expert. You must shoot from 200 yards, 300 yards and 500 yards.

- From 200 yards you shoot 10 rounds slow fire off-hand (standing position) & 10 rounds slow fire kneeling.
- From 300 yards you shoot 10 rounds rapid fire, 5 sitting/5 standing & 10 rounds rapid fire, 5 kneeling/5 prone

- From 500 yards you shoot 10 rounds slow fire, prone position
- A perfect score is 250. To qualify at all, you must score a minimum of 175 to 209 which earns you the Marksman Badge.
- To qualify as a sharpshooter you must score 210 to 229
- To qualify as an expert you must score a minimum of 230 or above

Each morning after morning chow we marched the mile and a half to the range. After we spent the morning doing "Snapping In," or classroom training, we would march the mile and a half back for noon chow. After noon chow we would march the mile and a half back to the range for more "Snapping In," and classroom training and then the mile and a half back for evening chow. After evening chow time was spent as Commanders Time. However, each DI on duty determined how we would spend Commanders Time.

On Wednesday morning and afternoon we repeated the same training we went through on Tuesday, "Snapping In," positions, Classroom training on Sight Picture, Triangulation, target alignment, windage and elevation, holding and squeezing. Repetition of everything we were taught was a way to burn it into our brains. Repetition of firing positions was teaching muscle memory.

After we finished our training schedule on Wednesday we marched back the mile and a half to our barracks for evening chow. Gunny Wolfmule held Mail Call Wednesday after evening chow. When my name was called, Gunny had me open the package I had received from Detroit, Michigan. Inside the box was my Timex Watch I had gotten as a present from my best friend and his dad as a going away gift, when I left for the Marines.

Gunny told me the reason he had me send for my watch, was to make sure there would never be a reason why Platoon 2227 was not on time for any event, class or training from this moment forward. He sent me back into the Platoon waiting for the mail call to continue. Everyone was very careful not to touch the DI's hands when retrieving their mail. Of course there were times when the DI would push his hands into yours, causing you to touch him and then you paid the price. It was all part of the plan to mess with you while at boot camp and it was important for you to know that.

The rest of the week, our PMI had the Platoon looking pretty good in all the firing positions, and it certainly made sense to have us "Snapping In" before qualifying with our rifles. It was important to be flexible enough to be steady at "offhand, sitting, kneeling and prone positions. A high-power rifle fired at distances of 200, 300 and 500 yards isn't an easy task without proper instruction.

Commanders Time while at the range varied depending on the DI on Duty. Some nights we would Close Order Drill if it was Sgt James. When Sgt Martinez had the Duty, we would write letters or read our Marine handbook. When Gunny Wolfmule had the Duty, he was insistent that our Platoon compose a platoon song that we could sing when we were performing Close Order Drill or for when we were on the obstacle course. We tried, but never got the job done. We did pay for it with push-ups.

Lights out at 2200 at taps, reveille was 0500 every day. Morning routine was the same, head call, PT, shit, shower and shave, field day barracks, morning chow, march to the range. The first week of "Snapping In" began in the afternoon on Monday and ended on Saturday at 1730 as we took the mile and a half trek back for evening chow.

I made it a point during the Commanders Time to write my mother a letter to explain my phone call and thanked her for sending me my watch so quickly. I gave her a short overview of how Boot Camp was going and told her we were at the rifle range getting ready to qualify for Marksmanship Medals.

I wrote that we would be at the Rifle Range for two weeks, with the first week we were trained at what was called "Snapping-In." This training would get us ready to actually start shooting our M-14's and know how to actually hold, sight-in our weapon and make sure we were on target.

Next week we would actually begin firing our weapons for real and fire our M-14's for score to earn our Marine Corps Shooting Badge which is what every Marine is taught to do in order to qualify as a United States Marine.

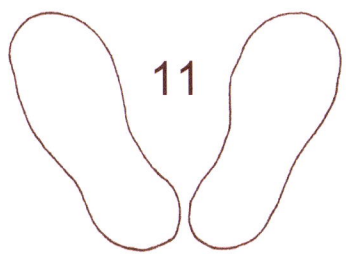

11

Rifle Qualifications

Sunday morning began week nine. The same morning routine as the week before, reveille at 0500, head call, PT, shit, shower, shave, and morning chow, but Sunday at the range was different than MCRD. Church Services didn't start until everyone returned from morning chow instead of going to chow with each Church Denomination Formation. There were only two Services on Sunday at the Range, a Christian Service and a Jewish Service.

Commanders Time, for those not going to Church include cleaning rifles, reviewing the Marine Corps manual, writing letters, shining boots, and personal hygiene. After noon chow on Sunday we were marched over to a classroom where we were taught how qualification will work now that "Snapping In," is over. We also went over the Safety Rules which we would review every day, repeat when asked and there were signs all over the Range to remind us.

The Safety Rules were:
- Treat your weapon as if it were loaded.
- Never point a weapon at anything you do not intend to shoot.
- Keep your finger straight and off the trigger until you are ready to fire.

- Keep your weapon on safe until you intend to fire.

These Rules had to be followed at all times and if stopped by a Drill Instructor, your PMI or any one on the Range, you were to repeat the Rules word for word. If you couldn't repeat them, you might spend quite a lot of time doing "Bends and Thrusts."

After classroom time, we spent the rest of the afternoon doing Close Order Drill with Sgt James in charge. After evening chow, the DI's held a class in the barracks explaining how the upcoming week was going to work.

On Monday morning of the second week, the routine was pretty much the same as the first week. The only difference from week eight to week nine was after slinging our rifles and marching the mile and a half to the range, we would begin shooting live rounds and find ourselves qualifying this week with the "Snapping-In" behind us. Two Platoons would fire on the line and two Platoons would Pull Targets.

There were 80 to 90 recruits on the line at a time made from two platoons. Two platoons would be on the line shooting, half a Platoon at a time, at the same time, and other two platoons would be pulling targets and working the  pits. Every recruit was issued a Range book that they would use on the line to log their shots.

 The Range book would be placed in your shooting jacket pocket when not on the line.

The first relay would move to the 200-yard line, strap their shot log to their leg, fix their sling and move into position to begin firing. Each recruit would load five rounds into a magazine and take up their firing position. The "Range Master" would ask, "All Ready on the Right? All Ready on the Left? Already on the Firing Line.?" If there was a problem on the line, one of the PMI's or DI would raise and waive a red Flag stopping the "Range Master" from giving the Command to Fire.

If the Flag was raised and was not being waved, the "Range Master" would say, "With five rounds, commence Firing."

After the five rounds were fired, The "Range Master" would yell "Cease Fire, Cease Fire, secure all weapons on the firing line." The DI's and PMI checked the hits on targets. There were a few adjustments, but not many. The same procedure was repeated each time there were rounds to be fired on target. Everyone on the line fired another 5 rounds and based on hits, minor adjustments were made again, and corrections placed in the shot log of each recruit on the line.

Each day we fired 20 rounds from 200 yards, 20 rounds from 300 yards and 10 rounds from 500 yards. We had a range book that we always carried with us. When we started on Monday, we would zero our sights and then begin shooting and adjust our sights for windage and elevation. The windage was determined by how hard the range flags were blowing. The elevation was set for 200 yards and when we found the elevation for offhand, we logged it in our range book.

We repeated the same for kneeling, from 200-300 yards, sitting for 300 yards and prone for 300 and 500 yards. You would make sure before you shot every position from each distance. You would zero your sights and mark up what the elevation was for each distance and then recorded each position at each distance.

After shooting our 50 rounds each, the first relay would depart the Firing Line, and the second relay of shooters would get on the Firing line at 200 yards and repeat the same procedure which would complete the shooting for the first two Platoons on Day one. After the two Platoons finished shooting, and the two Platoons Masking targets finished masking targets, all four platoons formed up and marched the mile and a half to noon chow

Noon chow was just as good as the meals we were getting at MCRD. When we finished eating, Sgt Martinez lit the "*Smoking Lamp*," and afterwards we made the mile and a half march back to the rifle range. Since our Platoon had already fired this morning, we were marched directly to the Butts to mask targets for the next round of shooters.

When you "masked" targets, you stuck a piece of tape over the hole where the bullet goes through the target and after raising the target back up, raise a disk to mark where the shot hit the target. If it was a bullseye, you would raise a white disk and cover  the bullseye "bull," which was black over the position where the round went through the Black Bull as on the face of a clock. If the round hit the Bull at the 3:00 side of the Black, the Disk would cover the 3:00 side of the target. Every other shot that was not in the "bull", was marked with a black disk over the position it hit the target. If the shooter missed the target all together, you would waive the red disk back and forth from side to side to signify a "Maggie's Drawers." NO HIT on target.

On Tuesday after morning chow, we were marched to the range and instead of shooting in the morning, we marked targets all morning. After pulling targets all morning, our Platoon marched the mile and a half back to our barracks area for noon chow. We stopped at our Barracks to leave our rifles and make a Head Call. After we finished noon chow we returned to our Barracks, retrieved our M-14 and "**Fell-In**" Platoon Formation where Sgt James lit the "Smoking Lamp."

Afterwards, the Platoon was called to "**Attention**" and then we were marched back to the Range to fire in the afternoon.

We made our way to the firing line where half of our Platoon took up their firing positions. Once on the firing line, we would automatically use the elevation from Monday and adjust up and down depending on hits, and for wind side to side. It was important to correctly site in your weapon and mark your Range Book correcting both elevation or windage based on your hits. Pre-qualification day was going to be on Thursday, and we needed to know how our weapon was sighted to be able to qualify. We had three days to get comfortable with our rifles and make sure we had the right elevations and windage setting for each distance.

I preferred to shoot in the morning because there was normally less wind to affect your shot. A five mile an hour wind could move your bullet from 300 meters, one to two inches off target if you didn't adjust to it properly. One of the most important things to know and to execute while shooting was to make sure you had a tight sling and a stable firing position from each distance. If done right, and your firing position was tight, you could site in your weapon, close your eyes, and after shooting and returning to your position after the recoil, have the same sight picture for the next shot.

Thursday Would be referred to as "Pre-Qual Day," and we would shoot as if it were qualification day. The score on pre-qual day was an indication of how you would do on qualification day. The Platoon that qualified the most recruits and had the highest scores would win the Rifle Range Streamer for their Guidon. If you went "UNQ" (Unqualified) on pre-qual day and didn't qualify on Qualification Day, your score hurt the Platoons chances to win the streamer and possibly the Honor Platoon.

Plus, those who do not qualify on Qualification Day do not graduate from boot camp with their Platoon. They have the choice to be reassigned to another Platoon and repeat the two weeks at the range, or they could be dropped from the Corps all together and take an "undesirable" discharge from the Marine Corps. Both ways hurt his Platoon towards winning the Streamer.

Tuesday evening after evening chow, Sgt James and Sgt Martinez worked with everyone on their Range book, making sure the markings were legible, and were within the range they should be. You see, there is a range that all rifles should be because all these rifles shoot pretty close to each other. For example, if my score was perfect on a target for elevation, no one should be four clicks higher or lower from the same distance. So while we are shooting, the DI's watched who was doing really well and used those marks as a basis to check. You would open your book and Sgt James would ask, from 300 yards who does not have say four clicks as an elevation? Raise your hand. Then they would check your mark and see how far you were off.

If you were not off more than two clicks either way, they weren't concerned, but if you were four to five off either way, it was a concern to watch for and check your scores. They did that for all distances, 200, 300 and 500 yards. Windage was next, they did the same thing, if you were more than two or three off either way it was a concern to watch on pre-qual day. By the time we finished reviewing the marks, it was getting close to lights out, so we were dismissed to get ready for hitting the rack. We did have time to write a letter if you chose to, I chose to hang out and get ready to hit the rack.

Lights out at 2200, Taps played, and everyone was sleeping within minutes except the On-Duty Fire Watch. We hadn't had mail call for the last two days so I figured we would probably have mail call on Wednesday. Again, I slept like a baby, and it seemed like the lights went out and then came right back on again. Wednesday morning reveille at 0500. Head call, PT, personal routine, then field day before having morning chow. After morning chow, the "*Smoking Lamp*" was lit before getting our gear ready for our march to the range.

After marching the mile and a half to the range, there was a change in plans for Wednesday morning. We were lined up and given a crash course on the .45 caliber pistol. We have had classes on the .45 and we took it apart in classroom settings but we had never fired it before. Wednesday morning we were allowed to FAM fire (familiarization) the .45 caliber pistol with two clips (seven rounds each) of .45 ammo, at 25 yards. We all had a chance to feel what it felt like to fire the standard side arm of the Marine Corps. We wouldn't need to qualify with the .45 while at Boot Camp, but with all the classes we attended and the fact some of us will be carrying .45's sometime in our career, this short version of small arms training was meant to get us familiar with the .45. We each took our turn on the firing line with the .45 and then went about getting ready to shoot another 50 rounds with the M-14 on the Rifle Range.

Since we spent time Wednesday morning FAM firing the .45, there wasn't time for getting our entire Platoon through the firing line. Only half the Platoon fired our M-14 Wednesday morning. We finished the second Relay after noon chow before pulling and masking targets once we were finished shooting. It was important to pay attention to the scores relevant to the elevation and windage settings.

It was apparent that reviewing our Range books the night before made a difference for scoring. As the 90 shooters online finished the 200-yard shoot, they adjusted for 300 yards. Again, reviewing the shot logbooks and making sure the scores were adjusted as well. One last check from 500 yards completed the adjustment. The scores were better than Tuesday, but now the second Relay of shooters got on the line and went through the elevation checks beginning at 200 yards, then 300 and finally, 500 yards.

The DI's and PMI were very satisfied that our adjustments were adequate, and everyone seemed to qualify based on preliminary results. Tomorrow would be pre-qualification day and after the scores were logged, the outcome would determine if we were ready for qualification. Hopefully the wind wouldn't blow in the morning because I would be on the firing line first relay.

Evening chow Wednesday night was the best we had since arriving at San Onofre. We had steak and mashed potatoes with green beans, dinner rolls and apple pie for dessert. We had iced tea or milk to drink, I picked the Iced Tea. After dinner, the "*Smoking Lamp*" was lit as we fell back into formation. We were told the mail call would go at 1830 in our barracks. The "*Smoking Lamp*" was turned off and we marched back to our barracks.

Mail call was held right on time. We crowded around and waited for our name to be called. The DI would hold the mail in his hand and wait for you to clap it out of his hands without touching him. I received two letters at mail call this day, one from my older brother Jim, and one from my mother. In my mom's letter, she brought me up to date about my dad doing a job in St. Louis, and how my sister and new husband were getting on. She also shared with me that my brother Denny and his wife Carol were having their second baby.

My brother Jim wrote wondering how things were going with me, and telling me how his life was different since he was transferred to Wisconsin compared to Detroit. He now living in Milwaukee, Wisconsin with his new wife and he told me how he thought I would be an Uncle by Summer. While I was reading my mail Gunny Wolfmule called me and the squad leaders to his room. We put away our gear and Reported to the room where our Platoon Commander and DI's were birthed. Gunny discussed with us how the next couple of days would go and what was expected from all of us.

After he dismissed us, he made his way into our Squad Bay to Inspect our Platoon before we hit our Racks. The Fire Watch was set and then lights were turned out and we heard Taps as our heads hit the pillow.

Pre-Qualification Day

Thursday, Reveille at 0500, followed by our normal daily routine before morning chow, and then the mile and a half march to the range. When we arrived at the Range, it was still dark, so our PMI had us "**Fall-In**" on the bleachers for one last class before we hit the firing line. He asked if we all had our shooting books. He then walked us through the procedure for pre-qualification day. There was no wind this early in the morning so there was no need to adjust much for "windage."

As daylight began there were two Platoons on the firing line and two Platoons pulling and marking targets. 45 shooters from each Platoon made their way to the firing line for the first relay and took their positions in front of their targets. The PMI from both Platoons and DI's made their way up and down the firing line handing out ammo to each shooter.

- Each Shooter would fire from 200 Yards, 10 Rounds offhand slow fire, (standing position) 10 Rounds Kneeling slow fire
- Each Shooter would fire from 300 Yards, 10 Rounds Rapid Fire, 5 sitting/5 offhand, and 10 Rounds Rapid Fire, 5 kneeling/5 prone
- Each Shooter from 500 Yards, 10 Rounds slow fire, prone position
- A Perfect Score is 250 points.
- To qualify at all for a Marksman you must score a minimum of 175.
- To qualify as a Sharpshooter you must score 210 to 229
- To qualify as an Expert you must score a minimum of 230 or above.

A total of 50 Rounds would be fired. The Target had the Bullseye worth 5 points, the four ring, 4 points, the three ring, 3 points, the two ring, 2 points, and the one ring, 1 point. A Maggie's Drawers is a "Miss" and is 0 points. The maximum score that a Shooter could score would be 250 Points.

At 200 yards we would load 10 rounds in two separate magazines. Each shooter was told to set their elevation and windage for 200 yards. I had already zeroed my sights, so I looked in my Shooting Book for 200 yards and added the clicks for elevation and for windage after looking at the range flags to see if the wind had picked up. The range master then told all shooters to take their position on the firing line.

The Range Master gave the Command, "With one magazine and ten rounds, lock and load." The shooters then put a magazine into their M-14 rifles and made sure the safety was set on safe. The Range Master continued, "All Ready on the right, All Ready on the left, All Ready on the firing line." The PMI's and DI's each had a red flag and when asked if ready on the right, they held their flags straight up in the air. If there was a problem they would wave their flag indicating that part of the firing line was not yet ready. The same on the left. When all flags were straight up in the air, the Range Master would then command, "With 10 rounds, commence firing!"

The firing line barked as each shooter began to unload their ten rounds down line at their target. As each round hit or missed their target, the target pullers would mark and mask each target after each round. After I fired each round, I marked my book as to where the round hit. I shot five rounds before even thinking about adjusting my sights. I was shooting off hand, and it was the hardest position to score on.

We had 15 minutes to put our ten rounds on target, so I didn't have to rush. When the target came back up the shooter would mark his shooting book with the score of each shot. This process would continue until the shooter expended all ten rounds on his target. Adjustments to elevation could be made if the shooter wasn't scoring on his target.

The first five rounds were two Bullseyes, one 4 ring, one in the 3 ring and one in the 2 ring. I know I was nervous, so that accounted for the first round being low on the two ring. Rounds three and five were in the Bull, so I knew I didn't have to adjust my sights, just be steadier before squeezing the trigger.

I continued to fire my next five rounds and marked each shot as my target was marked and masked. The second five rounds had one bullseye, three 4 rings and one 3 ring for a score of 39/50. I was shooting a little to the right, but I thought my windage was OK, I was just jerking a little. Not fantastic, but good enough to qualify.

When the 15 minute-time was up, the Range Master would command, "Cease fire, Cease Fire, secure all weapons on the firing line." All shooting would stop, and all weapons would be cleared and placed on "safe".

There was a time limit on pre-qualification day for each qualifying segment. You had 15 minutes at 200 Yards for 10 Rounds slow fire offhand, and 15 minutes for 10 Rounds slow fire kneeling. When we moved to the 300-yard line, you had 10 minutes for 10 Rounds rapid firing, 5 rounds standing/5 rounds sitting and 10 Rounds rapid firing, 5 rounds prone/5 rounds kneeling. Then at 500 Yards, you had 15 minutes for 10 Rounds slow fire prone position.

On pre-qualification day more time was allotted so you had a chance to mark your score in your shooting book to keep track of your score and track your elevation and windage. On qualification day, at 200 Yards, you would only have 5 minutes to fire 10 Rounds each segment, from 300 Yards you would have only 10 minutes to fire 20 Rounds for all four segments and at 500 Yards you had 10 minutes to slow fire 10 Rounds prone.

As I completed firing all my segments on Pre-Qual Day, I was pleased with myself as I had qualified with a score of 217 out of 250 which was a score for Sharpshooter. I would get another chance to improve my score tomorrow on Qualification Day. When the first relay of shooters finished, we had only one shooter who missed qualifying by one point. The second relay of shooters in our platoon, all qualified.

After the morning shoot was completed, we marched to noon chow. When noon chow finished, Sgt Martinez lit the "*Smoking Lamp*," before he marched back to the range to work the BUTTS, marking and masking targets for the afternoon shoot. The DI's and our PMI came down into the butts after the firing line was secured and sought out the one person who didn't qualify. They identified four other shooters that barley qualified.

Each of those five were instructed to bring their shooting book and report to the PMI at the bleachers as soon as they were finished pulling targets and released by the range master. After the first relay of shooters began firing after chow, the wind had started to pick up so I knew those shooting in the afternoon would have more difficulties qualifying than we had in the morning.

As our PMI walked by my target while I was waiting to mask and mark my shooter, I asked him if we would have final qualifications tomorrow in the morning or in the afternoon?

He told me normally whatever times you shot for pre-qual was the same time you would shoot on qualification day.

I became more at ease knowing that we would be shooting in the morning instead of the afternoon. If we had to shoot after lunch, our windage sets would be off and we would run the risk of having more non-qualified shooters. If we would have had pre-qualification in the afternoon, we would not be as comfortable because of the wind. Since we will shoot in the morning, we will have an advantage over the two platoons shooting in the afternoon.

When our time in the BUTTS was ended, we were told to "**Fall-In**," and were marched back to our barracks. The one non-qual and the other four low shooters were sent over to the bleachers to meet with our PMI. They wouldn't be seen again until it was time for evening chow. As the rest of the platoon marched back to the barracks, we spent the rest of the afternoon cleaning our weapons. Before going to evening chow, we stood a rifle inspection and if you didn't pass, the whole platoon would suffer and the payback to those who failed inspection would be rewarded with a blanket party.

Luckily, every recruit passed his rifle inspection, and then we marched over to evening chow. The five recruits who were left at the range showed up as we were lined up to go to chow. They were all alive, no visible bruises anywhere and no signs of bloodshed. They just spent two additional hours of instruction and getting help to build their confidence. The DI's were very convincing in their explanation of the consequence of failing to qualify on the final qualification day.

After chow, back at our barracks, the recruit who failed to qualify and the other four recruits cleaned their rifles as the rest of us reviewed our shooting books and helped each other understand and rehearse how to remember where to start in their book at 200 yards and so forth. We continued to work on our shooting books until 2030 (8:30 pm) when the "*Smoking Lamp*" was lit and then we were given Commanders Time to write letters, read mail, and get ready for lights out.

I took time to write a letter to my friend Zane and asked about his girlfriend Susan. I didn't want to think about my old girlfriend Linda who hadn't written to me since being at Boot Camp. I didn't want to think about what she might be up to at this time. Keeping my head clear and staying on course was my plan for the day. As normal, taps were played at 2200, and lights were put out and the Fire Watch was set.

Reveille went at the normal time of 0500 and after PT, morning head calls, showers, and barracks clean-up, we marched to morning chow. This was one of the most important days in our time at Boot Camp. Qualification Day on the Rifle Range with the M-14 rifle. This day gave each recruit the satisfaction of accomplishing what the Corps is actually all about. Besides the physical attributes of being a Marine, to qualify as either a Marksman, Sharpshooter or Expert, is what being a Marine is all about.

Those who do not qualify today will either be dropped from their Platoon and required to redo the two weeks at the rifle range with a different Platoon or will be given an "undesirable" discharge if it is determined they don't have what it takes to earn the title, "United States Marine." There were five recruits in our Platoon that had to worry about qualifying tomorrow, at least let's hope they do. So do the rest of us that qualified on pre-qual day.

The DI's and the PMI would keep close tabs on each of those five recruits on the firing line as well as the rest of us. It was fortunate we were shooting in the morning before the winds have a chance to pick up and I know it may sound unimportant, but the wind could have a negative effect on our sight picture or cause us to shoot lower scores than on pre-qual day.

As we were marched to the rifle range, we were in good spirits and the DI's were confident we were the best Platoon in our series. The rifle range would be but one of the tests we needed to pass to prove it. As we filed onto the firing line, the sun was coming up in the east and the targets were now fully visible. I placed the Platoon Guidon into the Flag stand outside the 200 Yard Firing Line. The ammo was passed out to each shooter as they came to the line. We were ready to prove we had what it took to be part of the history which makes the Marines so revered.

It was quiet on the firing line from 200 yards, until the Range Master shouted out, "Ready on the right, Ready on the left, Ready on the firing line." He continued, "Shooters, with 10 rounds, lock and load", and when the Firing Line was ready he commanded, "Shooters when your targets appear, fire at will." The silence ended with the volley fire of M-14's barking as each shooter was trying to find the bullseye on the target. The first volley of 10 shots of qualifying ended with the Range Master commanding "Cease fire, Cease fire, shooters, secure the firing line." After the ten rounds were expended, the whole process was repeated, and each shooter needed to shoot another ten rounds from a different firing position.

After the first relay of shooters were finished firing, we were instructed to police up all of our brass and then secure off the firing line. When the firing line was cleared, the second relay moved up to the line and the entire procedure was repeated until all the shooters from both platoons had completed qualifying from 200 yards.

Before moving to the 300-yard firing line, the second relay shooters were instructed to pick up all the spent brass laying around the firing line and place the brass into a number of

garbage cans located along the firing line. The brass was re-used as the Marine Corps would re-load spent brass, so we had plenty of rounds to shoot with.

Everyone then moved back to the 300-yard firing line and the entire process was repeated with the first relay as the Range Master shouted out, "Ready on the right. Ready on the left. Ready on the firing line. Shooters, with ten rounds, lock and load. When your targets appear, fire at will." Again the silence ended with the crackling of rifle fire as each Marine was attempting to find the bullseye. After ten minutes, the Range Master shouted, "Cease fire. Cease fire. Shooters, secure the firing line." This process was again repeated as each shooter had to fire another ten rounds from a different firing position.

Again, after the first relay of shooters finished firing their 20 rounds from two different firing positions, and finished picking up all their brass, the second relay moved up to the line and the entire procedure was repeated. When the second relay from both platoons had completed their qualifying from 300 yards, everyone cleared their weapons and after all the brass was picked up, we were instructed to move to the 500-yard firing line.

Once everyone had moved down range to the 500-yard Firing Line, the first relay of shooters was instructed to move up to the Line. With sights realigned and windage calculated, ammo was passed out to the shooters on line. Again, the Range Master began his instructions. "Ready on the Right. Ready on the Left. Ready on the firing line. Shooters with a magazine of ten rounds, lock and load. Shooters, you have ten minutes to fire your ten rounds from the prone position down range. When your target appears, shooters, fire at will."

Again, the silence was broken with the popping of M-14's all up and down the firing line. From 500 yards with open iron sights, the target seemed a long way off, but was visible with the naked eye. With each squeeze of the trigger, the round flew downrange at 2,800 feet per second to find its target. If it was a bullseye, a white disk would cover the center of the target to signify a bullseye.

A small white round piece of paper one inch in diameter would mark where the round went through the bullseye. When the bullseye was hit, it would be marked like a clock, where the round passed through the target is how it was marked. i.e. if the round hit at the 3 O'clock left of center, it was reported as "bullseye, right at 3 O'clock." Or, if it was low of the center but still in the bullseye, it would be reported as, "Bullseye, 6 O'clock low."

When all shooters were finished or the time of 10 minutes passed, the Range Master would shout, "Cease fire. Cease fire. Shooters, secure the firing line." All the shooters who hadn't fired their ten rounds ceased fire and unloaded their weapons. All the shooters made sure their weapons were empty and they opened the breach and set the safety on. We moved off the line and secured all weapons and picked up all of the brass.

Again, after the first relay of shooters finished policing up all their brass, the second relay moved up to the line and the entire procedure was repeated again until all the shooters from both platoons completed their qualifying from 500 yards. All shots were recorded for each target, and it would only take about 15 minutes to know if we had any non-quals.

The two Platoons who had just qualified on the Firing Line together with the other two platoons who were marking targets in the Butts, were marched the mile and a half to noon chow. The morning shoot went without a hitch, the weather was sunny and bright and there had been no wind to speak of.

After noon chow, the two platoons that fired in the morning would replace the two platoons in the butts and the platoons in the butts would go to the firing line to qualify. The other two platoons would follow the exact same procedures in the afternoon on the firing line as the two morning platoons followed, and the morning platoons would follow the same procedure in the butts as the other two platoons followed.

As we arrived at the BUTTS, I again planted our Platoon Guidon in the Flag stand provided just outside the BUTTS area. Platoon 2225 made their way down the walkway to take their positions on their targets. There were always two men to a target, one pulling the target up and down and the other to actually mark and disk the target. Our Platoon followed and took our position up at target 42.

The Range was set up for 90 shooters at a time On-Line, but not any of the four Platoons in FOX Company had 90 Recruits in their Platoons. The Range Master had a Master Log as to how many Recruits would be shooting On-Line at a time. For the second relay, there were only 83 Recruits shooting on relay number one and 84 Recruits shooting on relay number two. That is why we stopped at Target 42.

I wasn't on a Target, I was supervising with our PMI and when the Firing Line began shooting I watched as our Platoon marked and masked targets. The 2nd relay went through the same shooting procedures as we did on the first relay. When all the shooting was finished, we secured from the Butts, and "**Fell-In**."

By evening chow, we would know which Platoon had the best scores and would earn the streamer for their guide-on. While our Platoon was pulling Butts, it was rumored that we had 100% of our Platoon qualify with good scores. The determining factor for earning the streamer would be 100% qualification of the entire Platoon. If there is a tie, the highest score, or the highest average of all shooters. We will have to wait to find out, but if we win, I can guarantee we will enjoy our last day at Camp Pendleton.

We marched back to our Barracks to clean our rifles before evening chow. Once back in front of our Barracks, Gunny Wolfmule said, *"Smoking Lamp"* is lit. He continued, "Well, you shit birds finally learned to do something right and together. Good job." We were surprised we heard positive remarks from our senior Platoon Commander, it was actually the second time we were complemented. The first time we heard positive comments was after our seventh week inspection.

Those who were not smoking were dismissed to get in the Barracks and start cleaning their rifles. Those smoking would be sorry if anyone of them failed rifle inspection before going to chow. If I'm not mistaken, that was the shortest "*Smoking Lamp*" session I can remember. We all field stripped our cigarettes and went in to clean our rifles. The word was passed down that the inspection would take place at exactly 1815 in the Barracks in front of our Racks. It was my job to make sure everyone was ready at exactly 1815 when Gunny Wolfmule and Sgt James came into the Barracks.

Our DI and Platoon Commander passed by each recruit and inspected each rifle. The Gunny up the right side, and Sgt James up the left side. Amazingly, again everyone passed rifle inspection. The reason it was amazing is that at no time in nine weeks had we ever had a 100 % perfect inspection of any kind with Gunny being the inspector. There was always at least one guy screwing up. When inspection was completed, we were told to **"Fall-Out"** for evening chow. We secured our M-14's and made our way outside to **"Fall-In"** for evening chow.

After evening chow the Gunny lit the "*Smoking Lamp*" again, and it seemed we were being rewarded for 100% qualification on the range. I knew if we ended up earning the rifle range streamer we would be given some extra slack that we hadn't experienced for the past nine weeks. After the smoking lamp was turned off, the word came down to get our rifle and cartridge belt and **"Fall-In"** for close order drill. Sgt James put us through our paces on the grinder until 2000 (8:00 pm). It was getting dark when we **"Fell Out"** and made our way back to our barracks. Taps at 2200 Friday night.

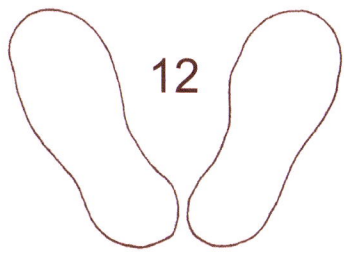

Guidon Full of Streamers

Reveille at 0500 Saturday morning. After our morning head call, PT, and our normal hygiene, we turned in our linen as part of barracks clean-up. In our Platoon morning formation, both DI's and Gunny Wolfmule were in attendance. Gunny had me bring the Platoon Guidon forward and he attached the Red Rifle Range Streamer to our spindle. He then had me fall back in formation. He paid us a compliment for getting 100% on the range and winning the Red Streamer for our platoon. He then had Sgt James march us to morning chow. The Red Streamer looked pretty good on our Guidon and we made sure the other three Platoons saw the Red Streamer fly atop our Platoon Guidon.

After Saturday morning chow, Gunny read out the scores by each Recruit. We had 100% Qualification and the highest score in our Platoon was 240 out of 250 shot by Pvt Havranek. I shot a 232 out of a possible 250, and our Platoon had 18 Recruits qualify as Expert, 29 Recruits qualified as Sharpshooter and 32 Marksman.

After Gunny lit the "Smoking Lamp," we were told to turn in our linen and pack all of our gear into our footlockers. I was instructed to make sure the Barracks was in cleaner condition than before we arrived. Then have the Platoon bring down their footlockers and have them "**Fall-In**" Platoon Formation and place their footlockers and buckets at their feet.

After the "House Mice" got their gear down to formation, they were told to clean the DI quarters and then "**Fall-In**" with the Platoon. The Squad Leaders and I went back into our Barracks to make sure it would pass Gunny's Inspection. Our Barracks was spotless, so I Reported to Gunny that our Barracks was ready for Inspection.

As we stood in Platoon Formation with our Guidon flying with the Red Streamer, Gunny and Sgt James Inspected our Barracks. We passed with flying colors, and after the Inspection was over and everything but our rifles were out of the Barracks, Gunny Ordered us back into the barracks to unlock our M-14's from our rifle racks and return to our Formation. Once everyone was down stairs and back in formation with their rifles, he had us sling arms and stand behind our footlockers. Since I couldn't carry my footlocker, bucket, rifle and the Guidon, Sgt Martinez again took charge of our Platoon Guidon until we returned to our Quonset huts back at MCRD.

Off to the right of our Barracks there were eight Cattle Car Trucks parked to take us back to MCRD. Our Platoon loaded the first two Cattle Cars since we earned the highest scores on the Rifle Range and earned the Red Streamer. Once all four platoons of FAX Company were loaded, the Cattle Car Trucks moved out of Camp Pendleton and we were on our way back to MCRD. The caravan of Cattle Car trucks was escorted by a Marine staff car and the California Highway Patrol.

The drive to MCRD was just over an hour from Camp Pendleton, and after passing thru the main gate of MCRD, we stopped directly behind the 2nd Battalion Mess Hall where we loaded up to go to Camp Pendleton two weeks earlier. We were ordered to unload from the cattle trucks and "**Fall-In**."

With our M-14's slung over our left shoulders and our footlockers and buckets laying at feet in front of us, Sgt

Martinez took charge of the platoon. With the Platoon Guidon in hand he marched us back to our Platoon Street.

Each squad returned to the same Quonset Hut they occupied two weeks earlier and found their same Rack. On each bunk was a rolled-up mattress with a pillow in the middle, two blankets, 2 sheets, and one pillowcase.

Sgt Martinez placed our unit Guidon in its stand outside the DI Duty Hut and gave the Platoon one hour to lock our M-14's on our Racks, stow our footlockers, make-up our racks and "**Fall-In**" on the Platoon Street.

Everyone worked frantically to get their Rack made, place our towels and laundry bags at the foot of our Racks along with our cartridge belts. Those done first helped those who needed help. Exactly one hour from the time we were given the order to get squared away, we heard Sgt Martinez count down, 15, 14, 13 …….. 5, 4, 3, 2, 1. Low and behold, every swinging dick was at his spot on the Platoon Street at "**Attention**" before he counted down to zero.

Sgt Martinez then walked into each hut and inspected how well each squad had stowed their gear and squared away their bunk. He went into one hut after the other and when he was finished, he stood at the head of platoon and said, "**Guidon**", "**Fall-In**" **the Platoon for noon chow**". I answered, "**Sir, Aye Aye Sir**." I then went over and retrieved the Platoon Guidon and told the Platoon to "**Fall-In**" for noon chow. The Platoon "**Fell-In**" Platoon Formation on the Platoon Street and waited for Sgt Martinez to march us to noon chow.

It was nice to be back in familiar surroundings and while we waited for our turn to enter the Mess Hall, we studied our Red Notebooks. As I stood in line, I was thinking how different my life had become. When I first arrived here at MCRD, I was unsure what to expect, I was scared, but I knew they couldn't eat me. I thought I was in pretty good physical shape, but after that first night I questioned how I was going to survive. I was just another Boot who was reminded, he was just an undisciplined, civilian puke.

However, now that we have the Rifle Range behind us, I have qualified as an Expert Rifleman. I have carried the Platoon Guidon for eight weeks and have learned the importance of leadership. I've stood out amongst everyone in my Platoon. I have excelled in everything I have been asked to do and exceeded, even my own expectations.

I believe once I came to accept what it was our DI's wanted from us, other than the mind games, Boot Camp became like double sessions I used to go through in High School during football season. Our Platoon has shaped up to almost qualify as Marines, and I am beginning to like this Marine Corps.

When it was our turn to finally get in line for chow, as I stood in front of the mirror, I was looking at a different person than I was ten weeks ago. I snapped a perfect Salute and said with confidence, "**Good afternoon Sir**," and cut my Salute away sharply. Noon chow turned out to be wonderful for our first meal back at MCRD.

After we finished noon chow, we marched back to the Platoon Street and the "*Smoking Lamp*" was lit. We were allotted 15 minutes to smoke and then the smoking lamp was turned off. We were ordered to get our rifles and cartridge belts and "**Fall-In**" for Close Order Drill.

Once the entire platoon was on the Platoon Street with rifles and cartridge belts, Sgt Martinez commanded, "**Right Guide, assemble the Platoon on the grinder**." I answered, "**Sir, Aye Aye Sir**," then told the Platoon to "**Fall-Out and Fall-In** on me on the **Grinder**." I then went to "**Port Arms**" with the Guidon and ran to the Grinder with the rest of the Platoon following and when we got to the Grinder, the Platoon "**Fell-In**" Platoon Formation on me.

I picked a spot on the Grinder, came to "**Attention**" and stuck out my left arm. Pvt Havranek stood at "**Attention**" touching my left hand with his right shoulder, looking to his right and aligning with me to form a straight line with 1st Squad. The 2nd Squad Leader "**Fell-In**" behind Havranek the 3rd Squad Leader behind Pvt Surma and the 4th Squad Leader Pvt Earle, behind Pvt Hesch. The rest of the Platoon "**Fell-In**" their assigned Squad and automatically went to "**Dress Right Dress**. Sgt Martinez went to the front of the Platoon and gave the Command, "**Ready Two**" then "**Cover.**"

It was important that we had the opportunity to practice Close Order Drill as often as possible because we were scheduled to compete for the Close Order Drill Competition next Wednesday morning to see who would win the coveted Close Order Drill Streamer.

We drilled all afternoon on the Grinder until it was time for evening chow. There was a difference in the quality of performance when we drilled between Sgt Martinez's cadence and Sgt James' cadence, so we knew that Sgt James would be the DI for the Drill Competition. After returning to our Quonset Huts we locked up our rifles and stowed our cartridge belts then returned to Platoon Street before going to evening chow.

After evening chow, when we returned to our Platoon area, the "*Smoking Lamp*" was lit, and Sgt Martinez was relieved from Duty by Gunny Sgt Wolfmule. After the "Smoking Lamp" was out, the Gunny had the Squad Leaders and the Right Guide report to the Duty Hut. When we all reported to the Duty Hut, he again congratulated us for winning the Red Rifle Range Streamer and asked what we thought our chances were of winning the Gold Streamer for Close Order Drill competition?

All five of us were very confident that we would win the Gold Streamer to place on our Guidon as the entire platoon had come together and were motivated to be the best Platoon on the depot. He was pleased with our attitude and dismissed us to get the Platoon ready to go to evening classes. Once we left the Duty Hut, I mentioned to the Squad Leaders that I thought the Gunny was pleased with us and I wouldn't be surprised if we received another "*Smoking Lamp*" before taps.

To our surprise, we were scheduled to attend a class on Saturday evening, so Gunny had us **"Fall-In"** and he marched us to a class on Marine Corps history. The class was on the history of the Marine Corps uniform from the beginning in 1776 up to and including today. When the class was terminated, Gunny marched us back to our platoon area and as I suspected, he lit the *"Smoking Lamp"* before holding Commanders Time.

Gunny had the Duty Saturday night and held a Hygiene Inspection. Each recruit stood on his footlocker as the Gunny passed by checking our feet and between our toes to make sure our feet had no problems. Each Hut stood at **"Attention"** on its footlocker until all four Huts were finished with the inspection and then given free time until taps.

Week Ten

Sunday of week 10 after Reveille, we were back in our old routine, PT, Head Call, morning hygiene, make our Racks, and those going to Church Services **"Fell-Out"** and made their way to their Denomination Formation for morning chow before going to Church. The rest of the Platoon continued to clean-up our Platoon area before going to morning chow.

Upon finishing Sunday morning chow, we spent the morning on the Platoon Street either writing letters, shining boots or dress shoes, cleaning our rifle, reading the Marine Handbook and just enjoying Commanders Time. By 10:30, all recruits had returned from Church Services, Bible classes or Lectures, and joined in Commanders Time. At 1130, all recruits returned their personal gear back to their Hut and the Platoon "**Fell-In**" and Gunny marched us to noon chow.

I would like to take a moment to make a comment about the food I have been eating and enjoying since arriving at MCRD in September. Now after the nine weeks we have been eating Marine chow, I must admit, the food was actually very good. Even the chow at Camp Pendleton, while at the rifle range, was delicious.

At breakfast, each day, we had eggs, cooked many different ways, and you took them the way they were cooked, there was bacon, sausage, and sometimes ham. They also served fried potatoes, grits, cereal, oatmeal, pancakes, waffles, fruit, juices, toast, occasionally donuts or pastries, coffee or tea, milk, or water. Before entering any Mess Hall at all the Battalion Mess Halls at MCRD, there was a sign over the door as you walked in the Mess Hall that said, "**Take all you want, But eat all you take**." Mess Sgt's took a very dim view of recruits who took food and didn't eat it or clean their trays.

Noon chow always gave us many choices, sandwiches with cold cuts, hot dogs, meat loaf, pork chops, chicken, vegetables, potatoes, soups, pasta, coffee or tea, cold drinks or juices, desserts, but always choices. Evening meals consisted of beef of some sort, roasts, steaks, meat loaf, pastas, stews, chicken, fish, potatoes, vegetables, soups, Jello's, milk, coffee or tea, water and assorted desserts. Whoever ran the mess hall, did one hell of a job making these delicious meals for so many guys every day.

There were very few meals that I did not enjoy, and the food was nutritious, always hot, and the cooks on the line were always generous with their helpings. There were a lot of conversations regarding how much you could take without even saying a word. Don't get caught going through the chow line twice without permission, and the longer you were at the Depot, the more you learned how much food to take at each meal.

Now that we have completed 9 weeks of training, and made it through the Rifle Range, we were beginning to look like a unit. The discipline, the self-confidence and the military bearing began to pay off and we only had two weeks left before we graduated and earned the title of United States Marine.

While marching from the Mess Hall after noon chow during week nine, Gunny Sgt Wolfmule held up the Platoon on the Grinder, and made a change in Squad Leaders. He had Pvt Gagnon return to the 2nd Squad and replaced Pvt Earle. He didn't give any reasons, didn't hit anyone, just had Gagnon move to the 2nd Squad and had Pvt Earle fall back in his position in the Platoon. I thought it was a good move because Gagnon made a good Squad Leader.

When we returned to the Platoon Street, Gunny lit the "*Smoking Lamp*" for a period of 15 minutes. Those not smoking were told to return to their Huts and get their rifles and cartridge belts and get ready for Close Order Drill. After

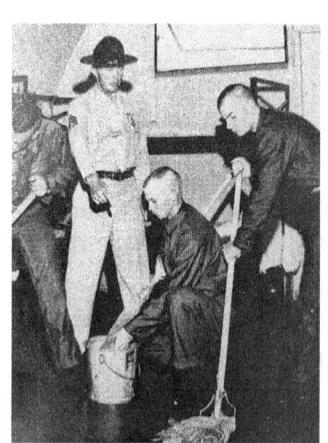

Gunny turned off the smoking lamp, we spent the rest of Sunday on the grinder practicing close order drill until evening chow.

Monday, Nov 14th

On Monday, now that we were back at MCRD, the old routine continued. Reveille, head call, PT, normal hygiene, and this morning Gunny had the Duty. Before we went to morning chow, he made sure we gave each Quonset Hut a special clean-up since we had been gone for two weeks.

After morning chow, the *"Smoking Lamp"* was lit and then we were to **"Fall-In"** on Platoon Street. Sgt James marched us to a classroom where we participated in a class on Marine Corps Uniforms. We would be issued the rest of our Dress Uniforms soon, and the class was to make sure we knew how to wear our uniforms correctly. The class lasted almost two hours.

When our class was finished, we were given a Head Call then marched to a row of Warehouses behind the Movie Theater. When we arrived at the Warehouse we would be measured for all of our Dress Uniforms. Sgt James had the Formation execute a **"Left Face**," and then had us unlace our boots, remove them and place them in front of us in Formation.

Sgt James had us file by Squads into the warehouse where we were issued three pair of black dress socks. Sgt James had us remove our black socks we wore in our boots and place a pair of dress socks on our feet. We were

instructed to place the pair of socks we took off in our pocket and place the other two pair of dress socks in our back pocket.

The first thing we were issued was a pair of black dress shoes. We each stood on a pedestal with five steps. The one in the center was about three feet off the ground, the two on either side were two feet off the ground, and the outside two were one foot off the ground.

Once our feet were measured, we tried on a pair of shoes. Once we were fitted with

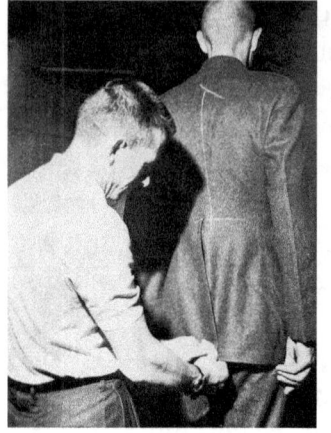

a pair of Dress Shoes, we stepped off the front of the platform. We wore the shoes the rest of the morning as we tried on six different sets of trousers, Dress Greens, Tropical, and Khaki. There were individual Taylors marking the waist, the rear, the crotch, the bottoms with a white marker. Each article of clothing had a tag with our last name and Platoon number.

We were also fitted for our Dress Green Blouse, and Overcoat. They were fitted by a Taylor who would mark them up and again each item had a tag attached with your name and Platoon number.

We were also fitted with two Dress Shirts, and two Khaki short sleeve shirts. We were fitted with our Combination Barracks cover with grommet, two black cover

straps, three changeable covers, Green, Tropical and Khaki and three Garrison covers, Green, Tropical and Khaki. All covers were placed in a bag with a tag, with our name and Platoon number attached.

The fittings for the entire Platoon took the rest of the morning. The bag containing our covers was tagged with our names and Platoon number, and we carried them with us as we left the Warehouse. We were then told to tie our boots together and place them around our neck and with our Dress Shoes on our feet, we then "**Fell-In**" a Platoon Formation. Sgt James marched the Platoon back to the Platoon area still wearing our Dress Shoes and when we arrived, he had us deposit our issue of covers in our footlockers. Sgt Martinez also told us to untie the boots from around our neck and place our boots under our Rack next to the other pair.

We continued to wear our Dress Shoes for the rest of the day to break them in. We wore our shoes to noon chow, and when we finished eating, we were marched back to our Platoon Street. Sgt James relieved Sgt Martinez, and told us to keep our Dress Shoes on. Sgt James had us get our rifles and cartridge belts and we spent the entire afternoon on the Grinder marching in our Dress Shoes.

Sgt James was determined to get our Platoon ready for the Close Order Drill competition between our four Platoons in FOX Company which was to take place on Thursday morning. We continued to Drill marching in our Dress Shoes until it was time for evening chow.

After evening chow on Monday, we returned to our Platoon area and after Sgt James lit the "*Smoking Lamp*," had us return to our Huts, take off our Dress Shoes, and put on our Boots. We were to get our shoe shining gear, sit on our buckets and shine our Dress Shoes, our Combination Cover and also clean our rifles. We could either sit on the Platoon Street or stay out of the sun and sit in our Quonset huts.

In the Marine Corps, the brim of our Combination Cover needs to be spit shined just like our new Dress Shoes. The brim of our Combination Cover and the strap that is part of the Combination Cover is rough leather not patent leather and needs to be shined by hand. We had been spit shining our boots for weeks now, so it wasn't like we didn't know how to spit shine our Dress Shoes. But, our Combination Cover Brim and the strap may be a little bit tricky.

Sgt Martinez joined the Platoon on the Platoon Street and between both he and Sgt James we were given advice on the best way to spit shine our Combination Cover Brim and strap. We were told we had to have our Dress Shoes, and our Combination Cover spit shined for Final Uniform Inspection by next Tuesday.

I had an advantage over most of the Recruits in my Platoon regarding spit shining. I had an older brother who was in the Marine Reserves and I when I was in High School, my brother would have me help him get ready for his weekend Reserve Duty by shining his shoes and polishing his Brass. Sgt James looked at the progress I was making on my shoes as well as my Combination Cover and was impressed.

There is a secret to spit shining either your shoes, boots, Cover Brim our strap, because spit shinning is nothing more than friction caused by continuously making small circles on the leather with polish and a wet soft cloth filling in the pores of the leather. It takes time and patience and continuously making small circles until the cloth becomes dry. Then you dip it in the polish again with more water and continue, repeating the process until all surfaces are shining like patent leather.

I spent one hour on my new shoes and one hour on my Combination Cover and was making progress on both. When new shoes have never been spit shined before, it helps to add polish and brush them to start, with a base. Once the leather has been spit shined, it becomes easier to keep the leather spit shined since the pores of the leather have been filled in.

The same process used on shoes and boots is used on the Combination Cover Brim as well as the strap. You have to have patience and continue to make small circles over and over and over filling in the pores on the leather. As Sgt

James walked back and looked at how well I had done with my strap and cover, he asked me where I learned to spit shine? I told him my story.

I was surprised he stood next to me and listened to my story on how I learned to spit shine my shoes and boots. When I had finished, he told me to keep up the good work and to teach as many Recruits as possible how to do it right. Pvt Havranek was sitting next to me on our buckets and overheard what I had shared with Sgt James. He watched how I did my cover and strap as well as my shoes and picked it up right away.

The sun was beginning to go down, so we knew it was getting close to Commanders Time. We had been on Platoon Street shining shoes, covers and straps for over two hours. Sgt Martinez walked all through the Platoon Street helping recruits with their shining assignments. Sgt James announced Commanders Time, and lit the "*Smoking Lamp*," so I put my shoe shining stuff away, stored my Dress Shoes under my Rack and put my cover in my footlocker. I went out to the Platoon Street to smoke a cigarette.

While I was smoking, Sgt James called me into the Duty Hut. I put out my cigarette and field stripped it and positioned myself in the doorway. I was getting ready to knock on the Duty Hut door when Sgt James saw me and told me to enter.

I centered myself on his desk and reported, "**Sir, Pvt Rilley Reporting as Ordered Sir**." He told me to "**Stand Easy Pvt**." He began by telling me what a great job I had been doing as the Platoon Right Guide, and shared with me that I had been chosen as the Platoon Honor Man! He said Gunny would talk to me more about it tomorrow when he assumed the Duty.

He then shared with me the Events coming up the remainder of the week. He told me on Thursday morning we would be competing with the other Platoons in FOX Company for the Close Order Drill Streamer. He also told with me that on Saturday morning we would be holding the final PT Test for the PT Streamer as well as participating in the required CMC Test which was necessary for each Recruit to pass in order to graduate from Boot Camp.

He asked me how I thought the Platoon was feeling and if there were any issues with the Platoon that he should be aware of. I answered, "Sir, the attitude of the Platoon was good, the Platoon was motivated since winning the Rifle Range Streamer, and the Platoon was confident about the Close Order Drill competition." I also shared with him that marching to his Cadence, the Platoon would perform better, and we had a better chance of winning with him in Command. He informed me that all competition has the Platoon Commander in charge, but he thanked me for my input.

I felt pretty good that Sgt James asked me my opinion, and even better that he listened to my input. Since I had missed the "**Smoking Lamp**," because of being called to the Duty Hut, Sgt James gave me permission to lite one up before returning to my Hut for Commanders Time. Now I was really feeling good about myself and how Sgt James had confided and talked to me. I thought things were going to be very enjoyable for the last two weeks of Boot Camp as long as we didn't screw up any of the upcoming competition with the other Platoons.

Commanders Time seemed to go very smoothly Monday evening and the entire Platoon had changed and grown in many ways. There was no longer any grab ass when left to work on our own. There was a much more serious atmosphere with everyone taking ownership in being squared away. I also think everyone was enjoying the feeling of accomplishment. When it was time to turn in, you could have heard a pin drop, it was so quiet. Taps sounded really special that night for some reason.

Tuesday morning after our normal routine and returning to our Platoon Area after morning Chow, Sgt James told us to "**Fall-Out**," with our dirty clothes, our buckets, Wisk and our scrub brushes. We were marched to the wash rack to do our laundry. We washed everything but one set of dirty utilities, which we would take to the Dry Cleaners after we got paid. We would wear starched utilities on Thursday for the Close Order Drill Competition.

After all of our laundry was hung on the clothes lines, we returned our buckets, Wisk and scrub brushes back to our Huts, and Sgt James marched us over to get paid. We went through the same procedure with the Disbursing Officer as we had every pay day. We dropped our $2.00 in the Bucket for the DI's Fund and afterwards carried our dirty utilities to the Dry Cleaners. We pre-paid the $2.00 to the clerk and got our laundry ticket, and then headed for the PX.

Since we only had two weeks left of Boot Camp, there wasn't much that we needed, but I bought another can of Kiwi shoe polish, two packs of Lucky Strikes, and another pack of razor blades. When I checked out it cost me $1.75. We were marched back to the Platoon Street to put our purchases in our Foot locker. Sgt James sent me to the clothes line to see if our clothes were dry yet from our morning laundry detail.

I reported back to Sgt James that our laundry was still wet and probably wouldn't be dry until after noon chow. He told me to pick two other Recruits to relieve the two who were on the clothes line watch and get the Platoon ready for noon chow. I answered "**Sir, Aye Aye Sir**," and picked Evanoff and Pvt Wilson to relieve the clothes Watch and had the Platoon "**Fall-In**" for noon chow.

Gunny Wolfmule arrived just as we were getting ready to march off to the chow hall and relieved Sgt James of the Duty. He marched us to noon chow. Our Platoon was starting to gain lots of confidence and we began to act like "Salty Recruits."

As each Recruit stood in front of the mirror outside the Mess Hall, the Salutes were giving were as sharp as anyone saluting on the Depot.

Chow was delicious for some reason and Gunny even commented how good chow was as he lit the *"Smoking Lamp."* Once our 15 minutes were up and all cigarettes were extinguished we returned to our Platoon Area to take our laundry off the line. We folded our clothes and put them in our footlockers. Gunny had us get our Rifles and Cartridge belts and we spent the entire afternoon on the Grinder doing Close Order Drill.

Before we began our four hour Drill Practice, Gunny had us in Platoon Formation, I stood to the right of t 1st Squad Leader at Attention with the Platoon Guidon by my right side. The rest of the Platoon stood at **"Attention"** with their rifles at their right side. Before we began to march, the Gunny gave the command, **"Right Face,"** and after execution and facing right, I would execute another **"Right Face,"** without a command and make my way to the 4th Squad and execute a **"Left Face."**

We were now in a Column of fours still at **"Attention"**, and t next command would be, **"Right Shoulder Arms."** The Platoon would execute the four counts necessary to move their rifles to their right shoulder. With the next command of **"Forward March,"** we stepped off with our left foot. As I stepped off with my left foot, I strutted more than marched as I led the Platoon forward.

As we moved forward, I would focus on a point somewhere in the distance to make sure the formation would march straight until given the next command. When marching in a column formation, I was always positioned in front of the 4th Squad Leader. When we were in the Platoon Formation, I was always to the right of the 1st Squad Leader.

Gunny put us through our paces. The four hours we spent on the Grinder weren't wasted, but they probably weren't our best performance. Not that we didn't know the movements when given the command, but Gunny's cadence just isn't as crisp as Sgt James, so at times not every heel hits the deck at exactly the same time. There's a special sound made when every heel is clicking at the same time. The sound of 79 boots hitting the deck at the same time, or 79 men moving as one, is a sight to see.

The Close Order Drill Competition wasn't the Gunny's first rodeo, so he ran a routine sequence of movements that he felt would be part of our Drill Card of movements we would have to perform later in the week. Once Gunny thought we had enough, we marched back to our Platoon Area and Gunny had everyone lock their rifles to their Rack, hang up our cartridge belts and "**Fall-Out**," for evening chow.

As we made a "Column Right" to position ourselves in front of the 2nd Battalion Mess Hall for evening chow, Gunny put us "**At Ease**," and told us to review our Red Notebooks as I placed the Platoon Guidon in the flag stand. Gunny stopped me and said, "We have an important day on Thursday, do you think the Platoon is ready Pvt."

I stood at "**Attention**," and answered, "**Sir, Platoon 2227 is ready for anything Sir**." He smiled and told me to get back in Formation.

On Wednesday morning we again followed our normal morning routine, head call, PT, our normal hygiene, hut clean-up and being marched to morning chow. Sgt Martinez had the Duty on Wednesday and after morning chow we were marched to a class on the "Code of Conduct" with the class being taught by a Veteran Sgt who had been in Vietnam, as a prisoner of war and had escaped.

The class lasted an hour and a half, and was most interesting, especially when he allowed for questions. Afterwards, Sgt Martinez marched us to the Barber Shop to get haircuts. We got haircuts twice a month, and this would be our last haircut before graduation. Now that we were getting ready to graduate, our haircuts weren't so severe, the sides were still cut close, but the top wasn't cut as close as when we arrived that first night.

Once haircuts were completed, Sgt Martinez marched the Platoon over to the Dry Cleaners where we picked up our starched utilities which we were to wear on Thursday morning for Close Order Drill Competition. When we got back to the Platoon area, we were instructed to hang our starched utilities on our racks.

We still had an hour and a half before noon chow, so Sgt Martinez had us get our rifles and cartridge belts and we spent the rest of the morning practicing close order drill on the Grinder, waiting for noon chow. We looked pretty good marching in Platoon formation with rifles smartly squared away on the right shoulder.

Before going to noon chow, we returned to our Platoon area and locked our rifles to our Racks and hung our cartridge belts on the end of our Racks. We marched smartly in formation, and it was unmistakably clear, we had our shit together.

After we finished noon chow we returned to the Platoon Street and Sgt Martinez lit the "*Smoking Lamp*" and we spent the rest of the afternoon sitting on our buckets on the Platoon Street shining our boots and cleaning our rifles getting ready for tomorrow morning's Inspection.

After evening chow, Sgt James came on board and took over the Duty. Mail Call was held and afterwards we spent another two hours on the grinder with Sgt James. That evening during Commanders Time we again starched our utility covers and finished shining our boots.

Thursday morning routine was the same as every other morning except, we did everything with a smile on our face and a bounce in our steps. Thursday morning chow was amazing, pancakes, maple syrup, bacon, sausage, scrambled eggs, fruit, juice, toast, donuts, milk and coffee. I remember the breakfast menu because this was a special day, competing for the "Close Order Drill" Streamer.

After morning chow, we changed out of the utilities we were wearing and dressed in our starched utilities. We bloused our trousers smartly, and made sure our boots were perfect. Each Squad Leader assisted the recruits in their

Squad making sure they were totally squared away before falling in and being checked over by myself and the DI's before our scheduled time on the Drill Field.

Platoon 2227 was scheduled to be the second Platoon to take the drill field and compete in the Close Order Drill Competition. To our surprise, Sgt James, who was our Senior DI', came out of the Duty Hut wearing the Black Leather Platoon Commanders Belt instead of his usual green cartridge belt.

All competitive Events were to be commanded by the Platoon Commander, not a Drill Instructor. Here was Sgt James acting as our Platoon Commander. How this came about wasn't for us to question, Sgt James was going to be in charge of the Platoon for "Close Order Drill." His cadence would make the difference and give us the best chance to win this competition.

Our Platoon was the second to be judged, so we stood just off the Grinder on the edge of Platoon Street waiting for the Command to "**Fall-In**." As soon as Platoon 2228 had finished their performance and marched off the Grinder, Sgt James yelled out the Command, "Platoon 2227, "**Fall-In**."

We had practiced this scenario many times, and Sgt James had picked out a spot on the Grinder four steps off a straight line left in the asphalt, the last time it was sealed. I saw where Sgt James was standing and headed towards his position. I calculated a distance of about fifteen feet to the right of Sgt James' position, approaching him from behind. I made a quick left turn on the line four steps in front of Sgt James and counted off seven steps as I ran.

In practicing for Final Inspection, I knew seven steps would put me just past Sgt James so he would be lined up in the middle of the Platoon Formation once the entire Platoon "**Fell-In**." When I stopped, I faced left, which was forward, towards Sgt James' position at "**Attention**," with my left Arm straight out palm down, head looking straight ahead. Pvt Havranek as the 1st Squad Leader "**Fell-In**" to my left, moving so he was touching his right shoulder to my left fingers, looking to his right to align with my position at Attention. The entire Platoon "**Fell-In**," as practiced and automatically went to "**Dress Right Dress**."

There were three judges standing off a short distance from Sgt James to judge the Drill Competition. One officer and two staff NCO's. Before Sgt James Commanded us to "**Fall-In**," the Officer In-Charge handed Sgt James a set of 3 x 5 cards with the commands he was to give and the order with which he was to give them in. The first command on the card was to have your Platoon "**Fall-In**."

We would be judged on the speed we "**Fell-In**," the actual distance the Platoon was positioned in front of Sgt James, as well as how close to the center of the Platoon Sgt James was positioned. On all three points, we aced the results. Sgt James then had the Platoon execute the 20 commands listed on the 3 X 5 cards following the initial command of "**Fall-In**.".

Sgt James followed each of the commands on the 3 X 5 cards in the order they were written. The Judges each had clip boards with the same commands listed in the order they were to be executed. We were judged on how we executed each command and whether someone was out of sync or made a miscue or mis-step. Not only did our Platoon complete all commands properly and in the time provided but we only committed one minor mistake throughout the entire program which cost us one deduction. After the last command, the Platoon was again in Platoon Formation, standing at "Attention" with our rifles at our right side. Sgt James Saluted the Officer In-Charge ending our Close Order Drill participation.

Once the Judges departed, waiting for the next Platoon to compete, Sgt James stood in front of our Platoon and told us, "Job well done." He then told us he would turn the Platoon over to the "Right Guide to follow his Orders. He then said,

"**Right Guide**," Carry out my last Order and "**Carry-On**." I answered his Command, "**Sir, Aye Aye Sir**."

I "**Fell-Out**" of the Formation and took a position to the left of the Platoon and gave the Command, "**Platoon, Right Face**." I then ordered "**Right Shoulder Arms**," and once the Platoon was at "**Shoulder Arms**," gave the command to "**Forward March**." I marched Platoon 2227 back to the Platoon Street, and once back on Platoon Street, I gave the command to "**Halt**," "**Order Arms**," "**Left Face**," and then "**Fall Out**."

After locking up our rifles, everyone returned to the Platoon Street. Sgt Martinez was in the Duty Hut and Gunny arrived to join him. Sgt Martinez yelled out for the "House Mouse to the Duty Hut," and the Platoon yelled out in unison, "**Sir, House Mouse to the Duy Hut Sir**," and the four House Mice scrambled to the Duty Hut.

Gunny had them make fresh coffee and clean up the DI Duty Hut. Sgt Martinez told the Platoon to study our Red Notebooks until it was time for noon chow. We still had over an hour before we went to noon chow, so we stood "**At Ease**," for the next hour studying. One week from today it would be Thanksgiving and then Graduation.

Sgt James came walking from the Grinder. Apparently, he stayed around and watched the other two Platoons perform their Drill Cards. He had a smile from ear to ear. Platoon 2227 had won the Close Order Drill Competition and earned the right to have the Gold Close Order Drill Streamer placed on our Guidon!

As you can well imagine, Sgt James handed the Gold Drill Streamer to Gunny to be placed below the spindle of the platoon Guidon next to the Red Rifle Range Streamer. I held the Platoon Guidon at "**Port Arms**" as the Gunny placed the Drill Streamer on our Guidon. He had a smile from ear to ear and after I returned to "**Attention**" with the Guidon by my right side, Gunny told the Platoon… "You did a Great Job today, and you have made me very proud of you."

Gunny had us **"Fall-In"** in Platoon Formation and marched our Platoon to the MCRD Grinder to show off our Guidon before marching us to noon chow. There were a number of new Platoons on the Grinder learning how to March. We knew they were mostly new because they did not have their trousers bloused or their top button unbuttoned. We felt pretty damn good and we looked as good as we felt.

We marched around MCRD until it was time for us to head over to noon chow. As a reward for our accomplishment on this day, after noon chow, the "*Smoking Lamp*" was lit and stayed lit for more than 20 minutes allowing some smokers to have at least two cigarettes.

Once we finished our cigarettes, we had another class on Marine Corps History. Sgt James marched us down the middle of the grinder to show off our proficiency in Drill, as well as the two streamers on our Platoon Guidon as we made our way to class. We turned every one's eyes as we marched to Sgt James' cadence. Especially the newer Platoons. I remember what we looked like when we arrived at MCRD and were just new boots, and how impressed we were with the senior Platoons marching so amazingly well, when we first arrived. Now it was our turn to show off.

After our class as we headed back to our Platoon area, Sgt James had us call out cadence as we marched. Not only did we look good, we sounded good as well. The entire Platoon had their chests sticking out just a little more than normal, our heads were held just a little higher, and our stride just a little smoother.

Thursday evening Gunny and Sgt Martinez had the Duty and after we completed evening chow, we attended classes on Guard Duty. Our series was to hold Guard Duty this upcoming weekend. Platoon 2225 had the Duty Friday night, 2226 had the Duty on Saturday night, Platoon 2227 and 2228 were to share the Guard Duty Sunday night. We were scheduled to attend classes on Thursday evening on how the Chain of Command works along with the 11 General Orders for standing watches.

After Thursday night classes, we returned to our Platoon area and were rewarded again with the "*Smoking Lamp*" being lit. Afterwards, the rest of the evening was spent on Commanders Time shining our Dress Shoes and the Brim of our Covers.

Friday of week 10 started off as every other Friday in boot camp. Reveille, head call, PT, personal hygiene routine, strip our linen off our racks, morning clean-up, and then marched to morning chow. After morning chow we were marched back to Platoon Street where Sgt Martinez lit the "*Smoking Lamp*." Sgt James took over the Duty from Gunny. Sgt Martinez told us to get our sea bags, make sure we had at least $5.00 in our pocket, and "**Fall-In**," on Platoon Street. Sgt James then marched us to the warehouse where we had been fitted for all of our Dress Uniforms.

We carried our sea bags over our left shoulders as we marched across the Grinder on our way to the warehouse. We entered the warehouse in single file by Squad and one by one received our altered uniforms and placed them in our sea bags. Besides the uniforms we placed in our sea bag, we each received one Dress uniform on a hanger, a Dress Green Blouse with belt, one pair dress green trousers, one tropical dress shirt, and one tie. We already had our Dress Green Cover in our footlockers.

There was a small brown bag attached to the hanger which contained the belt buckle for the green blouse, two black eagle, globe and anchor collar insignias, and a tie clasp. There was a large Eagle, Globe and Anchor insignia for the combination cover, a smaller insignia for the garrison cover, and two black Barracks cover strap screws. The small brown bag was attached to the hanger with our name on the tag.

We were instructed to place all of our new uniforms in our sea bag which included our overcoat, the second dress green blouse, a second pair of green trousers, two tropical trousers, two khaki trousers, one additional tropical shirt, two khaki shirts, and one additional tie.

When the entire Platoon received their clothing, we "**Fell-In**" with the sea bag over our left shoulder and the hanger with one full Dress Green uniform in our right hand. Sgt James told me he was marching us to the Dry Cleaners to have the Dress Green Uniform cleaned and pressed, as our uniform smelled like moth balls.

When the Platoon was halted outside the Dry Cleaners we were in a column of four. Sgt James called me forward and told us to drop our sea bags at our left foot. Then he told us to remove the little brown bag with our uniform accessories and place the brown bag in our right trouser pocket.

Sgt James then took the Guidon from me and had the 1st Platoon follow me into the Dry Cleaners in a single file and hand the complete uniform to the clerk in the Dry Cleaners to be cleaned and pressed. We were to pay the clerk, get a receipt and Fall back In formation. When I came out of the Dry Cleaners, he handed the Guidon back to me. When everyone had turned in their uniform and returned to formation, we picked up our sea bag and were returned to the Platoon Street. We locked our sea bags with our rifle on our racks and then Sgt James marched us to noon chow.

Once we finished noon chow, Gunny Wolfmule joined up with us and we spent the remainder of the afternoon at the Obstacle Course to practice for our PT test being held on Saturday. Sgt Martinez had a clip board to record our times and scores to ensure we all would pass our PT Test. The platoon practiced pushups, sit ups, bends and thrusts, fireman's carry, pull ups, 100-yard run, 3-mile run and the rope climb, all the events we would be competing in on Saturday.

The Squad Leaders made sure that while at the con-fidence course, every member of our Platoon passed the necessary exercises in the times required to graduate as well as breaking the times and numbers that may allow us to win the Orange PT Streamer. Besides competing for the streamer, Gunny made the point to tell us it was a necessity for each Marine in each platoon to pass the required CMC PT test to graduate boot camp.

It happened that day because we spent a longer time on the confidence course than we were scheduled to. We were late for evening chow. The confidence course is located close to the 3rd Battalion area as well as their Mess Hall, so Gunny Sgt Wolfmule marched us outside the 3rd Battalion Mess Hall and requested permission to eat evening chow there since we missed our chow time at the 2nd Battalion Mess Hall.

The 1st Sgt in charge of the 3rd Battalion Mess gave Gunny Sgt Wolfmule permission to have his Platoon cut in line and enjoy evening chow in his Mess Hall. Gunny addressed our Platoon and said, "We have been given permission to have chow in the 3rd Battalion Mess Hall. I am telling you to be on your best military bearing, use your best manners and when you enter the mess hall, take what you want for dinner, but eat all you take. You will have 20 minutes to finish chow. Do you understand me?" The platoon screamed, "**Sir, Yes Sir**."

We formed into two single file lines, I placed the Guidon in the flag stand to the side of the entrance, and as we were in line to file through the chow line, each Recruit stopped at the Mirror and gave a smart crisp Salute and said, "**Sir, Good Evening Sir**," and smartly brought our hand back down to our side and made our way into evening chow. As each Recruit said, "**Sir, Good Evening Sir**," the volume was loud and proud and could be heard throughout the entire area in front of the Mess Hall.

The entire Platoon finished chow within the 20 minutes we were given to eat. The food was delicious, breaded pork chops, steamed potatoes, gravy, green beans, dinner rolls, apple pie, milk, coffee, tea or water. The 3rd Battalion served delicious food, and it was just as good as the food we had in the 2nd Battalion Mess. I believe each Mess Hall served the same food at every meal, every day.

When chow was finished, Gunny lit the "*Smoking Lamp*," and when we returned to the Platoon Area, we spent time reviewing all the events we will be competing in on Saturday. Sgt Martinez and Gunny had kept score of each Recruit as we ran through events that day to see how we stood within our Platoon based on times and repetitions. Gunny was fairly impressed with our times and said so in front of us.

Everyone was tired after spending the afternoon on the obstacle course but, it was amazing how much everyone had changed since the first day of boot camp. I must have gained 15 pounds and it was all muscle. I looked much different physically since beginning Boot Camp. I was tan from the sun and my face was fuller. I could do 200 push-ups without even breathing hard. I could only do about 25 when I first arrived and was winded.

We had another class scheduled after evening chow to review our responsibility when we took over the Watch, which Platoon 2227 was scheduled to stand on Sunday evening. Once the class was finished, Sgt James and Sgt Martinez went over all the details we needed to know about how the Guard Duty Watch would go over the weekend.

The Training Series from DELTA Company graduated this morning. That left our Training Series from FOX Company the Senior Training Series on the Depot. We will be the next Series to Graduate Boot Camp. Being we are now the Senior Series, our Series has the Duty for the weekend starting with Platoon 2225 standing Duty Friday night from 2000 until 0600 and then Platoon 2226 Saturday night and Platoons 2227 and 2228 will share the Duty on Sunday night.

The Platoon on Duty had the following Roster:
- The Officer of the Day - Fox Company Commanding Officer

- Sgt of the Guard
- Cpl of the Guard,
- 8 Walking Guard Posts – Relieved every 2 hours
- 2 Messengers

The Guard Detail would go on Duty at 2000 hours each night. The Walking Posts would be relieved every two hours, 20000 – 2200, 2200 – 2400, 2400 – 0200, 0200 – 0400, 0400 – 0600. Guard Duty Terminates at 0600. Sgt of the Guard, Cpl of the Guard and Messengers stand four-hour watches.

Uniform for all Guards will be Starched Utilities, Starched Cover and Spit Shined Boots. Sgt of the Guard and Cpl of the Guard wear a cartridge belt with a .45 cal. pistol with holster. Walking Posts wear cartridge belts with M-14 Rifles. Messengers just wear cartridge belts.

After class ended we were marched back to the Platoon Street and before starting Commanders Time, Sgt James spent the next hour discussing what we could expect tomorrow competing for the PT streamer. He went through the List that Sgt Martinez kept on his clip board for each Recruit as to their times and repetition numbers. Sgt James made a point to remind all of us to support each other throughout the competition and help motivate those who needed encouragement.

Sgt James had the Platoon take showers before beginning Commanders Time. We needed to clean up after doing physical training on the Obstacle Course. After showers, we spent the rest of the evening shining shoes, writing letters and relaxing during Commanders Time before hitting the Rack.

Platoon 2225 assumed the Guard Duty Watch at 2000 on Friday evening as we enjoyed Commanders Time. Lights out and Taps at 2200.

Saturday morning Reveille again at 0500, head call, PT, personal hygiene, field day our Huts and Platoon area then, morning chow. After morning chow the *"Smoking Lamp"* was lit and afterwards we dressed in our red PT shorts, yellow sweat shirts, white tennis shoes and utility covers and "**Fell-In**" on Platoon Street. The Platoon was marched over to the Obstacle Course to the area where the PT Competition was to be held.

All four Platoons from FOX Company were competing and there were numerous permanent personnel from MCRD to score each Recruit and each Platoon as we began our final PT Test. Having the scores kept by outside personnel made sure the scores were correct and there was no cheating by anyone. ONLY Recruits passing this Test would be able to Graduate Boot Camp. The PT Test was the first part of qualifying and the second part was the CMC Test.

The morning session was the PT Test done in our Red PT Shorts and Yellow Sweatshirts. Every recruit had to do a certain number of exercises and earned points based on the number of exercises completed in the time allotted. Each recruit had to score at least 250 points in order to graduate Boot Camp. There were individual awards

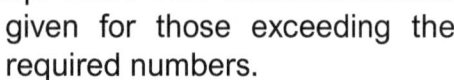

given for those exceeding the required numbers.

We competed with each Platoon for the fastest time in the 100-yard run, who could do the most pushups in two minutes, most bends and thrusts in two minutes, most sit ups in two minutes, and who had the most pullups in them. There was an award called the 300 Club, which was awarded to those recruits who accomplished numbers in excess of the requirement and earned a total of 300 points or more.

After the morning session, we broke for noon chow. We returned to our Huts and changed out of our PT gear and into our Utilities then marched to the 2nd Battalion Mess Hall for a light lunch. After chow there was no *"Smoking Lamp"* and we were marched back to our Huts to unlock our M-14 Rifles and cartridge belts. We then returned to the Obstacle Course for the afternoon session which was the CMC Test.

Upon arriving back at the Obstacle Course, we were issued Back Packs, Helmets and Canteens. The CMC Test was broken down into two parts. We began by climbing the 30-foot rope, which had to be completed in under 60

seconds. We rang the bell at the top of the rope support and climbed back down.

We were carrying our own M-14 Rifles when we started the CMC Test, but after an hour we **"Fell-In,"** and Gunny Wolfmule gave our Platoon the command to **"Stack Arms.**" To complete the rest of the CMC Test we were issued Mock Aluminum Rifles that were the same size and weight as our M-14's. We were never given a reason why we started with our own M-14's and then switched out for these Mock Rifles.

Sgt Martinez held a class on what to expect and how we were to finish the CMC Test. We had to climb a 30 foot rope with no knots, we had to run and jump over a six foot ditch, we had to do 60 step-ups in one minute, and then do the Fireman's Carry.

The Fireman's Carry was running 25 yards, picking up a fellow recruit and carrying him back the 25-yards in under 3 minutes.

The hardest event was working as a team and getting the entire platoon over a ten-foot wall and climbing a four-story platform and then back down the rope ladder leaving no one behind. Then we had to complete the three-mile run, while running in Platoon Formation in under 25 minutes.

The last event for the CMC Test was the 3-mile run. Once the CMC test was completed, we returned the Mock Rifles, packs, helmets, canteens and then **"Fell-In"** and unstacked our rifles. Sgt James, Sgt

Martinez and Gunny Wolfmule had been DI's for a number of years, and by what they observed during the day, there was no doubt in their minds that Platoon 2227 was the best Platoon in the Series.

After unstacking our rifles, we stayed in Platoon Formation and Gunny put us "**At Ease**" and lit the "*Smoking Lamp*." While we were enjoying our cigarettes, I was surprised that we were allowed to have small talk among ourselves without getting yelled at. I made sure that while we were given the opportunity to talk while in formation, we kept the volume down and there was no grab ass going on while we enjoyed the privilege.

Now that the competition was over, we waited patiently to see what was next on the days agenda. From time to time while we stood there in our formation, Sgt James or Sgt Martinez would walk up to where I was standing and look up at the top of our Guidon and comment how good the PT Streamer would look with the other Streamers on the top of our Guidon, under the Spindle.

Finally, Gunny approached the Formation and called us to "**Attention**." He was holding the Orange PT Streamer behind his back and with a giant smile, told me to come forward. I stood in front of Gunny Wolfmule and came to "**Port Arms**" with our Guidon so he could attach the Orange Streamer.

With the PT win, our Platoon was the probable winner for the Series Honor Platoon. Gunny was in a very good mood and could also sense Platoon 2227 would be recognized as the best Platoon on station, which is a feather in the cap of all three DI's. He told me to "**Fall-In**" the formation and brought us to "**Attention**." He faced the Platoon and said, "Great Job."

The PT competition and CMC Test took up the entire day, and afterwards all four Platoons from FOX company marched to the 2ⁿᵈ Battalion Mess Hall for evening chow. We were the last series to go through the mess hall, so after everyone was fed, the mess NCO yelled, "Seconds on the chow line." Everyone looked at their DI's for permission, and once it was given, we then rushed up and went through the chow line again.

It was quite a sight to see the mad rush to get a second helping of chow and not be yelled at or disciplined. Now that we were the senior series on station, and given permission to go through the chow line twice, everyone took advantage and were allowed to take their fill. Remember, "**Take all you want, but eat all you take**."

I just sat in my seat at the table and watched the others in my Platoon make their way to get a second helping of evening chow. The mob formed into a line and went through the chow line again. I just sat there waiting until the line was almost finished and then I got up, fell in line and took another piece of fried chicken and a dinner roll as well as another piece of blueberry pie.

Chow ended around 1830 and Sgt Martinez marched us back to the Platoon Street. Sgt Martinez lit the "*Smoking Lamp*", and we stood in formation on the Platoon Street. Our stomachs were full and the thrill of our accomplishments was written all over our faces.

Week ten ended with Platoon 2227 winning two more Streamers, to add to the Guidon, that we won at the Rifle Range. Our Guidon now donned the Red, Gold and Orange Streamers with two more available for us to win. There was a Green Streamer for Highest Test Scores on the Test we took earlier on, at the beginning of Boot Camp. We unfortunately didn't win the Green Streamer, that honor was won by Platoon 2228, but we found out later we were second.

Our platoon won the Red Streamer for the Rifle Range with 100% qualified recruits. Gunny told us we had the highest score shot by one of our Platoon's Recruits but, we wouldn't know who that was until Graduation Day. Our Platoon won the Gold Streamer for Close Order Drill, and our Platoon won the Orange Streamer for PT.

On Tuesday, we would be standing our Final Inspection before Graduation. If we scored the highest, we would win the White Streamer. The Honor Platoon was determined by which Platoon performs at the highest level across various competitions throughout the training cycle. This included excelling in areas like knowledge, final drill, rifle range, physical fitness tests, and combat fitness evaluations. Essentially, demonstrating superior overall performance compared to the other Platoons in their Company.

Saturday night, after evening chow, was fairly relaxing and Gunny gave us two separate "*Smoking Lamp*" times. One after evening chow, and one before Commanders Time. So, after evening chow, besides Close Order Drill, we spent most of our time spit shining shoes, and shining the Brim of our cover, as well as cleaning our rifles. Some Recruits were better at shining their shoes and the brims of their Garrison Covers than others. It was important that the Squad Leaders and I give assistance to those who struggled to shine both their cover brims or their shoes.

Week 11 now came to an end and we had accomplished quite a bit this week. Saturday was a long day and I couldn't wait for lights out at 2200. One joyful note, I adopted Taps as our nightly lullaby.

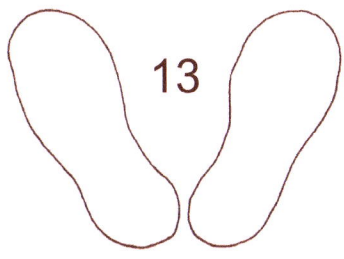

Final Inspection

Sunday morning again began after Reveille with PT, head call, hygiene, and those interested went to Church Services. Depending on the service you went to, you would "**Fall-In**" to that formation, i.e. Catholic held one formation, Lutheran had one formation, Methodist or Protestant had another formation, and there was also a Jewish formation.

You would "**Fall-In**" with the denomination of your choice and first go to morning chow then attend their service. After services, you would find your way back to your Platoon Street and enjoy what was left of the Commander's Time. Our Platoon would finish morning clean-up before we went to morning chow and then spend Commanders Time on the Platoon Street.

I spent my time spit shining my Cover, then my Dress Shoes and lastly I would clean my rifle getting ready for our Tuesday, Final Inspection. Even though I never carried a rifle, I would be inspected with my rifle at our Final Inspection with the rest of our Platoon. The Squad Leaders and I went up and down the Platoon Street helping anyone who was having trouble shining either their Combination Brim, their shoes, or issues with their rifles.

As we enjoyed Commanders Time, those Recruits who attended Sunday Services returned to enjoy what was left of

Commanders Time. Everyone worked feverously to get their shoes spit shined and the hardest task was getting the brim of their Combination Cover shined. We normally go to noon chow on Sundays around 1130, but now that we are the Senior Series, we weren't scheduled for noon chow until 1245. So this Sunday, we had an extended Commanders Time and afterwards Sgt Martinez marched us to noon chow.

Normally after we returned from noon chow on Sunday, we would continue training and today was no exception. Sgt James arrived while we were at noon chow, and would share the Duty with Sgt Martinez on Sunday afternoon after the Platoon was marched back to the Platoon Street.

Sgt James held a class on Guard Duty which we would be Standing on Sunday beginning at 2000. (8:00 pm). We would be sharing the Duty with Platoon 2228, and I was picked to stand the first Watch as Sgt of the Guard and then I would be relieved by the Right Guide from Platoon 2228 at 2400.

Pvt Havranek was standing the first Watch as Cpl of the Guard and would be relieved by the 1st Squad Leader of Platoon 2228. Our Platoon would assume the Duty at 2000 hours and would be relieved by Platoon 2228 at 2400 Midnight, including the Walking Posts and Messengers. We had the short Watch because of our status with FOX Company.

The Guard Duty Class ended at 1400 and after we made a Head Call, We "**Fell-In**" and rehearsed how our Final Inspection would be held. Sgt James had the Platoon "**Fall-In**" and had me leave the Guidon in the Platoon flag stand and grab my rifle and "**Fall-In**" with the rest of the Platoon. I was informed that on Tuesday when we "**Fall-In**" for Final Inspection, I would not carry the Guidon but would "**Fall-In**" in the Right Guide position, with my rifle instead to stand Inspection.

When we "**Fell-In**" we were marched to the Grinder and the first thing we did was go through the "**Manual at Arms**" for almost a half hour. Then we "**Opened Ranks**," and Sgt James played the role of the Inspector along with

Sgt Martinez, and walked through all four Ranks putting us through the Inspection routine. When he stopped in front of me, he made me do the Manual at Arms twice before having me come to "**Inspection Arms**." I executed both perfectly and Sgt James had a little smile on his face as he moved on to Inspect Pvt Havranek.

We ran through practice until 1800 then "**Closed Ranks**" and marched back to Platoon Street, locked up or rifles and got back in formation for evening chow.

251

I grabbed the Guidon out of the flag stand in front of the Duty Hut, and we marched with pride to evening chow. Platoon 2228 was in front of us, so we followed them through the chow line, spent our 20 minutes eating then Sgt James had us "**Fall-In**" and lit the "*Smoking Lamp.*"

We assumed the Duty at 2000 hours sharing the Sunday night Guard Duty with Platoon 2228. After I was posted as the Sgt of the Guard, I posted the Cpl of the Guard and the 16-walking posts. The OOD was Lt. Basiz and he made his way to the Duty Hut where he signed-in the Log Book that he was checking the Guard, and all was well.

Since the Sgt of the Guard Post was located in the Platoon Duty Hut, Gunny Wolfmule made sure I closed out the Duty Log Book properly at 2400.  Reporting that there were no incidents or issues to report for our Watch, was as important as properly standing the Watch itself. I turned the Sgt of the Guard Watch over to the Platoon 2228 Right Guide. The OOD Relieved me and Posted the new Sgt of the Guard. I signed the Log Book noting that Platoon 2227 had been properly relieved. My notation affirmed Platoon 2228 relieved us properly.

Gunny Wolfmule made sure that our Platoon had been instructed well, and it seemed our watch standing was almost perfect. Everything went off without a hitch. The most important parts of watch standing were uniforms, reporting each post hourly, Changing of the Guard and entries in the duty log books.

Monday morning, week 11, we were the last Platoons going to chow. Normally we always ate morning chow prior to 0800. However, this morning we happened to be outside the Mess Hall for morning Colors.

We heard the Bugle play, "**Attention to Colors**," which was always played prior to morning Colors. Sgt Martinez brought the Platoon to "**Attention**." Sgt Martinez saluted the flag as it was being raised and the Bugle played "**Colors**."

After morning chow outside the Mess Hall, Sgt Martinez lit the "*Smoking Lamp*." Upon returning to the Platoon area, Sgt Martinez had the platoon form up on Platoon Street and stand "**At Ease**." While in formation the voice of Gunny Sgt Wolfmule was loudly heard from the DI Duty Hut and commanded, "Private Rilley report to the Duty Hut." The entire Platoon responded to his command loudly and in unison, "**Sir, Private Rilley Report to the Duty hut, Sir.**"

I made an "**About Face**" from our formation, made my way to the DI Duty Hut, and stood centered in the doorway. I pounded on the Pine and said, "**Sir, Private Rilley reporting as ordered, Sir.**" Gunny answered, "Come in here, Pvt." I entered the DI Duty Hut and centered myself on the desk where Gunny Sgt Wolfmule was seated and reported, "**Sir, Pvt Rilley reporting as ordered, Sir**." Gunny Wolfmule told me to "**Stand At Ease Pvt**." The Gunny then told me what a fine job I had done last night as the Sgt of the Guard.

The Gunny continued, "Pvt Rilley, I am pleased to inform you that you have been chosen as the Platoon Honor Man for Platoon 2227. You will also be promoted to the Rank of PFC, (Private First Class). With that being said, I need you to come with me this morning to get fitted for a set of Dress Blues for Graduation." He then stood up and offed me his hand and said, "Congratulations Pvt Rilley." I shook his hand and said, "**Sir, Thank you Sir**." He told me to wait outside on the Platoon Street. I answered, "**Sir, Aye Aye Sir**," and did an "**About Face**." I ran out of his Hut and onto the Platoon Street with pride in my heart and a smile on my face.

When I was back on the Platoon Street, Sgt James walked up to me, shook my hand and said, "Congratulations Pvt on being chosen as the Platoon Honor Man. You deserve it and you earned it." I answered, "**Sir, thank you Sir**." He then turned to the Platoon formation and told the Squad leaders, **"Fall-In"** on the Grinder. As the Platoon left to form up on the Grinder, I stood fast and waited for Gunny Wolfmule. Sgt James had chosen one of the "House Mice" to carry the Guidon.

Gunny came out of the DI Duty Hut and said, "Come with me Pvt." We made our way across the Base to the warehouse where we were issued our Dress Uniforms the week before. Upon entering the warehouse, the Gunny approached the Supply Sgt in charge and said, "Fit this Marine with a set of Dress Blues for Graduation Day with all the accessories and make sure PFC Chevrons are sewn on as well."

I was beaming with pride, not only was it an honor to be chosen as the Platoon Honor Man, but Gunny referred to me as a Marine. The Supply Sgt responded "Aye Aye Gunny," and had me stand on a mark on the floor and measured me up for my Blues. When he was finished making the necessary measurements, the Supply Sgt asked, "How soon do you need these Blues ready Gunny?"

The Gunny answered, "Can you have them ready by tomorrow afternoon?" The Sgt responded that he would have them finished, pressed, and ready by 1400, Tuesday. The Gunny thanked him and also asked that he put together a full set of PFC Chevrons for all my uniforms. The Supply Sgt reassured Gunny it would be done.

The Supply Sgt told Gunny the Blues would be ready Tuesday afternoon and he would have them at the Dry Cleaners in the Gunny's name. The Gunny thanked the Sgt and they shook hands and he and I left to make our way back to our Platoon area. As we walked back together, the Gunny was asking me how I liked the Marine Corps so far and what part of boot camp did I find most challenging.

I told him the Rifle Range was the most challenging, I shared with him that I found getting the entire Platoon to work in harmony and be in sync as one, instead of 79 individuals, was challenging as well. He told me I was very astute and said, "Those were the two things the DI's found most challenging as well." As we continued walking, we ended up at the PX where Sgt James had taken the Platoon while Gunny and I were gone.

When we arrived at the PX, I saw our Platoon Guidon in the flag stand and wondered who was chosen to carry it in my absence. Before I walked into the PX, the Gunny told me not to buy a garment bag to carry my Dress Greens because I would get a better garment bag with my Dress Blues. He also told me I was allowed to buy a Duffle Bag if I wished to carry my personal items in. I thanked him for his courtesy and advice.

Sgt James told the Platoon they were allowed one half hour to complete their purchases. Most guys that smoked were purchasing cigarettes, they were only $1.00 per carton. I bought a Duffle Bag, a carton of cigarettes and a bottle of All Spice After Shave.

When I finished my shopping, I placed my cigarettes and the After Shave in the Duffle Bag I had just bought, and went out to where the Platoon was to "**Fall-In.**" I retrieved the Guidon out of the flag stand and asked Havranek who carried the Guidon to the PX? He told me Sgt James had one of the House Mice carry it.

We "**Fell-In**" and marched to the Dry Cleaners to pick up our Dress Green Class "A" Uniforms for the Tuesday, Final Inspection and Graduation. I was thinking, I get to wear my Greens for Inspection, but they would stay in the plastic on Graduation Day because I'd be wearing Dress Blues instead.

After picking up our Dress Greens from the Dry Cleaners, Sgt James marched us back to our Platoon area. We were told to take your purchases into our Huts, hang your greens on your Rack, and put purchases in your footlockers. We were to get out your ink kits to mark your names on the collar of the green blouse, the belt, the trousers, the neck of the shirt, the tie, and the sweat bands of all your covers that we placed in your footlockers last week. If we purchased a

Duffle Bag, we were to put your name on the outside of the Duffle Bag under the handle.

Sgt James wanted us to get our Dress Greens ready for Inspection on Tuesday morning. He had the 3rd and 4th Squads assemble into the 3rd Squad Hut and had Pvt Gagnon hang his Greens on his Rack. Sgt Martinez went into the 2nd Squad Hut and had Pvt Surma hang his Dress Greens on his Rack and Gunny went into the 1st Squad Hut and had Pvt Havranek hang his Dress Greens on his Rack. Each DI and the Gunny showed everyone how to put the insignias on the lapels, the belt buckle on the belt and how to attach it to the blouse. He showed us how to put the Combination Cover together and attach the large Eagle, Globe and Anchor Insignia on the Cover.

Gunny and the DI's had a cloth bag full of National Defense Ribbons and the Shooting Badge each Recruit earned on the Range. We were shown how to put the Ribbon and Badge centered over the left breast pocket. We spent the rest of the afternoon and later after evening chow working on assembling our uniforms, spit shining our shoes and Barracks Cover Brim and cleaning our rifles.

The hardest part of putting our uniform together was stretching the Barracks Cover over the metal grommet or halo bar. Stretching the material tight enough to make a saddle look of the Barracks Cover. The last thing they had us do was remove the quartermaster or lacquer coating that covered the Dress Green belt buckle. The quartermaster was sprayed on the Brass to prevent tarnishing from air, humidity, and oils from our skin. Once this lacquer was removed, it was then our job to keep all of our brass shined with Brasso.

We were all getting excited to be near the end of a grueling 11 weeks of boot camp. We were short timers even though we were just recruits. We just have to get through this short week to finish up Boot Camp. In spite of that our spirits were high. For some reason Monday was a long, long day and it seemed the day would never end. We were excited to get to the final inspection and get closer to Graduation.

We had an extended Commanders Time because of getting uniforms and gear ready for Final Inspection which we would be experiencing late Tuesday morning. I was beat, but too excited to sleep. The news that I was picked to be the Platoon Honor Man, being issued a set of Dress Blues, walking and talking with the Gunny like we were friends, all made my day. Lights were out, TAPS had played, but I just stared up at the springs on the rack above me. The next thing I remember, lights came back on, as I heard Reveille.

Rcvcillc on Tuesday seemed to be as smooth as any day of training over our 11 weeks. Everyone was anxious, but self-confident, excited but with a positive attitude. PT was fun this morning, with Sgt James making jokes as we exercised. Hygiene went smooth, and clean-up was seamless. Sgt James marched us to morning chow, and he was pumping everyone up about our Final Inspection later that morning. Morning chow seemed to be especially tasty this morning and you could feel the energy and the positive attitudes as we finished chow.

The "*Smoking Lamp*" was lit while in formation outside the Mess Hall. We were marched back to our Platoon area to get ready for Inspection. When we returned, we were given another Head Call. As we were finishing up, we saw Platoon 2225 marching to the Grinder as they were the first to be inspected. They didn't look as confident as we were, so already we felt better. They did look good in their Dress Greens though. Although we competed with the other Platoons in FOX Company, the other three Platoons looked good now that we were getting ready to graduate.

The other Platoons looked like Marines when they marched. They stood tall, and I am sure they felt the same excitement and satisfaction by what they had accomplished during their time at Boot Camp, as our Platoon. I am sure individually, there were recruits in other Platoons that were as squared away as well as anyone in our Platoon. After Boot Camp is over I will probably be stationed with some of these guys and we will become friends.

We hustled back to our Platoon area to change out of our utilities and into our winter Class "A" Dress Greens. Everyone helped everyone get dressed and squared away. When we were dressed each Squad Leader held uniform inspection with their squad. I walked through each Hut and reviewed their uniforms as well. I carried a fingernail clipper so I could clip any *"Irish Pendants"* off any uniform. I checked their buttons, their military alignment, their ties, their Ribbons and Shooting Badges, looked at their shoes and the Brims of their Covers.

Our platoon was truly all squared away and ready for Final Inspection. Gunny Wolfmule had the Platoon get their rifles and "**Fall-In**" on Platoon Street. He told us this day would determine if we were going to be the Honor Platoon or not. He emphasized very strongly that he was confident that Platoon 2227 was the best Platoon in our Company and would pass our Final Inspection without a glitch. When Sgt James came out of the Duty Hut, Gunny told him, "Get the girls on the Platoon Street."

Once in Formation on the Platoon Street, Sgt James marched our Platoon to a spot on the Grinder where we would be Inspected. We went to "**Dress Right Dress**," and once in position waited for the Inspection Team. The Inspecting Officer was Captain Wallace from the 3rd Battalion Headquarters along with the 3rd Battalion 1st Sargeant.

Gunny Sgt Wolfmule called our Platoon to attention as the Captain approached and stood in front of Gunny Wolfmule. Gunny Saluted and reported, "Sir, Platoon 2227, ready for Inspection." Captain Wallace returned his Salute and said, "Very Well." Gunny Sgt Wolfmule made an "**About Face**," and commanded, "**Platoon 2227, Open Ranks, March**."

The first squad took two steps forward, the second squad took one step forward, the third squad stood fast, the fourth squad took one step back. Each squad then "**Dressed Right Dress**" automatically aligning their squad so everyone was exactly in line. (Each recruit looked to his right, extending his left arm so the right shoulder of the recruit to his left moved to touch his fingers and made sure he was lined up perfectly even.) The squad dresses off the Squad Leader.

Gunny Sgt Wolfmule walked to the first squad and faced the Squad Leader to make sure the 1st squad was aligned. Then he walked to the second Squad Leader, then the third and then the 4th to ensure all squads were aligned. After he was assured each squad was aligned, he walked back, even with the first squad, then ordered, "**Ready, Two,** then **Cover**." When "**Ready two**" was given, all hands fell to your side and your head snaped forward.

The second command, "**Cove**r" means the second squad lines up directly behind the man in the first squad, the third behind the second squad, the fourth behind the third squad. When done properly, each Platoon is exactly lined and covered and perfectly squared off. Gunny then marched back to the center in front of the Platoon and faced the Inspecting Officer. Gunny then Salutes and Reports, "Sir, Platoon 2227 is Ready for Inspection."

Captain Wallace returned his Salute, and says, "**Very Well**." He then marched toward the 1st Squad and stood in front of the first man in the first squad. He was followed by the 1st Sgt and then by Gunny Wolfmule. The first man he stopped in front of was me. I am standing at "**Attention**," and I automatically came to "**Port Arms**, then **Inspection Arms**." Captain Wallace took my rifle out of my hands and begins to inspect the sites, the receiver, the barrel inside and out, the stock, the butt plate and then returned my rifle to me. I closed the bolt, pulled the trigger and returned to "**Order Arms**."

Captain Wallace then says to me, "Good morning Private." I answer, "**Good morning Sir**." he then asked me, "Pvt., what is your 4th General Order?" I replied, "Sir, this

Recruits 4th General Order is, "To Report all calls from posts more distant from the Guard House than my own, Sir." He then asked me my 7th General Order. I replied, "Sir, this Recruits 7th General Order is, "To talk to no one except in the Line of Duty, Sir." As he was looking my uniform up and down he then asked, "Who is the Commanding Officer of Marine Corps Recruit Depot, San Diego, I replied, "Sir, the Commanding Officer of Marine Corps Recruit Depot, San Diego is Major General Bruno A. Hochmuth, Sir."

Captain Wallace then made a "**Right Face**," took one step and stood in front of Pvt Havranek and faced him as Havranek came to "**Inspection Arms**." As he Inspected Havranek's rifle, the 1st Sgt stood in front of me and watched Captain Wallace Inspect Havranek. After returning his rifle,

Captain Wallace asked Havranek a couple of questions and then moved on to the next Recruit. He continued Inspecting the entire 1st Squad. Before Inspecting the 2nd Squad, he walked behind the 1st Squad and Inspected the back of our heads, our uniform, our shoes and then moved on to the 2nd Squad and continued Inspecting each recruit. The entire Platoon stayed at "**Attention**" during the entire Inspection.

After Inspecting the 2nd Squad, he moved on to the 3rd Squad and then the 4th. Upon finishing all four Squads, Captain Wallace returned to the front of the formation and told Gunny to "**Carry On**." As the Gunny Saluted him, he replied to Captain Wallace, "**Aye Aye Sir**."

The Gunny executed an "**About Face**," and was proudly facing our Platoon and gave the Platoon the command to, "**Close Ranks, March**." The first squad stood fast, the second squad took one step forward, the third squad took two steps forward and the fourth squad took three steps forward. The Platoon automatically went to "**Dress Right Dress**,", and once the Platoon was totally aligned, Gunny commands, "**Ready Two**," then "**Cover**." The entire Platoon "**Covers Down**," and again is in a perfect Formation of 79 proud and reformed civilians who were just days away from becoming real Marines.

Gunny then executed another "**About Face**," and faced the Inspection Team who reported to the Platoon Commander any information or comments he wished to pass on. The Captain read his Inspection results to the Gunny and told him his Inspection was complete. The Gunny saluted the Captain again, the Captain returned his salute then disappeared from the grinder. While we were still at attention, the Gunny addressed the Platoon.

He commanded, "**Platoon, Parade Rest**." He then looked us over and made his comments. "The Inspection went well, we received just one gig for the entire inspection. One belt was missing a loop. I was told by Captain Wallace this was the best inspection of a recruit Platoon he has inspected in over three years of Inspecting Recruits at MCRD. Congratulations, job well done!"

Gunny Wolfmule digested the comment by Captain Wallace "That this was the best Platoon he had inspected in three years." In the Gunny's 15 years in the Marine Corps, that was the most amazing comment he had ever heard. Gunny felt that because of that comment, we had won the White Inspection Streamer. Although a great comment by Captain Wallace, Gunny wasn't happy with the one gig we got.

The Gunny then said, "Pvt Hayes Front and Center." Pvt Hayes was in the 3rd Squad, and took one step forward, turned left and marched to the front of the Platoon and centered himself in front of Gunny Wolfmule and Reported, "Sir, Pvt Hayes, Reporting as Ordered Sir." Gunny asked him who his Squad Leader was, and Pvt Hayes answered, "Sir, Pvt Hesch Sir." He then told Hayes to return to his position in his Squad. He then said, "Pvt Hesch, Front and Center."

Pvt Hesch made a Right Face and then made his way to center himself in front of the Gunny and reported, "Sir, Pvt Hesch Reporting as Ordered Sir." Gunny told Hesch, you are relieved as Squad Leader, and after returning to the Platoon Area and changing out of your Dress Greens and into your utilities, Report to the Duty Hut. Put yourself in the "Sand Box" and give me 100 repetitions of Bends and Thrusts." Pvt Hesch answered, "**Sir, Aye Aye Sir**," and made his way back to his position in the Formation.

Gunny told Sgt James, "Dismiss the Platoon back to Platoon Street, have them return their rifles and cartridge belts, change out of their class "A" Dress Greens and back into their utility uniform. After the Platoon has changed into utilities, designate another Recruit to 3rd Squad Leader and make sure Pvt Hesch gives me 100."

Sgt James answered, "**Aye Aye Gunny**." Sgt James turned to the Platoon and made the "command", "**Platoon, Attention**." Sgt James then turned to me and said, "Guidon, once this formation is dismissed, have all the ladies on the Platoon Street by 1145." I answered, "**Aye Aye, Sir**." Sgt James then said, "**Platoon 2227, dismissed**."

We fell out, and everyone double timed back to their Hut, secured their rifles, took off their class "A" Dress Green uniform and put it back on a hanger, covered it with plastic and hung it on their Racks. We changed back into our utilities and "**Fell-In**" by 1145 on the Platoon Street. Pvt Hesch reported to the "Sand Box," and the rest of the Platoon "**Fell-In**," on the Platoon Street and waited for Sgt James to appoint a new Squad Leader for Pvt Hesch.

Once everyone was in formation on the Platoon Street, I went to the DI Duty Hut and reported, "**Sir, Platoon 2227**

all present and accounted for, Sir." Then I returned to my position on the Platoon Street. Sgt James walked out of the Duty Hut, Pvt Hesch was in the "Sand Box" doing his Bends and Thrusts and counting out loud. I assumed Gunny relieved Pvt Hesch as Squad Leader for the gig we received at Inspection for Pvt Hayes missing the belt loop on his uniform,

Sgt James said in a loud and positive voice that in his opinion, we won the Inspection but we had to wait for final results after Platoon 2228 finished their Inspection. He then assigned Pvt Dupree as the 3rd Squad Leader while Pvt Hesch continued in the "Sand Box." Sgt James put the Platoon "**At Ease**" and lit the "*Smoking Lamp*" and told us to study our Red Notebooks until it was time to go to noon chow.

While we were waiting to go to noon chow, Gunny walked out of the Duty Hut and told Pvt Hesch to "**Fall-In**" on the Platoon Street. Gunny turned to me and told me to go to "**Port Arms**" with the Guidon. He then placed the White Streamer under the Spindle of our Guidon. He turned to the Platoon, called us to "**Attention**" and said, "Platoon 2227, Good Job, you earned this Streamer and I believe you have also earned the "**Honor Platoon**" award as far as I'm concerned. We will find out Friday."

He continued, "The following Pvts "**Fall-Out**" and go into your Hut and bring me your Green Dress Blouse. Pvt Rilley, Pvt Havranek, Pvt Gagnon, Pvt Surma, Pvt Dupree, Pvt Earle, Pvt Gaines, Pvt Hayes, and Pvt Williams. These were the individuals who earned and will be Promoted to the Rank of PFC. Gunny wanted to get the PFC Chevron sewed onto their Dress Green Blouse for Graduation.

Gunny had two of the "**House Mice**" recruits to "**Fall-Out**" to collect the Dress Green Blouses. After he had all nine blouses, he had me and the two "**House Mice**" follow him to the Dry Cleaners where he had the PFC Chevrons sewn on. He was told he could pick them up on Wednesday afternoon.

While we were at the Dry Cleaners, Gunny asked the clerk if she had a uniform for GySgt Wolfmule? She returned with a black garment bag with Gunny's name on it. Inside the garment bag was a set of Dress Blues with a PFC Chevron sewn on both arms. There was also a plastic bag and a green cloth bag attached on the inside. The plastic bag contained all the accessories and the green cloth bag contained a set of PFC Chevrons for all my uniforms.

The accessories for Dress Blues consisted of a White Barracks Cover with a large Brass Eagle, Globe and Anchor for the front of the Cover, two additional Black Cover Straps with two Brass Strap Screws. A White Belt with a large solid Brass Buckle, one pair of White Gloves, 7 Brass Buttons for the front of the Tunic, 8 Brass Buttons for the sleeves, and 2 Brass Collar Eagle, Globe and Anchor Insignias.

The two "House Mice" waited for Gunny to hand me my Dress Blues and we made our way back to the Platoon area. Once back in my Hut, I took my garment bag and hung it at the end of my Rack next to my Dress Greens, and placed both the plastic and green cloth bag inside my foot locker.

The rest of the Platoon was reading their Red Notebooks and Gunny had us put our Notebooks away and "**Fall-In**" Platoon Formation and marched us over to noon chow, with our streamers flying high on our unit Guidon. It felt good for the Platoon to strut across the Grinder in full view of all the Platoons on the depot, on our way to noon chow. Sgt James made it a point to march close to where the new Recruit formations were marching on the Grinder and he intentionally guided our Platoon to pass closely by them. I remembered how much in awe I was when I saw a Platoon of Marines marching. We now looked like the Marines I saw on day one although we still had to graduate.

As senior series on base, we took our time marching to chow as Sgt James showed us off to every Platoon in sight. We actually were the last Platoon to enter the Mess Hall. I hated to leave our Guidon in the flag stand while eating chow. I was thinking someone may want to steal it because of all the streamers. It looked prodigious with four Streamers hanging from it.

As we sat eating noon chow slowly and relaxed, the Mess NCO called, "seconds on the chow line," and most of the FOX Company recruits in the Mess Hall got up and ran to get in line again. Everyone in our Platoon stayed seated and waited for Sgt James to give us permission before moving. Sgt James smiled and waited a few minutes before he nodded his head giving us permission to get in line for seconds as well.

On that day, Platoon 2227 really enjoyed noon chow, and for some reason it seemed like we had an hour to eat. Sgt James was in a very leisurely kind of mood, and after noon chow, we "**Fell-In**" outside the Mess Hall and Sgt James lit the "*Smoking Lamp*." While we were smoking, Sgt James walked through the Platoon making comments to recruits and asking questions of certain individuals.

He came and stood next to me and asked me what I thought of winning the "**Close Order Drill**" competition. I was careful how I addressed him and what comments I was going to make. I came to "**Attention**," to answer his question, and Sgt James said, "relax," "**At Ease, Pvt Rilley**," he continued, "I was just curious to know how good you think we are." I was as cautious as he was curious in how to answer or what to say.

Although I relaxed and stood "**At Ease**," I answered, "Sir, this Private believes Platoon 2227 is the best Platoon at this Depot, Sir." Sgt James smiled and said, "Well said, Rilley, well said, and walked away, and walked over to talk to the Mess Staff NCO who had come outside for a smoke himself.

When we finished our cigarette, Sgt James said, "Put 'em out and come to "**Attention**." He then marched us around the base to show off our Guidon. We went through the 1st and 3rd Battalion training area and then back to our Platoon Street.

We spent the rest of the afternoon on Platoon Street shining our Dress Shoes and cleaning our M-14 rifles. Wednesday morning we were to turn in our weapons to the armory along with our cartridge belts and bayonets. Sgt James informed the Platoon that after evening chow he would hold inspection on our M-14 rifles to ensure that when we deliver our rifles to the armory they would be spotless.

After evening chow and our rifle inspection, we held Commanders Time. Since we had won all the training streamers that were available to win except the streamer for testing, it was assumed that we'd win the Honor Platoon Streamer. Sgt James informed us that Wednesday would be our last full training day, being Thursday was Thanksgiving.

Wednesday morning Reveille was still at 0500 and the same routine we had been following since day one continued. PT, Head Call, hygiene, making our racks, morning hygiene, Platoon Area clean-up and then morning chow. Sgt Martinez assumed the Duty Wednesday morning and did not hold Hut Inspection. He was aware we had our sea bags locked to our racks with our rifles, and at the end of our racks had our Dress Greens hanging.

We were all surprised when Sgt Martinez lit the "*Smoking Lamp*" before morning chow. Again, since we were the Senior Series on the Depot we were last to enter the Mess Hall. We were standing outside when the Bugle blew "**Attention to Colors**." We were standing "**At Ease**" and Sgt Martinez brought us to "**Attention**." On the first note of the Bugle to "**Colors**," Sgt Martinez Saluted towards the Base Flag Pole across the Grinder from 2nd Battalion Mess Hall as the Garrison Flag was raised to the Bugle blowing morning "**Colors**."

When Colors were over, we again were in two single file lines. As we saluted the mirror, you could almost hear the snap of our arms. We then went into morning chow and enjoyed an amazing breakfast of waffles, maple syrup, bacon, sausage, scrambled eggs, fried potatoes, juice, coffee, milk, water and mixed fruit. Again, there was no reason to hurry as we were the last Platoons to eat, and Sgt Martinez didn't need to have the Platoon to the armory until 0930.

After morning chow, Sgt Martinez lit the "*Smoking Lamp*" again, and upon finishing our cigarettes, we were told to "**Fall-In**" on the Platoon Street with our rifles, cartridge belts and bayonets. Gunny Wolfmule came out of the Duty Hut and both he and Sgt Martinez will march us to the Armory to return our M-14's.

Before we were marched to the Armory, Gunny had Sgt Martinez march us to the middle of the Grinder and had us count cadence as we marched drawing attention to our Platoon as we maneuvered through the Platoons also marching on the Grinder. Sgt Martinez had the Platoon execute the marching Manual at Arms. As we marched at "**Right Shoulder Arms**," the command was given to "**Left Shoulder Arms**." We went from "**Left Shoulder Arms**," to "**Port Arms**," then back to "**Right Shoulder Arms**." I had my rifle slung over my back and carried the Guidon with Pride as normal in my right hand. I strutted across the Grinder on our way to the Armory.

The process of returning our rifles took all morning, as the other three platoons were turning their rifles in as well. Once all our rifles and cartridge belts were returned, Gunny marched us over to the Dry Cleaners so those getting promoted could get their Dress Green Blouses. I picked up my Dress Green Blouse as well, wrapped in a clear plastic bag. When the other eight Recruits getting Promoted to PFC picked up their Dress Green Blouse, they were covered in plastic and their sleeves looked good with the red PFC Chevron.

It started raining as we left the Dry Cleaners, so Sgt Martinez marched us straight back to the Platoon Street to hang up our uniforms so not to get them wet. As we marched to noon chow, we got soaked, but by the time chow was finished, the rain had stopped. The entire FOX Company spent the rest of the afternoon practicing for Graduation on the Grinder.

On our way to evening chow on Wednesday, Gunny had us march through the street just next to 1st Battalion berthing area before marching us to the 2nd Battalion Mess Hall. It was apparent Gunny wanted to show us off with the Streamers on our Guidon. After evening chow, the "*Smoking Lamp*" was lit for a half hour. We were allowed to smoke two cigarettes before Gunny had us "**Turn Two**" for Commanders Time.

All the Recruits were making sure our uniforms were squared away, our shoes were shined, and the Brim of our Combination Covers were spit shined as well. During Commanders Time, I was summoned to the Duty Hut. When I arrived, I Reported as I was supposed to, Sgt Martinez, Sgt James and the Gunny were all in the Duty Hut.

I stood at "**Attention**," and Gunny told me to "**At Ease**." He began by telling me what a good job I had done as the Right Guide and complimented me on my leadership skills and told me I should feel good about what our Platoon was able to accomplish. He told me not only did I earn the Platoon Honor Man Award, but I was also chosen to receive the Series Honor Man Award plus my Promotion to PFC.

The Gunny shook my hand and told me I would be wearing my Dress Blues on Friday at Graduation along with the other three Right Guides. Our Platoon would be the Honor Platoon. He told me it was a great accomplishment. Sgt Martinez and Sgt James also shook my hand and asked if I had received all the uniform parts for my Blues. I told them I hadn't put my Dress Blue uniform together yet. Gunny told me to go back to my Hut and bring my Blues and all the accessories to the Duty Hut. I said, "**Sir, Aye Aye Sir**." and went back to my Hut

When I returned to my Hut, Pvt Havranek asked me if everything was OK, and I told him everything was just great. I congratulated him for making PFC as he was getting his uniform ready for Friday. He asked me what was in the black

Garment bag. I told him I would show him when I returned. I took my Garment Bag and returned to the Duty Hut.

When I returned to the Duty Hut, I pounded on the door frame and asked permission to enter. Sgt James told me to enter. He took my Garment Bag and he and Gunny assembled my Dress Blue Uniform which consisted of the coveted Dress Blues Tunic, blue trousers, white belt, white barracks cover, brass belt buckle, white gloves, and PFC chevrons on the right and left upper sleeves, brass screws for my combination cover, 7 brass buttons for the tunic and 8 brass buttons for the tunic sleeves. I switched my National Defense Ribbon and my Expert Shooting Badge from my Greens to my Blues as well as changed out my combination cover from Green to White.

Once everything was squared away, Gunny had me put my Blues back in my garment bag and return to my Hut. Most of the guys in our Hut had their uniforms squared away from Final Inspection and were sitting on their footlockers shining their shoes when I returned. Havranek walked over to see what was in my black garment bag, so I unzipped it and showed him my Blues.

The Tunic was on a hanger with the blue trousers under-neath. There were some oohs and aahs from a few guys who were watching me show Havranek my Blues. Their reaction caught the attention of the other 18 guys in our Hut and they all wanted to see my Dress Blues.

So a couple of guys came over to my Rack to check out the Dress Blues I would be wearing at Graduation. When I showed them, some were happy and a few were jealous. Those who weren't positive didn't have anything to be jealous about, because those guys didn't win any recognition for graduation or didn't stand out in any way during training.

With the assistance of Sgt James and Gunny, everything on my Blues was assembled and my combination cover was at the bottom of the garment bag. I never took my Blues completely out of the Garment bag, but you could see how awesome they looked. I looked over PFC Havranek's Dress Green Blouse with the new PFC Chevrons sewn on and saw him smile and we shook hands acknowledging the fact that we had accomplished being the best we could be.

We finished putting away our uniforms, squared away the rest of our gear and got ready to hit the Rack. Again, lights out at 2200 and Taps closed out another exciting, rewarding day at Boot Camp.

Thursday was Thanksgiving, but Reveille was 0500 and we still did PT before morning hygiene, showering and shaving and cleaning up of our Quonset huts. As we were marched to morning chow, there was a slight drizzle in the air that wasn't there when we did PT. Because we were the last to go to chow, we hung around our Platoon area a little longer and while we were in line for breakfast getting a little damp, the Bugle blew "**Attention to Colors.**"

We were already in two single file lines when Sgt Martinez called the Platoon to "**Attention.**" Morning Colors took place with the Bugle playing "**Colors**" as we stood in line at "**Attention,**" and I actually had goose bumps hearing the Bugle play while I stood there. Although we will be Graduating in two days, we still ate breakfast by the numbers, filled our trays, made our way to our designated seats, waited to hear the command "Seats" and answered, "**Seats, Aye Aye Sir,**" before sitting down in unison. 20 minutes later we got up and left the mess hall and because of the drizzle, we didn't stay long enough for a cigarette, and marched directly back to the Platoon Street.

Around 1030, the rain stopped and the sun came out. All four Platoons in FOX Company "**Fell-In**" on the Grinder for Graduation practice. We went through the ceremony, practiced "**Pass In Review,**" and ran through the procedure for retiring the Unit Guidons. Normally the day before Graduation, the Graduating Series hosts Family and Visitors Day.

After we finished noon chow, the rest of the day we were on Commanders Time, spending the afternoon in our Huts relaxing, shining shoes, and the brim of our covers, writing letters, and reading mail. Those who had Family in town for Graduation were allowed to spend the afternoon visiting with their Family. Those who didn't have visitors just hung around the Hut and Platoon Area.

Although we were in our Huts and relaxing, we were never allowed to sit or lay on our Racks. I sat on my footlocker and put a couple more layers of polish on my shoes and touched up the brim of my Combination Cover and stopped a few times to look at my Dress Blues.

I took the time to think about home and how my family would be celebrating Thanksgiving. I wondered at whose house they would be celebrating Thanksgiving this year and who would be at dinner. I was also wondering who was winning the annual Thanksgiving day football game between the Detroit Lions and the Chicago Bears? I also thought about my good friend Zane and his family and how they would be celebrating the day.

The afternoon was over at 1630 and the visitors had to leave the Base. They would be allowed back for Graduation at 1000 on Friday morning, and in the meantime, the Recruits returned to their Platoon Areas. There was a visitors area for families to meet as well as a Base Museum, but visitors never were allowed to eat or visit the Mess Halls on MCRD. Only Recruits and Training personnel were allowed in the Mess Halls or on the Grinder.

On this Thanksgiving Day, for evening chow, we would enjoy a full Thanksgiving dinner of turkey, dressing, mashed potatoes, gravy, vegetables, pickles, both green and black olives, dinner rolls, cranberries, sweet potatoes, pumpkin pie, mincemeat pie, whipped cream, coffee, tea and milk. Because we were the Senior Series and the last Platoons to eat, we were allowed to have as much Thanksgiving chow as we wanted.

When we were finished eating our fill, our Platoon was the last one to leave the Mess Hall. When Gunny returned us to our Platoon Street, he lit the *"Smoking Lamp"* for over a half hour which allowed most of us that smoked to have a minimum of two cigarettes.

We not only enjoyed a very relaxing day, the actual first relaxing day in 11 weeks, but our DI's were cordial, animated, and actually joked with a couple of the "House Mice" during the evening clean-up. Gunny Wolfmule and Sgt James visited with us while we enjoyed our smoke and it was the first time I allowed myself to let my guard down since arriving at MCRD.

Once Gunny turned off the *"Smoking Lamp,"* those who smoked returned to our Huts to get ready for our last Hygiene Inspection before Graduation. Gunny wanted to ensure there were no problems or issues with any of the Recruits.

We were Graduating in the morning, and the whole Platoon was in good spirits. The fact that we were actually the Honor Platoon of our Series gave us the gratification and satisfaction that we were now considered the best and put us in a good place with our DI's. Everyone in the Platoon should feel proud of themselves for what we had accomplished.

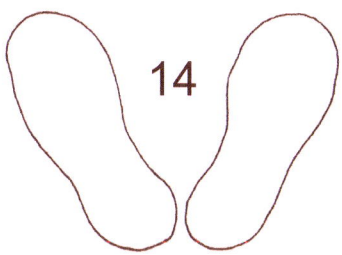

Graduation

Friday, Reveille was the usual 0500 and even though it was our last day, we still did PT, and did not change our routine as far as hygiene, clean-up or morning chow. We were marched back to the Platoon Street after we finished morning chow before the *"Smoking Lamp"* was lit. Once we finished our cigarettes, we were dismissed back to our Huts to get dressed in the Uniform of the Day for Graduation!

As I opened the black garment bag to take out my Blues, I noticed my Shooting Badge was not hanging over the left pocket as it was when I put them away. The upper right portion was broken and the Badge was swinging loose. Someone messed with my uniform. I took the shooting badge off my Blues and made my way to the Duty Hut to show the Gunny my Shooting Badge was broken and asked what I should do.

The Gunny looked over my Badge and said it couldn't be fixed, so he took a Sharpshooter Badge out of his desk drawer and gave it to me. He told me to find someone with an Expert Badge and take theirs and give them the Sharpshooters Badge. When I made my way back to my Hut, I didn't think that was fair, so I just put the Sharpshooter Badge on my Blues and got dressed for Graduation.

The Platoon stood at "**Attention**" on the Platoon Street dressed in the Class "A" Dress Greens with Combination Cover, spit shined shoes and actually looked like Marines. I was wearing my Dress Blues with all the trimmings, white Combination Cover, white belt, white gloves, spit shined shoes and my ribbon and Shooting Badge above the left breast pocket

Our Platoon "**Fell-In**" on Platoon Street. Gunny had me go from "**Attention**" to "**Port Arms**" with the Guidon as he hung the Blue Streamer for Honor Platoon on our Platoon Guidon alongside the Red, Gold, Orange and White Streamers. Once the Gunny was finished placing the Blue Streamer on our Guidon, I came back to "**Attention**" and the Gunny pointed out the Blue Streamer to the rest of the Platoon and said, "Congratulations."

He noticed I was wearing the Sharpshooter Badge instead of the Expert Badge and asked why I didn't change it out with another Recruit. I responded, "Sir, the Pvt didn't think it was fair to take away someone else's Badge for Graduation because mine was broken, Sir." He gave me a stern look and then he addressed the entire Platoon, "Each and every one of you should be proud of what you were able to accomplish. To win as many Streamers as you have is a credit to your hard work, your determination, your pride and your character. It isn't easy to win one Streamer let alone five which makes Platoon 2227 the Honor Platoon of this Training Series."

He continued, "I know I speak for Sgt James and Sgt Martinez when I say we are proud to be associated with each and every one of you and would be pleased to serve with any of you in the future. Today you Graduate from Boot Camp and have earned the right to be proud of what you have accomplished and will be recognized as you garnish the coveted Eagle, Globe and Anchor."

Gunny looked at his watch and it was time to get in position for Graduation Day Ceremony. Our Platoon as well as

the rest of FOX Company were marched to the area behind the Base Theater to be formed up by 1000. Graduation Ceremony will include the entire four Platoons in FOX Company as well as the Base Band. Once the entire Company was in Formation, at exactly 1000, Fox Company was marched through the Archway that is connected to the Base Theater, and we formed up on the Grinder centered in front of the Base Flag Pole which is located at the center of the Parade Ground.

With FOX Company in Formation, each Platoon had their Honor Man at the front of their Platoon carrying their Platoon Guidon. The four Honor Men are dressed in the Marine Corps Dress Blues, which designated them as the standout recruit

in each of their Platoons. The rest of the graduating Company as well as the Drill Instructors and Platoon Commanders were dressed in their Class "A" Dress Greens.

Platoon 2225 will be the first Platoon leading the way through the Archway followed by Platoon 2226, followed by a 4-man Marine Color Guard, then Platoon 2227 and finally Platoon 2228. Upon coming to the proper position on the Grinder, all four Platoons will "**Mark Time**," to make sure we were lined up properly. During that time the Marine Corps Base Band was playing marching music. Once the command was given to "**Halt**" the entire Company Formation made a "Left Face," which had us facing the guests who were seated in the bleachers, as well as the "Reviewing Officers."

The first part of the Graduation Ceremony and the tradition on Graduation Day is to have the Bugler play "**Adjutants Call**" followed by the Command "**Attention to Orders**." The Reviewing Adjutant reads or recites the "**Order of the Day**." The Base Chaplain gives the Invocation followed by The Commander of the Reviewing Officers. He then put the Company Formation "**At Ease**," before making his comments to the spectators and families regarding what the Recruits had accomplished to Graduate from Boot Camp.

After his comments, the Command of "**FOX Company, Attention**" was given and the entire Company came to "**Attention**." The next item on the Program was to have the Platoon Guidons be Retired. The actual Command was, "**Retire the Guidons**." At this Command, the four "**Right Guides**" one from each Platoon, take two steps forward, face either left or right, and meet in the center of the formation in front of the Color Guard facing the Reviewing Officers. When the next Command of "**Forward, March**" was given to the four "**Right Guides**" they Marched forward until they were on the marks, on the Deck, in front of the Reviewing Officers.

While the "**Right Guides**" were marching to the front of the Formation, the four Drill Instructors, one from each Platoon, marched from behind the Reviewing Officers to position themselves in front of the Reviewing Officers, while facing the Company Formation of Recruits awaiting the "**Right Guides**" to form up with their Guidons.

The "**Right Guides**" stopped in front of the DI's and while standing at "**Attention**," the "**Right Guides**" went to "**Port Arms**," with the Platoon Guidons, and each Platoon Drill Instructor took the Guidons from the "**Right Guides**." The Drill Instructors make a "**Right Face**," and retired the Platoon Guidons. The Platoon Right Guides, (the Honor Men), made an "**About Face**," and returned to their Platoons.

Once the "**Right Guides**" were back with their Platoons and the Guidon's had been Retired, the Parade Adjutant gave the Command "**FOX Company, Pass In Review**." The next Command given was "**Company**, **Right Face**," and the entire Company, executed a "**Right Face**," all at the same time. The Honor Guard executed a Right Facing movement. The next Command given was, "**Company**, **Forward**, **March**." As the Band began to play, the entire FOX Company stepped off with their Left Foot and marched forward. The entire Company was in step as they proceeded to Pass in Review. The entire time the Formation was marching, the Base Band played marching music, "Semper Fidelis," the "Washington Post" and the "Marine Corps Hymn."

As the 1st Platoon reached a designated spot on the Grinder, they executed a "**Column Left**," and continued until reaching another spot on the Grinder executing another "**Column Left**," which had them aligned just six paces in front of the Reviewing Officials as we passed by the Official Reviewing Party, the visitors and families. All four Platoons as well as the Color Guard executed the same movements as they Passed in Review in front of the Reviewing Officials.

As each Platoon passed by the Reviewing Officials, they were given the command to "**Eyes Right**," which had the 4th Squad continue looking forward and Squads 3, 2, and 1 snapped their head to the right looking at the Reviewing Officials, as they Passed.

As the last Recruit from each Platoon passed the Reviewing Officials, the Command of "**Ready Front**," was given and they snapped their heads back forward. When the Color Guard Passed the Reviewing Officials, the entire Reviewing Formation Saluted the Colors as they Passed by. When the first Platoon reached a designated position on the Grinder, they executed another "**Column Left**." When they reached the same space they began the Parade, they executed another "**Column Left**," and continued as the Band played the entire time the Company marched in Review.

The entire Formation continued to march past the same position they began at as they marched off the Grinder and formed up in front of the Base Theater in Company Formation.

The families, guests and visitors were dismissed to move to the Theater Area to observe the rest of the Graduation Ceremony.

The Base Theater was where the Award Ceremony for Graduation was to take place. After reaching the position in front of the Base Theater, all four Platoons were ordered into the auditorium one Platoon at a time, in a single file, by Squad to take up their positions in the Theater. Each recruit sat at attention waiting for the ceremony to begin. After all the Platoons were seated, the Adjutant's Staff along with each Platoon Commander sat on the stage. The entire Theater was commanded to come to attention while the Band played the Star Spangled Banner.

The ceremony had the Executive Officer of the base as the MC. After the initial announcements were made, each Platoon was introduced and was asked to stand while they introduced the Platoon Commander and the two Drill Instructors along with the Platoon Honor Man from each Platoon. After each Platoon was introduced, the recruits sat at attention while awards were presented.

The 1st Awards given out were to recognize the Platoon Honor Men, with special recognition given to the Series Honor Man. Each Platoon Honor Man was called on stage and received a Certificate of Honor, a Promotion Certificate to the Rank of Private First Class and had his picture taken with the Company Commanding Officer receiving his

Certificate. I received recognition as our Platoon Honor Man and also received the Series Honor Man award. I was asked to stay on the stage as the next award given was the Honor Platoon designation.

Gunny Sgt Wolfmule, Sgt James and Sgt Martinez joined me on the stage and the Company Commanding Officer awarded a

Certificate to Gunny Sgt Wolfmule and a Trophy. Both Sgt James and Sgt Martinez were given Plaques. Platoon 2227 was asked to stand and be recognized for winning the Red Streamer for the Rifle Range, the Gold Streamer for Close Order Drill, the Orange Streamer for PT, the White Streamer for Final Inspection, and the Blue Streamer for Honor Platoon. Our platoon won five out of the possible six streamers. The entire theater applauded our accomplishment. Pictures were taken and then we were released to our seats.

The next award was for the Highest Shooter on the rifle range who received a plaque and was promoted to PFC. Platoon 2227 had the highest shooter, it was PFC Mike Havranek. Mike made his way to the stage to receive his award and have his picture taken. The next award was for the highest score on the PT test, PFC Gilbert Gagnon, Platoon 2227 came forward to receive his awards. There were a number of additional Awards given for all Recruits who scored 300 points on their PT test.

All in all, Platoon 2227 had nine recruits promoted to PFC and we swept the award ceremony. There were another 21 Marines promoted to PFC from other Platoons. Each Platoon was able to promote up to 10% of their Recruits who stood out or distinguished themselves while at boot camp. All the Platoon Honor Men were Promoted to Private First Class.

Once the Graduation Ceremony was finished, all four Platoons stood and were orderly marched out in single file to "**Fall-In**" outside the auditorium. Each Platoon Commander took charge of his Platoon and marched them from the auditorium back to their Platoon areas. Once our Platoon was dismissed from Platoon Street, Base Liberty was given to share the rest of the day with families and friends who showed up for Graduation. Recruits were allowed to explore the Base and enjoy Graduation Day until 1800.

Gunny Wolfmule, Sgt James and Sgt Martinez were all on Platoon Street. Gunny Wolfmule dismissed our Platoon for the first time as Marines. Hearing him call us Marines made our chests stick out, our hearts pound, and brought a smile to our faces. We now have become part of history that is the United States Marine Corps.

Gunny stood in front of the Platoon and looked like a father that had just given birth to his first son, said, "Platoon 2227 it is my pleasure, and I am proud to address you all for the first time as U.S. Marines. I would be proud to serve with any one of you. When you are dismissed, you have been given base liberty until 1800. This was the first time in 11 weeks that you are free to enjoy the freedoms you have earned. Remember, you are now Marines, be sure to act the part. Report back to the Platoon Street by 1800 for evening chow. Marines of Platoon 2227, dismissed." The Platoon answered, "**Sir, Dismissed, Aye Aye Sir.**"

After hearing Gunny address us as Marines, the first person I shook hands with was PFC Mike Havranek. PFC Gibby Gagnon stood next to us and shook our hands and asked me what I was going to do for Liberty. He said, "Let's find a place to sit and talk if you have time." I told him I was looking forward to it. There were a number of other Marines in our Platoon that I felt close to who came over and shook my hand and told me congratulations and thanked me for helping them through Boot Camp. Everyone was cheerful now that Boot Camp was over.

I made my way back to my Quonset hut to drop off my awards before going on liberty. I put my certificates in my footlocker. I decided to stay in my Dress Blues instead of changing into my Dress Greens as I had earned them, and I wanted to be recognized for my accomplishments.

As I left my Hut, everyone I ran across either told me congratulations or shook my hand for making Honor Man. I was told a number of times how good I looked in my Blues as I made my way to the Base Enlisted Men's Club. To our surprise, the EM Club (Enlisted Men's Club) didn't open until

1630, so I walked over to the Base Bowling Alley where I was told most of the guys from our Platoon congregated.

I found my way to the Base Bowling Alley sometime after 1330 and since I chose not to attend noon Mess, I ordered a California cheeseburger with French fries and a coke. To be honest, that was one of the highlights of my day. Some of the graduating Marines that were over 21, ended up drinking 3.2 beer which was served at the Bowling Alley. No one under the age of 21 could drink on base, so I just enjoyed my coke.

I sat with Havranek, Gagnon and Evanoff and talked about my life in general after I moved back to Detroit and attended a different school. We talked about how strange it was to have Sgt Porta as our DI and Gagnon commented on Sgt Porta's brother Mike who didn't join the Marines when Gagnon and Evanoff did. We exchanged conversation about our families and friends we had in common. That was the only time in over 11 weeks that we actually had a personal conversation. What a difference now that Boot Camp was over.

Base liberty was over at 1800 and Marines that had family said their goodbyes and returned to Platoon Street with the rest of Platoon 2227. The entire Platoon changed out of our Dress uniforms and back into our starched utilities and spit shined boots. As a Platoon we were marched to evening chow. After evening chow, the "*Smoking Lamp*" was lit and we had Commander's Time for the rest of the evening to write letters, pack your sea bags or just relax. One thing you couldn't ever do was sit on or lay on your Rack unless it was time to sleep.

At 2100 Platoon 2227 was ordered to "**Fall-In**" on the Platoon Street in our utility trousers, t-shirts and shower shoes. Once everyone was in formation, Gunny Sgt Wolfmule put us at ease and lit the "*Smoking lamp*". Those that brought their cigarettes shared with those that didn't. He made an announcement of how proud he was of our performance during boot camp, and he was honored to be our Platoon Commander. He told us what we could expect in the morning and wished us all good luck in our Marine Corps career.

Those who did not smoke were dismissed, and those smoking were told after they finished their cigarettes, to field strip them and return to their Hut and finish up their activities and get ready to hit the Rack. Gunny Sgt Wolfmule took me aside and shook my hand again, he told me again what a good job I had done as the Right Guide, and for my leadership skills during boot camp. He handed me an envelope which contained a complete set of PFC Chevrons for all my uniforms and said, "Consider this a reward from me and Sgt James for a job well done." I felt very proud and very honored for Gunny to take the time to talk to me and to give me this gift. I said, "Thank you very much Sir, I will never forget you." He told me, "Hit the Rack Marine, I'll see you in the morning." I said goodnight and went to my Hut. Lights out and taps at 2200.

I laid in my Rack, too excited to sleep. I couldn't believe Boot Camp was all over. Those eleven weeks went by fairly fast considering. My mind went over the good, the bad and the ugly of the last eleven weeks. That first night getting off the bus and standing on those Yellow Footprints. As long as I live, I will never forget those Yellow Footprints.

Besides all the yelling that began from the time we got off the plane at the San Diego airport, the aspects of not knowing what to expect, plus the punching, the kicking, the pushing, the shock of cold showers and being up all night, I never thought I would survive the first day let alone eleven weeks. As I reflect back, I was fortunate that I knew something about marching before arriving and I am sure that helped me in being picked as the "Right Guide."

Everything we were taught about Marine History intrigued me. I thought about when I was a kid playing army, and John Wayne was always my Hero. I always loved watching World War II movies. History was my favorite subject in school as well, but who would have ever guessed I actually got to live my childhood dream being a Marine.

The most challenging parts of Boot Camp were the obstacle course, the towers, the rope climbs, the physical breaking us down and rebuilding us back up. I also wasn't the best swimmer, and was a little anxious when we began drown-proofing. The biggest lesson learned in the pool was to always relax and breathe. It was the unknown that affected me the most, but after executing anything we were told or ordered to do, and knowing what to expect, doing it over again wasn't bad at all. Most of it was actually fun.

The first day unbuttoning our top button and blousing our trousers, the first time wearing starched utilities, starching our utility covers, spit shinning our boots and wearing our Dress Greens for the first time were all triumphs that instilled self-confidence, and discipline.

The rifle range and snapping-in was quite an experience and learning how to shoot a high-power rifle is what being a Marine is all about. Although going to school to learn how to become an Air Traffic Controller is what I have been looking forward to. But if by chance I ever end up in combat, it's good that I know how to fire a rifle properly along with depending on the Marine who may be on my right or my left.

The last thought I remember before falling asleep was how proud I felt wearing my Dress Blues. Although I was very proud standing our Final Inspection in our Dress Greens, wearing my Dress Blues was an honor only a few of us got to enjoy. I know when I get home my parents and family as well as my friends will be impressed no matter which uniform I wear.

Saturday morning after reveille, we still did PT on the Grinder for the last time, and after hygiene, shower and shave, instead of making our racks, we stripped our linen and folded our blankets. Since we would be the last Platoons to eat morning chow, we spent the next hour or so doing our normal morning clean-up, after which we were marched to morning chow.

We were in formation outside the Mess Hall when morning Colors were executed, and Sgt James and Sgt Martinez saluted the large Base Garrison flag as we stood at attention. After Colors we entered the Mess Hall for the last time to enjoy Boot Camp chow. When morning chow was over, we would be marched back to Platoon Street where the "*Smoking Lamp*" was lit. Those not smoking were told to finish clean-up of our Platoon area.

After the "*Smoking Lamp*" was turned off, we were ordered to our Huts to make sure all of our gear was packed into our sea bags. Last Tuesday we received our last haircuts, and afterwards made our last trip to the PX. We were allowed to buy duffle bags to carry our personal articles in as well as buy a garment bag to carry our dress uniforms for traveling. So after packing our sea bags, almost every member of our Platoon had a Duffle Bag and a garment bag to carry besides their sea bag.

We were given instructions on how to pack our sea bags properly and efficiently with our uniforms, PT clothing, personal articles, extra boots, tennis shoes and all items from our footlockers. I filled my sea bag with my boots first and then filled in the spaces with socks, PT shorts, washcloths, utilities, skivvies, t-shirts, top coat, sweatshirt, extra covers, then my other dress greens, khaki's, tropical uniforms, towels, cover grommet, shoe shining gear, raincoat, and before closing my sea bag, I filled the space with my shoe polish, brasso, bottle of Wisk, the liquid starch, as well as my shoe shining rag.

In my duffle bag, I packed my dress shoes, shaving gear, shower shoes, personal letters from home and writing gear, extra handkerchief, cigarettes, and extra pad lock. The only items left to put in my duffle bag were the awards I received at graduation.

I had everything packed except my Dress Green Class "A" Uniform and my Dress Blues which I placed in my black garment bag that I received when I was issued my Blues. For transport to Camp Pendleton we would wear one pair of starched utilities, our starched utility cover and our work boots. After I was sure I had everything packed, I rolled my mattress with the pillow in the middle, folded my two blankets, and placed my two sheets and one pillowcase in the basket that the House Mice had outside each Hut. We stacked our buckets and left them inside each Hut. I locked my sea bag and placed it on the deck with my duffle bag next to it and hung my garment bag on my Rack.

We were given plenty of time to pack our gear and clean up our area including our bedding and mattress. When we were finished, we were to "Fall-In" on Platoon Street with all of our gear. It took about a half hour and to get organized with every swinging dick standing on Platoon Street without one of the DI's yelling at us to "Fall-In." The squad leader in each Hut had his squad take the basket with our linen and place it outside the Duty Hut. Once the entire Platoon was at attention on Platoon Street, I reported to the DI Duty Hut and notified the DI's that Platoon 2227 was all present and on Platoon Street.

Gunny Sgt Wolfmule came out of the duty Hut and addressed the formation. He told us before we were dismissed to board the cattle cars to Camp Pendleton, he and Sgt James would inspect each ut for the last time. It was around 0930 when the last area inspection took place. All four Quonset Huts were emptied and cleaned, there was nothing left in our Quonset Huts but the metal double bunk beds with a rolled-up mattress, a pillow and two blankets, a stack of our buckets, and in the middle and under each rack were two empty footlockers.

Each Hut was spotless and ready for the next recruit Platoon. All of our sea bags and personal gear was out of our Hut and on the Platoon Street and in a way the empty Huts

G/Sgt. R. W. Wolfmule
Platoon Commander

Sgt. J. G. James
Drill Instructor

was kind of anti-climactic after our 11 weeks of training. Of course we passed Gunny Wolfmule's inspection, and the *"Smoking Lamp"* was lit for the last time at MCRD as we waited for Gunny Sgt Wolfmule, Sgt James, and Sgt Martinez to address the Platoon and tell each new Marine their new M.O.S. He told us where we would be reporting after we finished ITR or BST training at Camp Pendleton.

There were two separate Trainings after Boot Camp. Those who were designated with the 0311 M.O.S. as their first and primary M.O.S. were going to BST Training (Basic Squad Tactics) at Camp Magarita at Camp Pendleton. There were 58 Marines going to BST Training. The remaining 18 Marines in Platoon 2227

Sgt. A. Martinez
Drill Instructor

were going to ITR Training (Infantry Training regiment) at Camp San Onofre, also at Camp Pendleton.

Gunny explained to us that once we had completed ITR

Pfc. T. S. Rilley
Platoon Honorman
and Blues Award

or BST training, we would receive a 20-day leave before reporting to our next duty station. One by one, Gunny read out each name and disclosed their MOS and where they would be going after they completed their 20-day leave. While Gunny Wolfmule read each name, Sgt James and Sgt Martinez delivered your set of orders and shook each of our hands and wished us good luck. When my name was called, Gunny read, "PFC Rilley, T.S. 7041, Report to NAS Memphis for Aviation Operations School." Sgt James gave me my Orders and shook my hand and wished me Luck.

When Gunny was finished reading all our names and having our orders delivered, he and I stood face to face and I said, "**Thank you, sir**." Gunny looked at me and said, "PFC. Rilley, you no longer have to call me sir, it's just Gunny Wolfmule from now on." I replied, "I understand the rank and the chain of command, Gunny, but you will always be Sir to me." Again he shook my hand and told me how proud he was to have me in his Platoon, and that I earned the position to be the Honor Man. His last words to me were, "Good luck, Marine!"

It was about 1100 when the formation was ordered to pick up our gear and again march behind the 2nd Battalion Mess Hall where the Platoon would split off and board the cattle cars for Camp Pendleton where we would continue our initial Infantry training. As the convoy of trucks left the Depot heading for Camp Pendleton I lit up a cigarette and I again began to reflect on my experience of the last 11 weeks at Boot Camp.

I remember my first jet airplane ride from Detroit to Los Angelas and the anxiety I felt when those first two DI's came aboard the plane in San Diego. That scary and uncomfortable bus ride from the San Diego airport through the Main Gate of MCRD. Who will ever forget those yellow footprints? I never will, nor will I forget the constant yelling, screaming and name calling.

I arrived at MCRD a young, skinny, scared civilian puke who had no idea what I was about to get into, how I would respond to what I would be subjected to, or if I would succeed or fail. Now I sat in the presence of 40 other Marines riding in the same cattle car, who shared and experienced all the same challenges that I faced every day. I accomplished more than I ever thought possible after that first day of having my head shaved, standing naked in the receiving building with

90 other guys, and after experiencing the coldest shower I had ever taken.

The pride I now feel with my chest sticking out just a little further, my shoulders back straight and strong, my attitude now is that of a man who can accomplish anything. I have learned the importance of discipline and built my self-confidence to a level I never knew possible. I was now on a new path and direction in my life that would have never been possible without the experience of what I was taught, what I have learned, and what I was able to accomplish in Marine Corps Boot Camp. I am extremely proud of the fact that I have earned the title of United States Marine!

I lit up my second cigarette as we made our way to Camp Pendleton. There were three weeks of training left before I would be able to go home on Boot Camp Leave, to show off the new person I had become and my new Marine Corps Uniform. Once I enjoy those 20 days Leave, who knows what the next three and a half years of my enlistment has in store for me.

In Closing...

This book was written to share my experiences of Marine Corps Boot Camp only, which I attended in 1966. I understand nothing stays the same in life. After 50 years most of what's left are life's memories. There is one thing I know for sure that hasn't changed, and that is if you enter the United States Marine Corps today, once off the bus that takes you through the Main Gates of either Parris Island or MCRD San Diego, your first stop will be the Yellow Footprints.

For those who read this book and were in the Marines, I am sure you can relate to the different stages of training, the yelling, the PT, morning reveille, the pushups, the runs, the Obstacle Course, the Rifle Range, the hours on the Grinder doing Close Order Drill, the classes on Marine Corps History, your Drill Instructors and Platoon Commander and their colorful language. The standing at Attention before getting permission to eat your many meals in the Mess Halls. Whether you were in the 1st Battalion, 2nd Battalion, or 3rd Battalion, you had to go through the exact same training schedule as everyone else who also stood on those Yellow Footprints.

The Marines don't give out Service Numbers any longer, you use your Social Security number. Some of the training has changed, maybe you never got hit in the solar plex, maybe you never got punched at all. But I know you did thousands of pushups, pullups and bends and thrusts. Pugil Stick training may have changed, but you experienced some kind of rifle combat training. You no longer live in Quonset Huts, but have beautiful brick Barracks. The Marine Corps has modernized in many respects, but they don't just give you the Eagle, Globe and Anchor, you still have to earn it.

Although there have been many changes made in the Marine Corps over the years, the Yellow Footprints are still there. The Obstacle Course is still there, you still wear the Dress Green Class "A" Winter Uniform, and the Summer Class "A" Tropical, uniform. The Dress Blues are still the best looking uniform wore by any member of the military. Marines still get goose bumps when they hear the Marine Corps Hymn played, or still stand tall when someone say's to you, "Semper Fi."

For those who wore the Eagle, Globe and Anchor, "You may not be as lean and mean, but you will always be a Marine." Those who served, "Thank You for your Service." For those that say, "I could have been a Marine, But….." Give it a rest.

OOOOH RAAAAH!

About
Timothy S. Rilley

Born and raised in Detroit, Michigan, Timothy graduated High School in 1965, attended Eastern Michigan University, and entered the U.S. Marine Corps in August 1966. He received an Honorable Discharge August 2, 1972.

Upon leaving the Marine Corps, Tim moved to Minnesota, raised his family and enjoyed successful careers in the automotive, insurance, and mortgage industries. He moved to Arizona in 2004 with his wife Debra and continued a career in the mortgage industry. Tim is currently retired.

Upon moving to Arizona, he was introduced to the U.S. Naval Sea Cadet Corps and served as the Executive Officer and then Commanding Officer of two separate units and served for a period of ten years. This program is probably the best kept secret for youth, both male and female. The program is dedicated to teaching young males and females what "Right Looks Like." This program is chartered by Congress and supported by the U.S. Navy, U.S. Coast Guard, and the U.S. Marine Corps.

He and his wife raised three children, one son and two daughters and currently has 13 grandchildren. Debra is a retired school teacher and is writing a series of children's books which will be published soon.

Having read years ago that, "To Whom Much is Given...Much is Required," he has always believed in giving something back as a reward for having so much given to him.

Timothy wrote the *"The Yellow Footprints"* to share his journey and his transformation from a civilian to a United States Marine. His time in the Marine Corps molded his life and taught him the meanings of Discipline, Self-Confidence, Goal Setting, and also how to adapt, overcome and improvise. He has used these lessons learned throughout his life.

Organizations he has belonged to and volunteered for:

Lions Club
Rotary Club
Cub Scouts
Boy Scouts of America
Sertoma Club
Kiwanis Club
Toastmasters
Big Brothers
Boys and Girls Clubs of America
Disabled American Veterans
Veterans of Foreign Wars
American Legion
Twin Cities Marathon Board of Directors
Make A Wish Foundation Board Member
Minneapolis Children's Heart Hospital Board of Directors
Sky Kids Inc. Founding member and Board of Directors
President of Estrella HOA Voting Committee President
US Naval Sea Cadet Corps,
Veterans Pride Battalion, Commanding Officer, Glendale, AZ
Sea Eagle Squadron, Commanding Officer, Yuma, AZ